Senghor

THEORY IN FORMS

Series Editors: Nancy Rose Hunt, Achille Mbembe, and Todd Meyers

Edited and translated by   YOHANN C. RIPERT

Senghor

*Writings
on Politics*

═══

*Léopold Sédar
Senghor*

═══

Duke University Press *Durham and London* 2025

© Editions du Seuil, 1964, for *Liberté 1: Négritude et humanisme*
© Editions du Seuil, 1971, for *Liberté 2: Nation et voie africaine du socialisme*
© Editions du Seuil, 1977, for *Liberté 3: Négritude et civilisation de l'universel*
© Editions du Seuil, 1983, for *Liberté 4: Socialisme et planification*
Project Editor: Lisa Lawley
Designed by Courtney Leigh Richardson
Typeset in Garamond Premier Pro by Westchester Publishing Services

Library of Congress Cataloging-in-Publication Data
Names: Senghor, Léopold Sédar, 1906–2001, author. | Ripert, Yohann C.,
[date] editor, translator.
Title: Senghor : writings on politics / Léopold Sédar Senghor ; edited
and translated by Yohann C. Ripert.
Other titles: Theory in forms.
Description: Durham : Duke University Press, 2025. | Series: Theory
in forms | Includes bibliographical references and index.
Identifiers: LCCN 2025013345
ISBN 9781478032847 (paperback)
ISBN 9781478029380 (hardcover)
Subjects: LCSH: Socialism—Africa, Sub-Saharan. | Negritude (Literary
movement) | Africa, Sub-Saharan—Politics and government. | Africa,
Sub-Saharan—Civilization.
Classification: LCC DT549.77.S46 A25 2025
LC record available at https://lccn.loc.gov/2025013345

Cover art: Léopold Sédar Senghor, based on a 1964 photograph.
National Archives of Brazil.

Cet ouvrage a bénéficié du soutien des Programmes d'aide à
la publication de l'Institut français. (The publication of this book
was made possible with support from the Institut français.)

publication supported by a grant from
The Community Foundation for Greater New Haven
as part of the URBAN HAVEN PROJECT

For my mother,   ELIANE RIPERT,

who planted the seeds of curiosity,

For my wife,   HANNAH SUN,

who nurtured this work with patience and love,

For my mentor,   GAYATRI CHAKRAVORTY SPIVAK,

who unveiled realms of thought I never knew existed.

Contents

Translator's Introduction
Yohann C. Ripert

Léopold Sédar Senghor was a paradox: a thinker who sought to reinvent politics and yet was horrified by the idea of becoming a politician; a poet who dared to reimagine the contours of a new racial identity and yet was often seen as an apologist for essentialized identity politics. Like the philosopher who escaped Plato's cave only to be forced to return to free fellow cave dwellers, Senghor was imbued with the vision of a world that he felt compelled to share with fellow postcolonial pioneers. Negritude was that vision.

As often as Senghor himself defined and redefined Negritude, other prominent thinkers have given it some of the most memorable, if problematic, definitions. Over time, catchphrases and forgotten texts by those who participated in the elaboration of both the word and the concept petrified Senghor's original vision into a frozen tableau. Yet, even when Jean-Paul Sartre, in his eloquent preface to Senghor's *Anthologie de la nouvelle poésie negre et malgache de langue française* (Anthology of new Black and Malagasy poets writing in French), a contribution that assured posterity for Senghor as both poet and politician, wrote that "Négritude is the root of its own destruction, a transition and not a conclusion, a means and not an ultimate end," he, too, challenged any easy definition. Though Frantz Fanon felt that Sartre "robbed him [Fanon] of his last chance" to regain power over Black consciousness, the psychiatrist's dismay only gave substance to what Senghor conveyed in poetics: Negritude is more than a racial movement. It is a peri-racial critique shaping a space around race rather than defining race itself.[1] Because "race is a reality" (page 3), Senghor writes, it seeks to generate narratives beyond core racial dialogues and engage with surrounding discourse production informed by race. Its goal is to constitute a repository of texts with diverse and sometimes conflicting voices to prevent the danger of imagining any kind of racial homogeneity. As its body of texts continues to grow, Negritude becomes more than the sum of its parts, going beyond empirical observations and into the conditions for knowledge and experience—influenced by and influencing what surrounds the performance of Negritude.

To be sure, the *Anthology* did not constitute a cohesive body of texts from which something akin to a philosophical practice could eventually lead to—or at least coincide with—political actions. Following almost to the letter the argument developed in the *Republic*, Senghor had made his own the idea that no philosophical or poetic work could find a solution for political issues, yet philosophical and poetic practices were necessary for the success of any political work aimed at the sustainability of the polity—a timeless lesson we have often forgotten. In Plato's text, more than a coincidence between philosophy and politics, the philosopher-king succeeds when philosophical practice and political practice become one; indeed, when the philosopher-king embodies a truthful attitude toward knowledge of himself and his relations with others. Almost straight out of the *Republic*'s playbook, Senghor, who went through the best training Plato prescribed for the future leader of the just state, poetry writing, began to question the kind of knowledge through which he came to know himself and others. Surely, the nascent idea of Negritude could not rest on the imaginary that André Breton and Paul Éluard provided, however they pleased him. Surely, the language with which they painted the world was not unbiased, however they reworked it. Caught in double binds, he saw only one option: to burn it all. Let us listen to Senghor recalling the scene: "At the Sorbonne, I became infected by Surrealism. Fortunately, I discovered Africa and Negro art through European ethnographers and art critics on the one hand, Negro American literature and especially poetry on the other. . . . Those discoveries were true revelations for me which led me to seek myself and uncover myself as I truly was: a Negro, morally and intellectually métissé with French. I then burned almost all my early poetry to start at zero. It was 1935."[2]

The moment is significant in the trajectory of a promising graduate from the prestigious École Normale Supérieure. In Janet Vaillant's important biography, the moment is symptomatic of an identity crisis for which psychology provides the explanation.[3] The child must become a man. Decades later, the poet recalls the memory more boldly: "1935: the year when I burned *all* my early poetry."[4] The theatrical gesture is uncharacteristic of a man known for his calm temperament. It is also a noble lie. No, Senghor did not burn his early poetry.[5]

Poetry, perhaps more than any other genre, relies on powerful imagination and language, and Senghor's commitment to language as a tool to unearth a repository of knowledge buried by colonial epistemic violence cannot be understated. The premise is not without problems. Which language to use to express what has been repressed by centuries of physical, psychological, and epistemic violence? It is this problem, the problem of language, that Senghor positioned as foundational for emancipation.[6] It is also the problem that most vocal critics of Negritude have seized upon to mount their assault against the movement. Thus, Ngũgĩ wa Thiong'o's criticism of Senghor's "anointment" by the Académie Française illustrates the argument made in *Decolonising the Mind* against neocolonial oppression through linguistic imperialism: There can be no African history, literature, or even politics, unless it is decidedly thought and written in a language indigenous to the continent. But what would it mean to—and what are the conditions under which one could—think, write, or translate Negritude into one or more African languages? Indeed, Senghor asks, "What language to choose from the multiplicity of languages and dialects? There are mother tongues and dynamic languages, languages that prey on others: Mandinka, Hausa, Yoruba, Fulani, Wolof" (page 8). The question, which is fundamentally a problem of translatability, underwrites the entire project of Negritude—and Senghor's work. In a sense, translation is a performance of Negritude. "Each generation, each thinker, each writer, artist, politician, must, in their own ways and for their own good, go deeper and expand Négritude, [overcoming] Négritude's predecessors" (page 141). This monumental task is as pertinent to our time as it was in Senghor's.

The aim of this translation is therefore twofold: first, to engage in the ongoing performative act of translating and reinterpreting Negritude across languages and generations; second, to foster dynamic interplay between seemingly disparate texts to critique a constantly evolving movement. This is why this collection juxtaposes political and poetic texts, polished articles and lesser-known spontaneous lectures, many translated for the first time, and some offered with a refreshed translation: to reveal the porosity between Senghor's politics and poetics driving decolonization toward a sustainable independence. By highlighting a feedback loop through all five decades of his intellectual journey, this arrangement allows readers to witness Senghor's mind at work. The unexpected discovery of Marx's manuscripts in the library of the French National Assembly, reflected in "Marxism and Humanism," sits alongside the poetic revelations of his Harlem stroll evident in "Negro-American Poetry." Meanwhile, "Balkanization or Federation" is both a response to and a necessary correlate of a poetic foundation transcending political and linguistic boundaries expressed in "Like the Manatees Go Drink at the Source." Two short pieces about art, "The Fodéba Keita African Ballet" and "For a Senegalese Tapestry," respectively written and spoken, capture Senghor's constant negotiation between nation building and transnational construction. The collection's chronological approach also brings to the fore a mutually reinforcing poetic and political vision challenging historical signposts and rigid periodization to demonstrate ongoing responses to global intellectual and political developments, always in motion. As such, both the early "The Problem of Culture in French West Africa" and the later "Francophonie as Culture" demonstrate an evolving stance on cultural identity and linguistic diversity that both precedes and follows independence while being enabled by the Year of Africa. Throughout, my translation philosophy aims to re-create these evolving dialogues at the core of Senghor's prose to engage readers in the ongoing process of crafting an interconnected poetico-political vision.

Through this approach, readers can appreciate how Senghor's evolving thoughts on culture, language, and politics contributed to his vision of true independence and societal transformation. Even though national resistance through protests, civil disobedience, and cultural reforms led to a political upheaval known as decolonization, Senghor knew that a sustainable independence required a literal revolution, a turning, like the Earth around the Sun. This revolution did not mean returning to a precolonial beginning but redoing a familiar route with renewed willpower—a re-volition. Indeed, such a revolution is not a radical transformation but a movement toward self-determination. For Senghor, self-determination means the freedom to determine one's history rather than merely escaping historical determinism—a premise that run through the poetic essay "Like the Manatees Drink at the Source." There, Senghor deftly navigates between myth and historical reality to demonstrate how the interplay of these narratives not only enriches literature but also empowers individuals to actively reclaim and reinterpret their past, crafting a self-determined politico-cultural identity. Indeed, because he is more interested in poetry and philosophy, his relationship with Africa's past is less reliant on historical evidence than on a personal, subjective, even sensual rediscovery of the continent, giving free rein to poetic imagination. One year after independence, Senghor posed a rhetorical question to the governor general of Nigeria, Nnamdi Azikiwe: "Governor General, did you not yourself call for Negritude, in 1934, in *Renascent Africa*, when you called for mental emancipation as a precondition for independence? Is it not true that the worst colonization is the colonization of the mind?" (page 103). As Frantz Fanon also noted in the early days of independence, from his vantage point in Algeria's painful struggle, the destruction of the mind, soul, and thought of the colonized subject is colonialism's deepest wound.[7] Despite the many divides between Senghor and Fanon, they are united in their shared effort to reconstruct the beings whose lives were shattered by the physical and epistemic violence of colonialism and the power of its ideology.[8] Fanon, a trained psychiatrist, sought to heal his patients by developing a radical theory of colonial psychopathology; Senghor, a trained poet, sought a different goal and means: to spark the imagination of the present, without which no future emancipation can be sustained. Negritude was only—and sometimes barely—one element of that spark.

This book, through its introduction and collected essays, illuminates the intricate relationship between Negritude and Léopold Sédar Senghor. Both often flow in parallel, as the translation shows, with essays alternating between drawing on and deviating from the movement, supporting the poet's philosophy without being wholly defined by it. Yet, like the vesica piscis formed when two circles overlap, they also intersect at pivotal turning points where Senghor's vision either diverges from or reinterprets Negritude. At these junctures, the poet-president charts his own course, informed, yet not constrained, by the movement's trajectory. In this introduction, I aim to pinpoint four moments of divergence and convergence, or turning points. The first turn, occurring in 1935, marks the birth of two entities: a new French word, *Négritude*, and a new Francophone thought, embodied by Senghor. This period witnessed a fascinating divergence: As Senghor began to shift his focus from poetry toward politics, Negritude moved in the opposite direction, from political discourse toward poetic expression. While the movement sought to articulate the power of racial identity through poetic writing, the poet embarked on a journey to theorize the political implications of *métissage*: a process not so much akin to mixing (mestizo, from the Latin *mixtus*) as it is to *weaving* (*tissage*, from the Latin *textere*) racial and cultural threads: a "mixthreading" that preserves each thread while forming an organized whole.

In the years leading up to the next turning point, Senghor's journey unfolded alongside a Negritude still searching for its identity—a process that reached a significant milestone in 1948, our second turning point. The year marks a pivotal moment when Senghor's path fully converged with Negritude as the movement became the voice of the *Anthologie de la nouvelle poésie negre et malgache de langue française*. Much like our present collection, the *Anthology* demands a comprehensive reading of both its preface and essays. It charts a decolonial trajectory toward sustainable independence—not merely independence in name, but a process liberated from the ideological and epistemic violence of colonialism. However, the turning point extends beyond this literary milestone. That year, Senghor advanced his vision of decolonization and cultural renaissance by establishing the Bloc Democratique Sénégalais (BDS, Senegalese democratic bloc), a political party, and *La Condition Humaine*, a journal bridging philosophy and poetry. Over the subsequent twelve years, Senghor and Negritude jointly confronted the challenges of subalternity, each leveraging the other's name and ideas to articulate a newfound agency for peoples marching toward freedom. The year 1960 stands as a symbolic milestone for freedom and marks the third turn in Senghor's intellectual journey. His ascension to the presidency might seem a departure from poetry and philosophy. Yet it is at this apex of political power that Senghor reappropriated Negritude, liberating it from racial philosophy and steering it back toward its linguistic roots. This reimagining set the stage for Negritude's evolution into Francophonie over the following two decades, a process that unfolded alongside what Souleymane Bachir Diagne aptly terms "state poïesis."[9] This evolution reached its culmination in 1981 when Senghor resigned from the presidency. This moment, far from signaling a retreat, represents our fourth turning point. Liberated from the immediate demands of state governance, Senghor fully embraced his philosopher-king aura. Building on his political experience, he now articulated a vision that transcended national boundaries, reimagining the postcolonial world through the lens of shared linguistic and cultural heritage: Francophonie. In Senghor's hands, the institution became more than a mere celebration of the French language; it evolved into a comprehensive philosophy of cultural exchange. This period saw Senghor grappling with the challenge he had long foreseen: how to forge a cultural identity that respects diversity while fostering cooperation among nations with shared colonial histories. His approach to Francophonie echoed the earlier development of Negritude, but with a crucial difference. While Negritude emerged as a tool of cultural assertion against colonial dominance, Francophonie became Senghor's instrument for building bridges in a postcolonial world. Just as Negritude emerged in French at the twilight of the empire, Francophonie represented a poetic return to the challenge of national language in forging transnational politics.

1935: Senghor Before Negritude

Christopher Miller's groundbreaking article revealed that the word *Négritude* first appeared not in Aimé Césaire's *Journal of a Homecoming* in 1939 but in his much shorter 1935 article in *L'Étudiant Noir*, "Nègreries: Jeunesse noire et assimilation" (Negronesses: Black youth and assimilation). This earlier appearance substantiates the political framing of a nascent Negritude, easily eclipsed by its poetic quest for a mythical origin.[10] According to Miller, there is a troubling comfort in inscribing Negritude within a poetic tradition that Aimé Césaire inaugurates, which addressed race without racism, a comfort that obscures the movement's emergence as a rallying cry for political action. But where Césaire frames the nascent concept with Marxist terminology, reading race through the lens of class and critiquing systemic structures of racial oppression, Senghor rejects using race as a colonial construct meant to systematize racism. Instead, Senghor attempts to move beyond entrenched binaries: reason and intuition, mind and soul, Black and White. In short, Aimé Césaire's Negritude emphasized a political stance rooted in Marxist theory, while Senghor's humanist approach sought to transcend racial binaries. Senghor's humanism presents a challenging counterpoint to current trends in Afro-pessimist thought and works emerging from diasporic geographies, like Sylvia Wynter's *After Man, Towards the Human*. While these approaches emphasize the enduring impact of systemic racisms and the limitations of traditional humanism, calling for the undoing (rather than mere replacement) of Eurocentric definitions of what it means to be human, Senghor challenges us to achieve horizontal solidarity through *métissage*. While his approach may appear idealistic in our current climate of renewed racial tensions and identity politics, it underscores the importance of reconsidering the fluidity and complexity of identity formation beyond rigid racial categories: of finding unity in diversity.

This perspective on fluid racial identity is evident even in Senghor's earliest writing. In his first-known publication, in the January edition of *L'Étudiant Noir*, "Humanism and Us: René Maran" (an essay meant to complement Jane Nardal's anticipated yet unprinted article, "For a Black Humanism"), he suggests, with the pronoun "us," the existence of a collective whose identity calls for a third option.[11] In the article, the figure of the métis subject opens the unverifiability of the experience of Blackness: "I am not a purebred Negro. Beautiful discovery! According to ethnologists, there is no more than 25 percent purebred Negroes in Africa. The remaining 75 believe themselves to be Negroes, and they are right. As a métis stated: 'Being a Negro is a psychological business, more than blood purity.'"[12]

Senghor's rejection of perceived scientific validity of ethnography in favor of the psychological subjectivity of *métissage* is not without political implications: How can individual experiences coalesce to form a collective, a people? Who is the *we*?

Unlike Plato's *kallipolis*, where governance is entrusted to political leaders trained in philosophical practice to determine the future of the state, Senghor turns to the formation of a collective from whom such governance—indeed a people—emanates. Not unlike Plato, Senghor shuns political action as the remedy for a life that the former wants just and the latter desires free, and in 1937, he swiftly declines an offer from the new governor general of French West

Africa, Marcel de Coppet, to become inspector general of education. That summer, the young graduate was invited to participate in the International Congress on the Cultural Evolution of Colonial Peoples in Dakar. Not missing the chance to go back home, Senghor accepted and gave an unexpectedly radical lecture on the necessity of indigenous knowledge for selfhood—a precondition for future self-determination. Titled "The Problem of Culture in French West Africa," the lecture focused not on colonized subjects but on the false premise upon which colonizers sought to educate them. The French aimed to select and groom some colonized men, like Senghor, in all French matters, preparing them to join a French collective—a romanticized idea that falsely promised acceptance on equal terms.[13] Yet, Senghor warned, shaped by decades of colonization and centuries of forced cooperation, colonized peoples had become essentially "bicephalous," a description that reappropriates W. E. B. Du Bois's "Double Consciousness." Du Bois articulated this as a space of psychosocial conflict and alienation experienced by African Americans. Senghor, however, envisioned it as potential for politico-cultural integration that would lead to a renewed social construction. While Du Bois emphasized the inner conflict resulting from forced dual identities, Senghor sought a *métissage* that willfully comprehended and interacted with the world through both colonized and indigenous knowledge. This perspective is further explored in Senghor's 1971 speech "The Problematics of Negritude," translated here, in which Senghor acknowledges Du Bois as yet another one of Negritude's forefathers, furthering the movement's Afro-American intellectual lineage. In 1937, the problem was not that the colonized had no culture, but that they had two: intertwined, complicit, and inseparable. The challenge was to find the conditions under which a bicephalic culture might coexist without overpowering or destroying its host. "*Survival* necessitates adaptation—indeed, *assimilation*. We cannot evade it. Our milieu is no longer just West African, it is also French. It is international. In short, it is Afro-French" (page 4). Still, Senghor's proposed educational path remained dichotomous and Eurocentric: "Scientific works, among others, would be written in French. Literary forms that express the racial spirit—poetry, theater, folklore—would be written in one's native language" (page 9).

Addressing a large gathering that included influential colonial administrators and many prospective decolonized constituents, Senghor did not foresee political independence.[14] Beneath a skillful political performance that sought not to burn bridges with French administrators while addressing the hopes of an African polity that viewed him as a prodigal son, Senghor hinted at a politics transcending mere empiricism. In a text that was to become the opening piece in the series *Liberté*, he laid the groundwork for racial reconstruction from which a political collective could be formed. Simply put, before Negritude, Senghor did not seek to retrieve an authentic Negro selfhood from ancestral roots. Instead, self-introspection through bilingual memories served a political project: to overcome the false dichotomy between a return to authenticity and a dilution into globality.[15] In so doing, Senghor stands out as one of the first intellectuals to view this bilingual and bicultural experience not as a legacy of colonial epistemic violence to be undone but as a means of resistance to be cultivated. He eventually conceptualized this idea under a theory of *métissage* to build the foundation of a decolonized people.[16]

While racial and territorial threads form the core of individualized identities, they seldom define the collective. "Race is a reality; racial purity is not" (page 3), Senghor asserts shortly after translating a Wolof proverb into French. As Ben Conisbee Baer notes, Senghor's needle-threading constitutes one of the most forceful hints at the formation of a French citizenship "detached from the requirements of cultural identity."[17] But for children to become the citizens of the future polity, they must "little by little . . . grow the circle of the universe around them, where they will act, tomorrow, as men" (page 4). This vision aligns with what I have called *peri-racialism*, a framework that shapes the structures influencing the spaces, narratives, and discourses wherein race occupies a central role, yet more powerful than explicit racial declarations. At the inception of his intellectual journey, Senghor sought a path to bring Blackness from the margins while aiming to decouple the center-periphery binary, carving a path that would be neither color-blind nor racialist. Over time, Negritude emerged as one such path: "ever larger concentric circles staggered upon one another, entangled with one another," ending politically with "a federation or an empire."[18]

Senghor's world was profoundly marked by his experiences of Eurocentrism before and during World War II, leading him to literary portrayals of a post-imperial worldly vision elaborated throughout and after the war.[19] Contrary to many of his Caribbean counterparts, including Aimé Césaire and Paulette Nardal—who returned to Martinique in 1941 to cultivate a distinct politics of resistance against Nazi Germany and the Vichy Regime while researching and writing about their local environment in *Tropiques*—Senghor stayed in Paris throughout the war years. There he engaged with fellow Africans brought together by his compatriots Alioune Diop and Ousmane Socé Diop as well as French administrators Georges Pompidou and Robert Delavignette.[20] By 1945, Senghor had become adept at navigating this complex dual existence, his insights shaped by this intricate dance between two worlds.[21] *Hosties Noires*, written concurrently with *Chants d'ombre* (though published three years later), thus refuses to choose between sacrifice and victimization, vindication and abstraction, loyalty and betrayal. In a sense, Senghor's new theory of *métissage* as mixthreading in the postwar period is a symptom of the refusal to choose between two poles productively intertwined in a nascent postcoloniality: aesthetics and politics. Ultimately, Senghor's political vindication of federalism as a sustainable pathway out of imperialism rises from his negotiations between self-rule and shared rule, racial identity and political responsibility—the former two hitherto investigated in literary writing. They find roots in the imagination of a postwar society where race and politics function as two converging circles unswervingly merging toward a unified ideal. Fortuitously, Senghor ascended to a role in the French Constituent Assembly, formally commencing his political career on October 21, 1945, as one of two (SFIO, French Section of the Workers' International) congressmen from Senegal. It would not be long before the two circles formed one.

1948: Becoming Senghor

Today, the annals of literary history earmark the year 1948 with the publication of Senghor's *Anthologie de la nouvelle poésie nègre et malgache de langue française*, with "Orphée Noir" (Black Orpheus), its (in)famous preface by Jean-Paul Sartre.[22] More often analyzed through Sartre's preface than Senghor's anthologizing, it is easy to miss the journey from West to East that the poet undertakes: from Guyana to Haiti, then Black Africa, ending in Madagascar. The poetic reversal of the Middle Passage timely commemorates the centennial anniversary of slavery abolition and the decree, "signed the same day," which established a free and mandatory education in the colonies.[23]

Beneath the poetic enterprise, politics seeps through every page carefully selected by the poet. Calls to "set ablaze my bloody lips," to "burn every flower and all my vain ideas" in the poem "Hurricane" go beyond just the desire to reiterate the burning of poetry hitherto written in French.[24] It fosters a connection with the legacy of the political revolution of 1848 that, Senghor tells us in his introduction, "has been more fruitful than we think." Since that revolution aimed to dismantle old monarchical structures to pave the way for sovereign nation-states, it is safe to say that in 1948, the anthology is indistinguishably poetically and politically motivated.

It is to Sartre's credit that he laid bare the relation between racial oppression and economic exploitation. But Sartre soon races through a step Senghor is not ready to make: the definition of a constituted collective—of Africans on the continent and the Black diaspora united against colonial oppression—which can be integrated into another collective, that is, workers united by class consciousness against capitalist exploitation. Indeed, in the twelve years between the *Anthology* and the moment of independence, the poet's imaginative energy turns to the political question par excellence: Who is the *we* that constitutes a people?

Though poetic writing made him aware of the nuance between individual and collective identity, the *we* he is called to represent in his political duties remains an ambiguously defined entity. Senghor finds himself caught between a desire to vindicate African voices and a proclivity not to racialize political agency. The tension is palpable in a piece written for *Réveil* in 1947, where the "tyranny of international capitalism" is denounced as the culprit for the racial discrimination and political shortcomings of the Fourth Republic constitution.[25] While articulating a vision for reconciliation between "European socialism and African collectivism," "modern techniques and African humanism," the goal remains to build a world "without distinction of race or religion." Senghor's impasse, which is symptomatic of what Jacques Derrida has termed "aporias," finds an opening in Marx's newly compiled and translated into French *Economic and Philosophical Manuscripts*, which the poet-congressman reads in the library of the French National Assembly and reflects upon in "Marxism and Humanism," here translated for the first time into English:[26] "For us, men of 1947, men of the aftermath of the two wars who narrowly escaped the bloody contempt of past dictators only to face the looming shadows of new dictatorships, what profit could we gain of those early works" (page 33). In these pages where Marx develops a critique of capitalism based on an analysis of the alienation of human labor through wage labor, he finds the material to reframe the question steering him toward independence: What are the conditions under which self-determination can be achieved? "Only in community with others, each individual has the means to cultivate his faculties in all directions," Senghor paraphrases from *The German Ideology*, and "only in the community, therefore, is personal freedom possible" (page 44). The role of community building in the development of individual capacities is exactly not Sartre's vindication of an immanent formation of a world proletariat. Workers' struggle may be universal, not their working conditions. The reading of Marx's early works reveals to Senghor the existence of a "reciprocal action" between material conditions, whose transformation falls to economic and political actions, and imaginative performance, whose empowerment falls to poetic and philosophical training. Thus, self-determination is the task of both the poet-philosopher and the politician: the former to imagine the community and the latter to forge a polity from which a people can emerge.

In February 1948, Senghor creates *La Condition Humaine* (The human condition), a journal whose title echoes Malraux's 1933 eponymous novel about the failed communist insurrection in Shanghai in 1927.[27] There, readers often encounter extended excerpts of "Negro-African" poetry, conveniently sourced from the *Anthology*, juxtaposed against political pamphlets.[28] A testament to Senghor's efforts to wield poetic creativity to amplify a shared experience of Blackness, the journal steers it toward a communal consciousness of West African workers' socioeconomic realities, like those in the Dakar-Niger Railway strike captured in Ousmane Sembène's *Les bouts de bois de Dieu* (*God's Bits of Wood*). Despite the strike's resolution in March 1948, Congressman Senghor had a front-row seat for the SFIO officials' refusal to engage with worker representatives, ongoing tribal politics, nepotism, and neglect of African interests. In a poignant letter penned to the party's secretary on September 27, 1948, Senghor expressed his disillusionment: "The Party is no longer, in Black Africa, structurally democratic or actively socialist. . . . It has sacrificed Marxist ethics and socialist practice to political tactics. . . . In the face of such deceit, I cannot but leave."[29] The BDS was created one month later. Influenced by Marx's late "Letter to Zassulitch," which suggested that the conclusions in *Capital* were valid only for Western Europe, Senghor set forth an "African Road to Socialism" that might bypass or mitigate the phases of capitalism.[30] Yet one thing is sure, he noted in his inaugural address to the BDS: "The consciousness of a world proletariat is not yet alive in our minds."[31]

Senghor's vocal antinationalism and the rise of Negritude throughout the decade both stemmed from the vision of a transnational solidarity that preserves the "original personality of each people."[32] His committed work for the Council of Europe at that time was driven by a parallel yet contrasting antinationalist goal where race is both medicine and poison.[33] Nominated to the United Nations Trusteeship Council in 1950, Senghor traveled to New York for the first time to urge the international organization to tame national sovereignty and empower local assemblies.[34] As he roamed the streets of Harlem, he could not but reflect proudly on a distinctive Negro American poetry: the Negro spirituals. Listen to "God's trombones" (page 53), wrote Senghor, alluding to James Weldon Johnson's eponymous collection of inspirational sermons by African American preachers reimagined as poetry. Yes, through centuries of physical and epistemic violence, "Black slaves had largely forgotten African languages and, to a smaller extent, African folklore," but they also "fertilized folklore even as some deep-rooted connections tethered it to their ancestral traditions" (page 48). Reading "Judgement Day" in a lecture whose exact details remain conspicuously undisclosed, the audience was urged to look past material conditions and seek something akin to divine mysticism.[35] "Negro imagination unfolds there" (page 52), Senghor wrote. Yet to read the poem for its content is to take the shadow for the prey. Undoubtedly, there is in the poetry of Johnson, as well as that of Langston Hughes, Countee Cullen, and Claude McKay, a racial affirmation of Blackness through an evocation of African folklore—and its transformation. After all, the "discourse surrounding Race inevitably intertwines with the discourse surrounding Africa" (page 62). But if, "rightfully so, Claude McKay can be considered the true inventor of Négritude" (page 58), it is because his poetry "rarely and discreetly evokes Africa"—and when it does, it is as a land marred by "destitution and savagery." Not unlike Sartre's, McKay's Negritude connects the racial struggle with the class struggle of the proletariat against capitalist exploitation. "In recent years," Senghor writes in the concluding paragraphs of the text, "Negro-American poetry has endeavored to overcome the discourse surrounding race, through union with God—or the proletariat" (page 63). Back home, it would become necessary to create the conditions under which a racial consciousness surrounded by political representation and economic potential would not just survive but thrive. Between 1948 and 1956, new electoral regulations enabled the BDS to clinch more victories in federalwide polls, each new seat amplifying new voices (some inspired by the Muslim brotherhoods), each shifting the balance from city to country.[36] Soon, Senghor was faced with the task of uniting them. Far from assuming a preexisting unity, the future poet-president drew from the rich history of African oral traditions, which he discovered then, to raise a postcolonial consciousness that was not yet racial but collectively already more than purely political. Indeed, "since Blacks are oppressed in their race and because of it, it is of their race that a consciousness must arise," Senghor repeated.[37] If Africans sought more autonomy, politics and economics alone would not be enough: Racial agency would have to play a central role, on both sides of the Atlantic and the Mediterranean.

The negotiated convergence of race and politics—consciousness of a distinctive racial personality and awareness of a shared political agency—intensified throughout the decade. In a book ardently promoting a single French citizenship for all members of the French Union, Doudou Thiam, future minister of foreign affairs of Senegal, depicts it as a "tendency," a "movement" toward an elusive "convergence between two humanities."[38] This stance, upheld by figures like Mamadou Dia, transcends a mere colonized desire to remain within the "French orbit" and contributes to Senghor's "federal solution"—a project whose seminal blueprint is translated here for the first time. It mirrors the growing incapacity to secure economic participation, contributions, and reparations from France—a feat the overseas legislators tirelessly advocated for—coupled with a simultaneous forging of the ideological framework of a peri-racial society: one not defined by race or embodying racial identity but operating in an adaptive agency where core racial realities would influence and be influenced by surrounding factors (political, economic, environmental, etc.).

In "For a Federalist Solution," published in 1955 in *La Nef,* the congressman warns that "member states have grown disdainful of the epithet."[39] Though both Dia and Senghor respectively argue in the pages of *La Condition Humaine* that there may not be a "real alternative to federalism," that "it would be pure folly for the territories to constitute themselves in so-called independent nations," the problem to which federalism is the solution is not the political system: It is the polity. Indeed, no "French" polity can be sustained, be it national or federal, for "the word has become a symbol of domination." The problem is not just, not even primarily, political. "The overseas territories, specifically those in Black Africa . . . share a natural connection through ethnic, geographical, and development factors" (page 69). If "African nationalism is willing to forgo the nation, not the African fatherland" (page 73), Africans may be able to forgo the colonial legacy of the nation-state altogether. Senghor's vision extends beyond political structures to encompass cultural production as a means of fostering collective consciousness undefined by national boundaries alone.

In two pieces published in *La Condition Humaine* concurrently with the article in *La Nef,* "Laye Camara and Lamine Dialhaté, for Art Is Not Partisan" and "Laye Camara and Lamine Niang, for Art Must Be Incarnate," Senghor thus promotes an aesthetic creativity that draws from the African oral tradition to foster a collective consciousness indispensable to and yet independent of the experience of a shared identity. This decolonizing project aims to infuse aesthetic creativity in political construction—an ideological effort Terry Eagleton describes as the "equivalent in the mental realm of the overthrow of priest and king in the political one."[40] Inspired by Marx's *German Ideology,* the poet-congressman sets his political agenda to transform the socioeconomic conditions (e.g., wages, pensions, equal pay, etc.) of the West Africans he represents in the French National Assembly against the backdrop of the transformation of a cultural production (e.g., poetry, novels, music, etc.) not just reflective of its society but a force capable of molding it. Focusing on one without the other cannot succeed. Concluding that the real transformation is not political and economic but lies in "the conscious awakening of the men that are here" (page 75), the "federalist solution" presents only one part of the necessary changes on the road to independence. "Like the Manatees Go Drink at the Source" would stage the other.

On the board of *Présence Africaine,* Senghor hastened the production of an African corpus. In 1955, no less than three prefaces introducing collections of

West African tales, Mongo poetry, and Malagasy epic were published by the journal.[41] But as Senghor worked to develop a literary corpus that would qualify as African, significant political changes were unfolding across the continent. On the political front, New Year's Day set the tone: Sudan, the largest state of Africa with one million inhabitants, attained independence. In March 1956, France withdrew its protectorate over Morocco and Tunisia, acknowledging their freedom from French rule. Yet the Algerian war intensified, and Senghor, along with 146 other congressmen, voted in favor of a French peacekeeping intervention.[42] His vocal opposition to policies that might undermine the integrity of the French Union, however, was not a symptom of his sentimental or colonial attachment to France. It was a far-sighted warning of a postimperial governance structure that could hinder West African integration. At the core of Senghor's vindication of a thread connecting metropole and overseas territories is a Marxian premise that to enact a sustainable change in material conditions and relations of production, what is needed is the expropriation of old means of ideological production, which *métissage* enables.[43] If Frederick Cooper has shown that French politicians did not seek to "carve up French West Africa so as to keep its territories poor and weak," the genius of Senghor lies in foreseeing that the most significant and long-lasting lever of autonomy transcends politics: It is ideological.[44]

The commitment to an ideological reorientation necessary to secure the sustainability of any future autonomous governance—not to mention independence—came to the fore at the First World Congress of Black Writers and Artists, organized by Alioune Diop under the patronage of *Présence Africaine* and heralded as a cultural counterpart to the more political Bandung Conference held just one year earlier. Taking place at the symbolically significant Descartes amphitheater of the Sorbonne from September 19 to 22, 1956, the event marked a desire to affirm the existence of a collective consciousness shared by all Black peoples throughout the world, independent of colonial history. Although Malagasy writer Jacques Rabemananjara assured his listeners that the organizing committee deliberately omitted "the truly political aspect of the problem," Alioune Diop counterpointed that one frequently overlooks "the natural link between the cultural and the political," a separation that often leads to a "crisis of consciousness."[45] Ostensibly, Senghor's lecture, "Spirit of Civilization or the Laws of Negro-African Culture," sought to theorize an objective cultural creativity among African peoples that the hyphenated and singular "Negro-African Culture" represents.[46] Yet in the unscripted discussions that occurred in the private Q&A following the speakers' presentations, the poet-congressman went beyond dubious generalizations on Negro-African arts and into a politically motivated artistic creativity as "prerequisite to overcoming our alienation."[47] This led him to further articulate the quandary at the core of Black emancipation: Neither a transnational solidarity constructed as a metonym for anticolonial struggle nor a nationalist freedom built on colonized politics would lead to a sustainable independence.[48] Senghor's approach to resolving this dilemma was unconventional and, to some, controversial. His desire to remain "within the French orbit" originated from his conviction that politics and economics alone could not address the core challenge of enhancing a collective's productive capacity in the postcolonial era. He believed in fostering "a true culture [that was] always [a] deracinalizing, active assimilation of foreign values," rejecting notions of an irreducible, racially homogeneous Blackness, through the political and linguistic practice of *métissage*.[49] Here, the concept of deracinalization stems from the Wolof phrase *Génn xeet*—literally, "to get out of one's race/ethnic group"—rather than the French word *racine* meaning "root." This linguistic nuance informed Senghor's (mis)translation of Claude McKay's "getting down to our native roots" as *"plonger jusqu'aux racines de notre race"* in *Banjo* as the concluding sentence of "The Problem of Culture in French West Africa." This nuanced understanding of the relation between race and root informed Senghor's broader views on racial identity and cultural politics. He cautioned against reducing racial identity and culture to a narrow politics of identity. While he acknowledged the importance of resisting epistemic violence, he warned that this approach risked leading to aesthetic insularity and political nationalism. It was this risk of racial essentialism and ethnic balkanization—a neologism he coined then—that led him to caution against policies that would "artificially divide territories into political, economic, and cultural entities that do not ignore the metropole but do ignore each other" (page 88). This did not negate the role of politics and economics or overlook the "social, economic, and even military frailties" of the colonies. It highlighted the need to aesthetically craft a renewed collective consciousness called Negritude, "rediscovered" from a repository clouded by centuries of epistemological violence.[50]

As Senghor noted in 1956, "the example stems from Europe where, in the nineteenth century, the nations on the continent, stirred by France, endeavored to become nations. They made themselves historians, archaeologists, philologists, ethnographers, to resuscitate their past and discover national virtues."[51] Arguably, "Balkanization or Federation," published in *Afrique nouvelle* in December 1956, is Senghor's blueprint for a political integration with France. But to prevent balkanization from eliminating the possibility of a shared historiography necessary to the formation of a collective, federalism alone is only a political answer.

To produce and then to sustain the collective, an aesthetic project is needed. This project, composed between 1948 and 1954, is *Éthiopiques.*[52]

Published in 1956, the compendium is concerned with the problem of representation, focusing not on the political but the cultural kind. Its postface, "Like the Manatees Go Drink at the Source," aims to radically alter recognizability and subvert the tradition of representation of words and images that perpetuates colonial epistemology and hinders self-determination.[53] How could it not, Senghor writes, for "after centuries of rationalism," what used to be a "transparent veil [is now] a wall" (page 80). Often analyzed for its elaboration of rhythm in Negro-African poetry, the postface exhorts a practice of naming to address the deeply ingrained epistemic violence in the process of world making. Simply put, naming—or renaming—is an essential step toward self-determination. Still, it would be a mistake to view the issue just as a matter of language. The postface calls for a new poetics, an ars poetica that aims to theorize a newly written and self-named Negro-African poetry.[54] "Our aspiration is humble: to pioneer, to pave the way for an authentic Negro poetry that does not foreclose being French" (page 84). If the "we" precedes and is simultaneously created by the process, it is because, as the title suggests, Negro-African poets will sustain independence by going toward—not returning to—an unspoiled source. Eventually, this "authentic Negro poetry" might as well be foreign to Wolof and French speakers. Consider the first verse of "Man and the Beast" that opens the compendium: "I name you Evening, / O ambiguous Evening, / fluttering leaf I name you."[55] This verse both names and is confounded by the act of naming. In "Kaya-Magan," the king's name changes in almost every verse, remaining elusive, while the poet ambiguously describes himself as "Prince of the North of South," "of rising-sun and setting-sun Prince," "both sides of a double door," and "tom-tom movement" that "commands future Africa." (Re)naming, then, is not merely a linguistic return but a political act for constituting a new polity by historically situated subjects whose emerging agency requires the continuous articulation of a new lexicon. As Jacques Chevrier notes, Senghor's (re) namings in the poems of *Éthiopiques* draw from Latin syntax (characterized by frequent inversions), Old French (incorporating archaic words), and African languages (with a translation glossary).[56] This nuanced articulation of multilingual representation echoing the past while allowing for future evolution, "*around which* the figure of the poem is organized," becomes a cornerstone in the formulation of Negritude.

The imminent political demise of French colonialism, alongside its desperate fight to retain power, and the resurgence of African aesthetics, arguably more vibrant in Europe and America than on the continent itself, temporarily challenged Senghor's universal aspirations. In 1957, reflecting the continental reality of decolonization, the journal *Condition Humaine* gave way to a publication better suited to the task ahead: *L'Unité Africaine.* Addressing prospective independent citizens and party members, Senghor continually warned against balkanization as a territorial fragmentation that could not rely on an innate collective consciousness for reconstruction.[57] Writing for a different audience in *Le Monde*, Senghor extolled an "autonomy of thought" and a "decolonization of the minds" related to yet independent from the political independence of Africa.[58]

Senghor's urgency to train the minds of future African citizens, embracing a novel form of transnational solidarity as a precursor to sustainable independence, is evident in both his policy recommendations to the National Assembly and in his philosophical discussions on African socialism. Olúfémi O. Táíwò thus notes that decolonization was "a matter of making a colony into a self-governing entity with its political and economic fortunes under its own direction (though not necessarily control)," a fact demonstrated by Senghor's interventions in the National Assembly, where he backed addressing economic disparities and illiteracy through political means.[59] Yet he harbored a deeper concern: that independence not grounded in, or aligned with, a decolonized ideological framework would ultimately prove unsustainable.

The alternation between political and aesthetic speeches and essays in this translation aims to bring this negotiation to the fore of ongoing debates about decolonization, the process of decolonizing, and their own different goals. There is perhaps no better illustration of the difficult negotiation faced by intellectual leaders like Senghor than the context of General de Gaulle's 1958 constitutional referendum.[60] While Sékou Touré's Guinea is often cited as an isolated, almost aberrant response to the West African decolonization, this seemingly unwavering position obscures the fact that most intellectual leaders struggled with endorsing the yes vote. Just a few weeks before the vote on September 28, 1958, de Gaulle traveled to Senegal, where the conspicuous absence of both Léopold Sédar Senghor and Mamadou Dia—the former engaged with "urgent family business" in Normandy, the latter in Switzerland for "medical treatment"—conveyed their refusal to succumb to a false dichotomy between colonial subordination and immediate independence, leaving the relatively low-ranked minister of the interior, Valdiodio Ndiaye, to oversee the presidential reception.

How could a no vote, leading to immediate independence, not exacerbate the political fragmentation or balkanization unless it were a part of a concerted effort?[61] Conversely, how could a yes vote not perpetuate delays in crafting policies steering the territories away from French rule—whether via an African federation, confederation, or union?[62] Denouncing the "nationalist virus" in an article for *Les Cahiers de la République*, Senghor substantiated his endorsement of the *yes* with more than just political arguments. One might lament the somewhat poetic justification of "friendship," "honesty," or "loyalty" or find hints of regrets interspersed throughout the text.[63] Yet he anchored his choice in Articles 76 and 86 of the constitution's text, which envisioned more than mere prospects of independence. By requiring that a "community member" aspiring to change their status "manifest a will" validated through a "local referendum," the process underscored a political objective grounded in fostering a cohesive Black collective—not undermining it. This rationale informed Senghor's ultimate justification for endorsing the yes vote, guided not merely by political expediency but by a will to foster African unity through a collective practice moving "freedom from" to "freedom to." Negritude is the attempt to make that move.

It should not escape us that Negritude was shaped by the dynamic relation between aesthetics and politics during this decade, more than it was by the *Anthology*. Indeed, Senghor eventually defined Negritude as "the sum of cultural values of the Black world" less than a year later, at the Second Congress of Black Artists and Writers, in Rome, on April 25, 1959.[64] As the decade turned, the movement faced the emerging realities of new nation-states stepping into political sovereignty. Far from meeting an ossifying death, it morphed in real time, becoming more institutionalized than essentialized. Under Senghor's presidency, it began to shape the national narrative, catalyzing a generation of engaged intellectuals like Ousmane Sembène, who challenged Negritude's boundaries. It also entered a new domain of national sovereignty: foreign policy. The diplomatic arena revitalized Negritude, ushering in a new chapter many had prematurely written off. The organization of the 1966 First World Festival of Negro Arts, creation of the Organisation Internationale de la Francophonie in 1970, and staging of the Négritude Colloquium of 1971, along with their politico-aesthetic inception and aftermath, embodied by texts such as "The Fodébo Keita African Ballet" and "For a Senegalese Tapestry," provided Senghor with ideological pivots to transform the spirit of unity, identity, and racialism that had been a cornerstone of the movement's early years. I have translated these texts here for the first time. In them, we see how the strategies Senghor adopted as the poet-turned-president were not merely political maneuvers but, in keeping with those of Socrates's philosopher-king, were rooted in an ideological ground prepared by years of poetic training. These texts are clear examples of how Senghor integrated his poetic sensibilities into his politics, infusing Negritude into burgeoning domestic policies and international relations, reinventing the birth of a nation claiming its historical determination.

1960: Poet-President

The Year of Africa, 1960, which saw seventeen African nations win their independence, stands out as one of the greatest historical shifts in the modern world, a landmark in anticolonial politics. Yet commemorating decolonization with a single year fails to capture the culmination of decades, if not centuries, of struggle and the full geopolitical and historical magnitude of the event, including the lingering consequences of centuries of exploitation and underdevelopment. Symptomatic of the inadequate metonym that 1960 represents, Senghor's election to the highest office in Senegal was an extended process that both preceded and followed that pivotal year.

To understand the complex realities surrounding the symbolic year, let us look at the extended process around Senghor's election, which began in 1959. Then, 302 years after the French set foot in a place they named Fort Saint Louis, the leaders of the future Mali Federation drew upon Articles 76 and 86 of the Constitution of the Fifth Republic to chart the federation's course to independence and fulfill Senghor's long-standing vision for a federated polity.[65] During a meeting with de Gaulle on November 27, Senghor recounted the general's personal advice to "build a strong state"—advice whose repercussions would resonate beyond the Year of Africa.[66] On April 4, 1960, a "transfer of competence" was ratified by Michel Debré, Mamadou Dia, and Modibo Keita, leading to the proclamation of independence on June 20. Tensions soon emerged, however, and just two months later, Senegalese leaders Mamadou Dia and Léopold Sédar Senghor denounced what they perceived as a coup by Modibo Keita, breaking up the Mali Federation, triggering a state of emergency that would last for the next two years. Senghor was sworn in as president of the Republic of Senegal on September 5, 1960.

Less than a year after his presidential inauguration, Senghor, addressing the governor general of Nigeria, acknowledged that "national independence [was] not an end" (page 98). As though the federal idea from which independence politically rose was now itself also in question, the text was reprinted in 1963 with the title "From Federation to the Civilization of the Universal." Was national sovereignty merely a stepping stone, "an uncharted territory we must survey" to facilitate a progression from a federative to a universal polity? Or could it serve as a foundation of a new kind of entity—one that neither dismisses nor depends entirely on traditional political structures?

These questions, which the translated texts in this collection compel us to reconsider, point to the agenda Senghor grappled with in his transition to poet-president: a modern philosopher-king whose raison d'être was to shape a social community into a willed political entity. The hyphen between *poet* and *president* aptly presents Senghor's unique position. His poetic identity allowed him to navigate the political landscape with cultural authority while his responsibilities as president were balanced by his poetic work operating beyond just the political realm. Recall that Plato's leader yielded "no ruling, law, or political authority in the usual sense," for the goal was to exceed the political project and retrieve the possibility of justice. What would happen if we were to rethink Negritude as a broader ethos akin to Plato's *dikē*—justice—led by its philosopher-king Senghor? It would reveal its vital role in postcolonial self-governance and elucidate a twofold necessity: the need for aesthetic practice in fostering a political cohesion that did not rely only on repressive apparatuses, and the importance of political practice in shaping aesthetic representation pointing toward something more than just a romanticized idea of Blackness. Because no independence can sustain itself indefinitely, this dynamic relationship between aesthetics and politics required constant adaptation, creating a feedback loop where political actions inspired new aesthetic interpretations, which in turn influenced political strategies.

The constant reimagination and recalibration of Negritude that are symptomatic of postindependence texts such as "Négritude Is a Humanism" and "The Problematics of Négritude" exposed the limits of the movement. Its foundational vision, "the sum of cultural values of the Black world," reconnecting continent and diaspora via a dreamed United States of Africa as is evident in "Culture, Development, Cooperation," soon faced "too many fact-based obstacles that [would] prevent their realization for quite some time: cold war, as well as racial, linguistic, and cultural differences."[67]

By 1962, ethnic and religious tensions within Senegal, coupled with broader geopolitical challenges, led to two significant policy shifts, casting a shadow on the promise of transnational collaboration. One, a ministerial circular by Mamadou Dia dated May 21, granted the state the power to nationalize groundnut production, effectively politicizing the economy to sidestep the divergent interests of ethnic and religious groups—especially the Mouride Brotherhood.[68] The other, a decree signed by Senghor, accused his premier of orchestrating a coup in December and set the stage for a new constitution enhancing presidential power.[69] The political and economic fallout have often obscured that it was that very year, 1962, that Senghor first outlined what eventually became Francophonie in a special issue of *Esprit*—further developed in "Francophonie as Culture" three years later.[70] There, the poet-president did not just introduce a concept he would institutionalize; he also elaborated on what it meant to decolonize when the legacy of colonialism had become so intertwined with indigeneity that distinguishing them became nearly impossible. In many ways, Francophonie, a linguistic *métissage*, a "double symbiosis between theory and experience, discursive reason and intuitive reason" (page 121), is Negritude's offspring.

By 1963, the poet-president could no longer ignore the ideological limits of postcolonial politics. He adopted a two-pronged approach: pursuing economic development contingent on external forces (e.g., environmental disasters, financial crises, monetary devaluation, aid assistance, etc.), and a decolonized imagination fueled by three decades of Negritude aesthetics. In "African Unity," delivered at the Organization of African Unity annual meeting in May and subsequently published in *Liberté 4,* Senghor made a poignant statement that underscores the aspirational nature of Negritude in the postcolonial imagination: "The vitality of our feelings, this passion, which is a hallmark of Africanness . . . was too often approached in a rhetorical manner. It is time to ground it on our *realities*."[71] In the first three years of independence, the poet-president had learned the hard way that a desire expressed in a text, poetic or political, is not to be confused with its fulfillment.

Recognizing these harsh realities, including "fanaticisms (racial, linguistic, religious)," "micro-nationalisms," and the limitations of the "European and American examples," Senghor addressed the Fourth UPS Congress just a few months later (Union Progressiste Sénégalaise, later renamed Parti Socialiste in 1976).[72] There, he denounced a lack of "creative imagination" and "spirit of innovation" without which sustainable independence would remain elusive. To overcome this deficit, Senghor argued, real decolonization required economic independence and intellectual freedom. "Truth be told . . . I should use the word *freedom*, which stands in opposition to the colonized situation and is the faculty to choose our ways. . . . More than political freedom, it is intellectual and spiritual freedom that cultural freedom needs: hearts and minds. In that sense, let's admit it, we are not yet decolonized."[73] Contrary to a literary historical narrative according to which Senghor was consumed by the lofty goals of a derelict Negritude inadequately suited to the economic, social, and political realities of postcoloniality, the poet-president championed economic development, revised the balance of payments, controlled budget planning, and so on. Indeed, *Liberté 4*, which highlights his pragmatic governance, bears the subtitle *Socialism and Planning*. In a policy address delivered on July 12, he extolled a "depoliticization of the masses," urging a shift toward the "primacy of economics" empowering a new decolonized governance: "Habib Thiam [minister of planning and development] will demonstrate, with data, that within a year—from December 1962 to 1963 . . . distortions and deviations from our plan have been largely corrected, and execution efficiency improved."[74] Indeed, the impartial economic metrics were increasingly prioritized over the more abstract notion of the nation-state, whose political unity was beginning to fray, heralding crises in nations like Algeria, Congo, and Nigeria.

With this profound understanding of the challenges ahead, Senghor's remarkable foresight of the coming wave of rebellions and civil wars that would sweep across the continent by the decade's end played a crucial role in helping Senegal remain relatively stable during this turbulent period. Beyond short-term political and economic gains, Senghor was focused on the long-term emancipation of minds. "I must reiterate, we are not yet decolonized," he emphasized.[75] The journey, he asserted, begins with acknowledging that "a well-formulated plan, reflecting our realities, is not enough. To a consciousness of our situation, we must add the *will* to transform it."[76] For that task to succeed—not just to decolonize but to engage in the process of decolonizing— what is needed is not merely a goal but a practice. "We must exercise our creative imagination."[77]

The 1966 First World Festival of Negro Arts emerged as a major showcase for this exercise, becoming a pinnacle of Negritude and a testament to postcolonial self-affirmation. Initiated during the 1959 Second Congress of Black Writers and Artists amid negotiations for independence and actualized after Senegal's constitution revision in March 1963, the event was steeped in political influences. Senghor, reliant on the United States for financial and cultural support, personally intervened in top-level political discussions, meticulously selecting artists and artworks for the Dakar showcase. On one occasion, he tasked Gray Cowan, a professor at Columbia University and eventual president of the African Studies Association, for expertise on "traditional African dances."[78] On another, he directly appealed to President John F. Kennedy to send American jazz artists, specifically requesting Duke Ellington.[79]

Fulfilling a wish expressed in "Ndessé or Blues," a wartime poem where the poet implored Ellington to play "Solitude," Ellington began crafting *Senegalese Suite.* Though the jazzman had never visited Senegal, he aimed to incorporate Senegalese musical motifs but ended up with an unconvincing essentialized representation. He soon altered the musical form from a suite of relatively independent pieces to an elaborate chord progression and titled it in French *La Plus Belle Africaine*, symbolizing a shift from national to continental framing. Ellington's composition became emblematic of the festival's struggle between its aspiration for authentic representation and translating such aspirations into aesthetic creation that could be shared beyond inherited artificial borders. In Dakar, his jazz throbbed with these musical and political tensions. Such, however, was not Ellington's first musico-political negotiation. The US government had, for years, endorsed Black artists for global tours, leveraging their art as a countercommunism weapon with an air of color-blindness and civil rights optimism.[80] Aware of the festival's political undertones, Ellington innocently noted in his journal: "When the time for our concerts come, it is a wonderful success. We get the usual diplomatic applause from the diplomatic corps."[81] Still, the musician challenged the contours of a stage that had in many ways been tailored for him.[82] Ellington's unconventional approach mirrored the need for cultural and political transformation in the face of disillusionment with the realities of independence. Unsurprisingly, the concert's inception was marked more by its initial shock than anticipated familiarity.[83] Just as decolonized nations were grappling with rediscovered identities and renegotiating their places in the world, so too was Ellington pushing the boundaries of what was familiar and expected.

Senghor had anticipated the compounding meeting of music and politics. If the art was to shock, so was Dakar's visual appeal to the festival's guests—to their expectation. In the months leading up to the festival, the poet-president engaged in massive urban development reforms and aspired to transform the medina into a Le Corbusier–like Radiant City—a transformation that led its residents to support the students' uprising and demonstration in the city two years later.[84] At the political cost of antagonizing the Muslim brotherhoods, he cleared the streets of Dakar of beggars and erected walls to hide impoverished neighborhoods.[85] The image strongly recalls the shielding of high-level diplomatic summits more than the openness of popular cultural encounters.[86] As one article in the *New York Times* noted, "For the 10,000 visitors who came to Dakar this month . . . Dakar itself appeared strangely un-African."[87] Both Ellington's music and Senghor's nation were doing exactly what they had been designed to do: Leave an unambiguous print. For the three weeks during which the festival allegedly paused the political life of the nation, at least in Dakar, both its figurehead and its participants presented a curated image of postcolonial Africa through artistic production—an image recently scrutinized by scholars on transnational identity making.[88] The event served as an experiment that, unlike Plato's *kallipolis*, was not confined to mere thoughts. By excluding most Senegalese from its celebration, it relegated art to being a luxury available only to the select few who could attend it—by geographical or financial means. The significant outsourcing of its production raised questions about the political resources needed to craft African aesthetics.

The three essays from 1966 featured in this collection approach such questions from diverse perspectives: Negritude, African art, and Francophonie. "Négritude Is a Humanism," delivered in Beirut in the wake of the festival, begins with an unresolved tension: "Négritude . . . is a rooting in and an affirmation of oneself" (page 105), states Senghor, yet simultaneously expanding it outside of the self and into a collective notion in another language: "It is nothing more than what English-speaking Negro-Africans call *African personality*." The rest of the essay is mired in tensions emphasizing that "to live ethically means to live with naturally opposing yet complementary forces." These tensions, initially perceived as clichés, morph into a political principle facilitating a "decolonization in sub-Saharan Africa . . . with minimal bloodshed and hatred" that "could extend to South Africa, South Rhodesia, and the Portuguese colonies if only the Manichean mind of Albo-Europeans would open to dialogue." The First World Festival of Negro Arts, a point of pride for Senghor, indeed facilitated interactions between African, European, and American artworks and artists, with diplomacy playing a pivotal role. Yet these "apparent contradictions," far from being symptoms of an irreconcilable divide, instead point toward a latent harmony, "*the harmony of a union*" (page 113), that political governance could tap into. Enriched by references to Bergson and Augustine that present him as a philosopher in the most Platonic sense—the one who accesses the "forms," a word he uses more than twenty times—Senghor reveals his objective: to create a harmonious political order through laws, policies, and institutions. Symbolically, the festival's African contemporary art exhibitions were displayed in the old courthouse, requisitioned for the occasion. A sign of things to come, Jean Collin, Senghor's advisor, noted institutional weaknesses in *Dakar Matin* shortly after the festival's conclusion: "Too many public institutions have taken a step back because of their weakness before their client and a concern for clientelism." Clearly, de Gaulle's counsel for a robust state found resonance.

As illustrated in the essay "For a Senegalese Tapestry" (page 128), Senghor also began to lean heavily toward a state-driven patronage of culture. When he inaugurated a state-run factory because "national art requires a nation," the institutionalization of aesthetic creativity was turned toward not artistic but a political realization that Souleymane Bachir Diagne has fittingly termed a "State poïesis."[89] If the manufacture is to decolonize the imagination, it is not for the masses who cannot afford artworks predominantly created for consulates, embassies, museums, and other institutions.[90] As James S. Coleman points out in *Sénégal Carrefour*, an official imprint of Dakar's Ministry of Information and Tourism at the time, the state remains the sole "purchaser of the tapestries used to adorn its many Ministries and Embassies abroad." This practice became further institutionalized when ratified into law on December 19, 1973, metamorphosing the manufacture into a public institution of an "industrial and commercial" character.[91] The new direction aligns with Negritude's foundational ethos: to perpetually recalibrate the play between aesthetic representation and political action, ensuring a postcolonial governance adapting to the necessities of its sustainability.

The rejection of Negritude by intellectuals such as Ousmane Sembène in Senegal, Wole Soyinka in Nigeria, and Stanislas Adotevi in Benin—evident at the 1969 Pan-African Festival in Algiers, where Adotevi famously declared the movement dead—represents the climactic reaction to this misperceived self-betrayal. If Negritude struggled to gather support after independence, it is because it shed, almost by political design, its once-mythical discursive qualities that empowered the Black imagination to think beyond the Eurocentric mythos. Reduced to a mere instrument of Senghor's policymaking, it descended from its pedestal, becoming a casualty of questionable decisions, including economic choices that paved the way for the 1970s—the "decade of decline." Indeed, the establishment and merging of large economic institutions in the late 1960s parallel what the Thiès tapestry factory, the Dynamic Museum, the Daniel Sorano National Theater, and other art and culture institutions did for a decolonized imagination: They ushered in a state patronage as politically potent as it was economically at odds with a world increasingly dominated by, and at the mercy of, unregulated finance capital.

It is in this context that Negritude was mobilized for one last vanishing Senghorian moment: filling the political vacuum left by this increasing technocratic turn. Spurred by political mismanagement, keeping Senegal economically weak and reliant on foreign aid, the turn emerged amid mounting challenges to both state authority and Senghor's leadership, especially as he gravitated toward a one-party system to solidify his philosopher-king dominance. As newly appointed experts turned to technocracy for an antinationalist panacea for African economic problems via neoliberal discourses and global institutional solutions, Negritude morphed into a cornerstone of Senegal's national identity and a tool for transnational construction, promoting development.[92] This time, however, the contradiction became untenable: Nationalism can accommodate transnationalism no more than econometrics can reconcile with aesthetics.

In "Francophonie as Culture," Senghor anchored the emerging institution within Blaise Pascal's rationalism that "grew and deepened, propelled by scientific progress, the subsequent development of technology and industry, and the burgeoning of interracial and intercontinental relations" (page 122). The essay champions rationalism—a term reiterated seventeen times—paralleling the rational and technocratic veneration of mathematics and other data-driven paradigms. Rhetorically, Senghor asked, "In our technocratic and practical world today, isn't it mathematics that sits at the heart of science and thus material power?" (page 121). At the Eighth UPS Congress, aptly titled "Economic Community as Framework for Development," Senghor drove the point home: "Despite ever more work to be done, our planners benefit from better statistics with every year that passes. So do economists and other experts."[93] Domestically, a fresh wave of experts and technocrats gained private access to the corridors of power, as evidenced by the 1969 foundation of the Club Nation and Development (Club nation et développement) and the 1970 inception of the Center for Study and Research on Socialism, culminating with the appointment of Abdou Diouf in February to the revived *primature* (a French word coined by Senghor for the prime minister's office). On the international stage it is the Agence de Coopération Culturelle et Technique (ACCT, Agency of cultural and technical cooperation) that emerges in Niamey in March as precursor to the future Organisation Internationale de la Francophonie.

Amid the rise of technocratic governance and its corresponding erosion of the state, the politics of Negritude would—once again—morph into aesthetics, aiming to fill the political vacuum with creative imagination. Only this time, Francophonie would provide Negritude with a new tool for Senghor's cultural diplomacy. The decade spanning 1970 to 1980 bore witness to the zenith of Senghor's intellectual production. Sixteen prefaces—more than in any other decade—are strewn among his literary output, spanning topics from ancient Greece to African history, Chagall's paintings, and Frobenius's life. Translations of his earlier poetic and philosophical writings made their debut in languages as diverse as English, Italian, Chinese, and Romanian. For his Francophone readers, approximately a hundred essays and speeches found their way into *Liberté 2* and *Liberté 3*, published in 1971 and 1977, respectively. Indeed, 1971 saw Dakar hosting a weeklong Colloquium on Negritude under Senghor's presidential banner and the patronage of the UPS. "The Problematic of Négritude," the inaugural address, cast a veil of doubt on projects whose objectives of progress, modernization, retrieval, and so on tacitly reproduced the very paradigms they sought to displace. "In our ideological struggle—for this is where the heart of the issue lies—we need both facts—which scientific research alone can give—and concepts—which form the other half of dialectical reasoning—simultaneously" (page 136). Senghor's framing of Negritude as an ideology subtly nudged the attending intellectuals and technocrats to think beyond technocratic solutions.

As Senghor explored the complexities of Negritude on a renewed stage made increasingly international by a nascent neoliberal global world, he acknowledged its diasporic origins and championed its American roots once more, this time reconciled through Francophonie: "[It is] as though we were not Francophones, as though we did not draw inspiration from Negro-Americans when we crafted the concept from Alain Locke's movement, at least partially, which he christened with a French word: *Renaissance*" (page 134). A substantial segment of the discourse delved into the American Black experience, from W. E. B. Du Bois to Mercer Cook, hinting at the diasporic strength of ideological resistance. While the president might have been inclined to shape Senegalese society through technocratic and structured laws and decrees, the poet now urged his readers (and possibly himself) to appreciate the unpredictable, the nonlinear, the moments of reflection, seeking unexpected connections both familiar and foreign.

Even as he navigated the demands of governance, Senghor's poetic voice remained strong, as evidenced by his 1973 collection *Lettres d'Hivernage*. Composed of thirty new poems, the compendium explores the play between the familiar and the foreign—to begin with a title built on a word "coined by the French colonial army" to describe the rainy season in sub-Saharan Africa.[94] This is not to suggest that Senghor's poetic works were a catalyst redirecting the state's institutional power away from a nationalistic vision. But there is a renascent poetic realization about the contradictory nature of neoliberal discourse that shifts the fight back onto the terrain of ideology.[95] By 1975, in the face of a neoliberal growth that appeared unstoppable, abetted by technocrats and further stressed by droughts and oil crises that strained "developing economies," Senghor's philosopher-king instincts kicked in. With his sights on his own *dikē*, Negritude, he was compelled—by political duties, his cabinet, and the legislature—to return to the task of crafting laws and policies to ensure a harmony of the state, however artificial. Gravitating toward Platonic ideals, Senghor gradually retreats from the political arena.

In line with this philosophical shift, *Éthiopiques*, a journal he created in 1975, resembled the politico-aesthetic journals of the decade leading to independence that supported grassroots movements, yet it published few articles on politics, on political work, or by politicians. By 1976, as Senghor wrote his "Elegy for Martin Luther King," he implemented yet another constitutional revision empowering the prime minister to conclude a presidential term should the sitting president step down, preparing for his resignation even further. Even as he prepared his eventual exit from politics, he continued to advocate for diplomatic ties based on an aesthetic worldview transcending narrow national interests. The soon-to-be-established International Organization of Francophonie emerges as the most visible shift from national to international responsibility. *Dialogue on Francophone Poetry*, a telling addendum to *Major Elegies* published just a year prior to Senghor's leaving office, reads as both an epitaph and a vision.[96] As Senegal grappled with the desolation of economic stabilization endeavors and fiscal recovery strategies, Senghor came full circle and returned to the imaginary world of Francophone poetry unhindered by national fiscal deficits. By the decade's end, not only did Senegal's borrowing ability dwindle, but its diplomatic representations, one of Senghor's proudest accomplishments, diminished. Senghor's *Dialogue*, a modern spin on Plato's dialogues, introduced an alternative to the neoliberal gridlock via four texts, charting a path toward the Civilization of the Universal. Amid the failure of modernized economic development, Francophonie emerged as a worthy venture with the potential to reshape inherited norms in an increasingly global world. It is no surprise that it dominated Senghor's subsequent (last) decade. Amid strikes and popular discontent, it is time to turn the page. Léopold Sédar Senghor resigned on December 31, 1980.

1981: Negritude After Senghor

Though the formal announcement came in the form of a written communiqué on December 3, Senghor planned his resignation at least a year in advance.[97] Politically, there is no evidence that the president used his last months in office to settle scores or ossify his considerable legacy. Poetically, the ostensible turn toward Francophonie aligns with a "philosophy of becoming" that Souleymane Bachir Diagne underscores to characterize Negritude's contribution to African thought. After all, "each generation, each thinker, each writer, artist, politician, must," Senghor writes, "in their own ways and for their own good, go deeper and expand Négritude, [overcoming] Négritude's predecessors" (page 141). On January 1, 1981, Senghor overcame himself. Francophonie overcame Negritude. Looking at the texts that constitute *Liberté 5*—the final volume in the series published during Senghor's lifetime—the influence of Negritude wanes with each subsequent year. Then as now, neither the word nor the concept has died. Instead, successive generations have embraced it, used it—sometimes against its own grain—to give rise to other movements: Antillanité, Créolité, the Black Arts Movement, the African Renaissance, and more. Negritude claimed its independence.

Though the relation between Negritude and Francophonie can be traced back to Senghor's earliest text of 1937 that inaugurates this collection, by the time Senghor left office, the two ideas had swapped ends and means. While the former unmistakably evolved in nonpolitical spheres, the latter had grown as an institution. When the poet-president was inducted into the Académie Française—an institution founded by Cardinal Richelieu to use language as a political instrument to assert transnational presence—on March 29, 1984, Negritude was conspicuously absent from Senghor's acceptance speech. Yet, in *Ce que je crois*, published that same year, Senghor contended that he "joined the Académie Française so that next to Francophonie, Négritude would join as well."[98] In May 1985, in a letter to Stelio Farandjis, chair of the High Council of Francophonie, Senghor elaborated on his motivation: "Our defense of the French language is not against the English or the Americans . . . but against the French of the Hexagon."[99] Proposing an overhaul of the archaic objectives set by the French Academy in 1635, which essentially tasked the grammarians with establishing "rules to the language and to make it pure," the mission was to develop a will to create a new Francophonie, rooted in direct engagement with innovative political, cultural, and social expressions—enabled by new scientific and technological innovations.[100] Such engagement, however, mandates substantial political commitment to tools of literacy and numeracy without which no creative imagination necessary for a sustainable polity—decolonized or not—can flourish. Hence, Senghor's vision encompasses more than mere grammar and structure; it encapsulates the political infrastructure mobilized by language building—a project both derailed and necessitated by the technocratic turn.

Throughout his half-century of intellectual, cultural, and political contributions, Léopold Sédar Senghor's wellspring was to imagine affirmative forms of agency that deliberately eschewed labels and epithets. Negritude is not simply a synonym for Black literature, African history, or diasporic psychology. Negritude cannot just be a definition. Its invitation to be elucidated is, in truth, a challenge to sculpt it, through which it becomes something else. That is why its originators profoundly contemplated its nomenclature. It was not—or not only—pure sophistry, pedantry, or surrender to a language that may or may not have been their own. It was the beginning of a journey to reverse the physical, political, and epistemological violence of colonialism and capitalism without legitimizing them by reversal (i.e., making them the end-all of all that is wrong with the world today).[101] On that journey, Senghor, along with many contemporaries, encountered numerous options. Federalism, African socialism, Francophonie, and even *métissage* are but attempts to build alternative futures, grounded not in regrets over what should not have existed, but in imaginings of what could. Senghor's final journey to Senegal was in November 1991, after which he returned to Verson. Among his very last speeches, "Normandity," not "Normanditude," still signals the poet's negotiation of that incalculable distance between ipseity and alterity—incalculable but inviting calculation. Could only a *normand* claim *normanditude*? The key is perpetual inquiry. So long as we keep questioning, we will be all right.

NOTES

1. I use *critique* in the Kantian sense of *Kritik*, a form of analysis that systematically examines the conditions, possibilities, and limits of human knowledge and understanding. In this context, my premise resonates with—and expands upon—the project undertaken by Gayatri Chakravorty Spivak in *Critique of Postcolonial Reason* and Achille Mbembe in *Critique of Black Reason*. My construction of the term aligns with Eve Kosofsky Sedgwick's "peri-performativity": a class of utterances that, "though not themselves performatives, are *about* performatives and, more properly, cluster *around* performatives." See Sedgwick, *Touching Feeling*, 67–90. Notably, the title of Plato's *Republic* represents not just a potential mistranslation by Cicero of the Greek term *politeia*, it has also overshadowed the work's subtitle, *Peri-dikaiosyne politikos*, which directly translates as "around political justice."

2. Senghor, "Letter to Maurice Martin du Gard, December 4, 1943," in Dormesaine, Fierro, and Masson, *Léopold Sédar Senghor*, 63.

3. Vaillant, *Black, French, and African*, 143–44.

4. Senghor, "L'inspiration poétique, ses sources, ses caprices," in *Liberté 5*, 27. The poet-president reiterated this in 1983 with "Tradition orale et modernité" (*Liberté 5*, 188).

5. An editor's note added to the 1970 speech, which was later published in *Liberté 5* in 1993, elucidates that these initial poems were eventually published separately in *Œuvre poétique*. In Plato's *Republic*, as noted by Karl Popper, the term *gennaios*, usually translated as "noble lie," more accurately conveys the notion of an "inspired lie" or "spirited fiction." These translations eschew the notion of nobility, instead emphasizing the grandeur and liberating potential of such a fiction. See Popper, *Open Society and Its Enemies*, 270n.

6. In *The Tongue-Tied Imagination*, Tobias Warner examines the dynamics surrounding the boundaries of literature, paying specific attention to the roles of translation and translatability. Warner suggests that the intersections and confrontations between Wolof and French languages act as "points of departure," fostering a unique "space in which to imagine literature otherwise."

7. Fanon, *Towards the African Revolution*, 171. Originally published as "Unité et solidarité effective sont les conditions de la libération africaine" in *Pour la Révolution Africaine* (Paris: Maspero, 1964), 196.

8. Another fortunate coincidence in literary history binds Senghor and Fanon: Jean-Paul Sartre penned the prefaces to their respective magnum opuses: Senghor's *Anthologie de la nouvelle poésie nègre et malgache de langue française* (1948) and Fanon's *The Wretched of the Earth* (1961). Despite challenging the authors' objectives, Sartre used his prefaces to critique colonialism as a system of institutionalized oppression. For a more in-depth exploration of Sartre's evolving stance on colonialism, including his prefaces to Albert

Memmi's *The Colonizer and the Colonized* and Patrice Lumumba's *Lumumba Speaks: The Speeches and Writings of Patrice Lumumba, 1958–1961*, see Arthur, *Unfinished Projects*.

9. Diagne, "La leçon de musique."

10. Miller, "(Revised) Birth of Négritude." I use the latest translation, by N. Gregson Davis and Abiola Irele, of Césaire's *Cahier d'un retour au pays natal* into *Journal of a Homecoming*. The word *Négritude* appears in both articles published by Aimé Césaire in *L'Étudiant Noir*: "Nègreries: Jeunesse noire et assimilation" (first issue) and "Nègreries: Conscience raciale et révolution sociale" (third and last issue). The two articles have been republished in *Les Temps Modernes*. Edward O. Ako goes as far as claiming that Negritude did not exist as a movement until Lilyan Kesteloot defined and popularized it. See Ako, "'L'Étudiant Noir.'"

11. Lewis, *Race, Culture, and Identity*, 62; see also Sharpley-Whiting, *Negritude Women*, 17.

12. Senghor, "L'Humanisme et nous," 1; translation mine. An original of the first issue of *L'Étudiant Noir* is kept in the Centre des Archives d'Outre-Mer, Aix-en-Provence (France), SLOTFOM V, box 21, FR ANOM 4005 COL 21. For an analysis of the essay, see Vaillant, *Black, French, and African*, 114–15; and Edwards, *Practice of Diaspora*, 185–86.

13. To some extent, the policy governing the Four Communes—a collective term for the oldest colonial settlements, Saint-Louis, Dakar, Gorée, and Rufisque—granted full French citizenship rights to their residents. However, various legal and societal barriers largely prevented them from fully exercising these privileges. For further exploration, see Diouf, "French Colonial Policy of Assimilation"; and Johnson, *Emergence of Black Politics*.

14. The evolving political imaginary of those who would later steer the continent toward independence faced significant challenges even in the postwar period, sometimes building paths not necessarily leading to political independence. See Cooper, *Citizenship Between Empire and Nation*; and Wilder, *Freedom Time*. See also Smith and Jeppesen, *Britain, France, and the Decolonization*; and Collis-Buthelezi, "Peter Abrahams's Island Fictions."

15. In a separate vein, A. L. Becker explores the concept he termed "lingual memory" in *Beyond Translation*.

16. Over time, the French word *métissage* has undergone many translations: hybridity, crossbreeding, mixing, interbreeding, and more. While the Spanish *mestizaje* often involved a caste hierarchy and a eugenic racial mixing, the perspective I suggest here leads to a new understanding of *métissage* as "mixthreading," challenging the colonial history of enforced mixity and embodying the aspiration to intertwine threads differently in a decolonized world. The textile woven by this new mixthread is also a text to be read differently. *Mixthreading* captures both etymological accuracy (the *mix* prefix echoes the Latin root *miscere*, the linguistic ancestor of *métissage*) and the weaving imagery (the *thread* reflects the *tissage*, representing the intertwining of different elements, cultures, or races to create a new tapestry). For an exploration during the Spanish colonization, see Rappaport, *Disappearing Mestizo*; and Twinam, *Purchasing Whiteness*. For Léopold Sédar Senghor's reflection on the topic in the 1949 essay, "De la liberté de l'âme ou éloge du métissage," see Marquet, *Le métissage dans la poésie de Léopold Sédar Senghor*. Françoise Verges argues that *métissage* should always be examined retrospectively, arising

from a forceful—yet anticipated—confrontation. See Verges, "Métissage, discours masculin," 79.

17. Baer, *Indigenous Vanguards*, 111–12.

18. Senghor reiterates the characterization of the African family as organized in "concentric circles" during his address at the First World Congress of Black Writers and Artists in 1956. This exploration can be found in Senghor, "Negro African Aesthetic," in *Liberté 1*, 202–17.

19. Further readings on this topic include Burbank, *Empires in World History*; and Mazower, *No Enchanted Palace*.

20. For anticolonial dynamics in the Caribbean amid World War II, particularly the pivotal role of literary creativity in fostering a resistance movement, see Ripert, "When Is Poetry Political?"; see also Joseph-Gabriel, "Beyond the Great Camouflage"; and Kelley, *Freedom Dreams*.

21. In "Review of *La paix nazaréenne*," Senghor praises Delavignette's novel for its attempt to overcome a French African binary through the act of writing. Published by Gallimard in 1943, the novel explores the experiences of a French colonial administrator's family as they relocate to Niger amid World War I, pursuing a transcendent and elusive peace built on individuals relinquishing their differences and crafting a shared history.

22. The impact and interpretation of Sartre's preface, particularly its influence on subsequent evaluations and scholarly discourse on Negritude, has been examined by Lilyan Kesteloot in "L'après-guerre, l'Anthologie de Senghor et la préface de Sartre." In the aftermath of Sartre's death in 1980, Daniel Maximin heralded "Black Orpheus" as a pivotal resource for the independence generation in "Sartre à l'écoute des sauvages," 63. Furthermore, Valentin Mudimbe acknowledges Sartre's significant role in elevating Negritude to a political and philosophical platform critiquing colonialism. See Mudimbe, *Invention of Africa*, 83.

23. Senghor, "Introduction," in *Anthologie de la nouvelle poésie nègre*, 1.

24. Senghor, "Ouragan," in *Anthologie de la nouvelle poésie nègre*, 149; Senghor, *Collected Poetry*, 4; translation modified. Dixon's otherwise excellent English translation mistakenly interprets the French word *embraser* (to set ablaze) as *embrasser* (to kiss). It is noteworthy that Senghor's brief introduction to the compilation, spanning just two pages, is situated immediately following Sartre's preface.

25. Senghor, "Les négro-africains et l'Union française."

26. The manuscript initially surfaced in Germany in 1932 as *Der historische Materialismus*. By 1933, selected sections were translated into French by Norbert Guterman and Henri Lefebvre, initially appearing in *Avant-Poste* and later republished in their collaborative work, *La conscience mystifiée*. Comprehensive insights into the history of the manuscript's publication and its various French translations can be found in Fischbach, *Manuscrits économico-philosophiques de 1844* and in Renault, "Introduction" to *Comment lire les manuscrits de 1844?* On the aporia of democracy, see Derrida, *Rogues*, 48. The argument is that democracy (also sovereignty, identity, etc.), as it is elaborated by a certain philosophical tradition, is the sum of irreducible contradictions and contains or produces the very forces that can compromise or undermine it, thus inviting a constant rethinking or rewriting of its praxis. See also Derrida, *Aporias*.

27. Malraux, *La condition humaine*. The journal's motto, "We say Revolution ... but not Revolt," resonates with the novel's attention to the varying attitudes to a revolutionary situation and interrogates how collective action can agree with individual free will. See Malraux, *Malraux*.

28. Tsitsi Jaji and Tobias Warner emphasize the importance of a comparative approach to *La condition humaine*. During this period, journals such as *Bingo* and *L'A.O.F.* witnessed an increase in readership and utilized distinct strategies to influence and engage readers, potentially as voters. While *Bingo* leveraged the impact of photographic content, *L'A.O.F.* employed pamphlet-like essays.

29. Janet Vaillant recounts that the SFIO government was not willing to engage in discussions with the representatives of the workers. Following the government's downfall and its replacement by the Auriol administration, Senghor advocated for a scrutiny of the colonial bureaucracy. See Vaillant, *Black, French, and African*, 228.

30. In 1881, Vera Zassoulitch corresponded with Marx to seek clarification on whether, according to *Das Kapital*, agrarian Russia needed to undergo the various phases of capitalist exploitation before aspiring to a socialist revolution. See Marx, "Lettre à Vera Zassoulitch."

31. Senghor, "Birth of the Democratic Senegalese Bloc," in *Liberté 2*, 51–59. This material is a condensed version of the formal "Report on the Method," which was presented during the inaugural congress of the BDS in April 1949.

32. Senghor, "Birth of the Democratic Senegalese Bloc," 57.

33. Senghor, "L'intégration des pays d'outre-mer." See also Senghor, "Eurafrica: Economic Unit of the Future" and "European Policy," in *Liberté 2*, 90–94 and 117–24. For an archival exploration of the role African intellectuals and politicians played in the integration process and its enduring legacy, see Hansen and Jonsson, *Eurafrica*; as well as Garavani, *After Empires*.

34. Mark Mazower critically revisits the ideological underpinnings of the inception of the United Nations, highlighting remnants of antiquated imperial and racial hierarchies in institution building. See Mazower, *No Enchanted Palace*. Additionally, Senghor's discourse at the UN is documented in the minutes of the 145th General Assembly meeting, 4th Committee, October 3, 1950. See *Report of the Trusteeship Council* (A/1306—A/C-4/SR-145), UN Digital Library, https://digitallibrary.un.org/record/813926?ln=en.

35. Johnson, *God's Trombones*. For further analysis, see Gates and West, *African American Century*.

36. For a foundational discussion on the evolution of political elections in the postwar period leading up to independence, see Morgenthau, *Political Parties*.

37. Senghor, "Half a Century of Negro Poetry Contribution," in *Liberté 1*, 134.

38. Thiam, *La portée de la citoyenneté française*, 157, 174.

39. Federalism was envisioned as a transitional solution, and Senghor predicted that independence would be a reality within a decade. This perspective is substantiated in a special issue of *La Nef*, which included contributions from individuals such as Gaston Monnerville, René de Lacharrière, Jean-Marie Domenach, Maurice Duverger, and François Mitterrand, all expressing doubts regarding the union's long-term viability.

40. See Eagleton, *Ideology*, 2.

41. See the following prefaces by Senghor: "The Realism of Amadou Koumba," in *Contes de l'Ouest africain* (Paris: Présence Africaine, 1955); "Bolamba," in *Chants pour mon pays* (Paris: Présence Africaine, 1955); and "Flavien Ranaivo," in *Mes chansons de toujours* (Paris: Chez l'Auteur, 1955), all reprinted in *Liberté 1*.

42. See Morgenthau, *Political Parties*, 82. The term "Algerian War" was formally adopted by the Assemblée Nationale on June 10, 1999, replacing the 1956 designation, "Peacekeeping Operations in North Africa." For more, see "La France reconnaît qu'elle a fait la 'guerre' en Algérie. L'assemblée vote aujourd'hui un texte qui enterre le terme officiel d''opérations de maintien de l'ordre'" [France recognizes it went to "war" in Algeria. Congress votes today to bury the official term "peacekeeping"], *Libération*, June 10, 1999.

43. In his 1945 article "Vues sur l'Afrique noire ou assimiler, non être assimilé," Senghor advocated for alterations to the French graft (*hair greffe française*) to foster a "prolonged education" in anticipation of sustainable decolonized growth. See *Liberté 1*, 39–70. Nearly two decades later, he continued to use the graft metaphor to explain how France is a part of African history despite being colonial. See chapter 11, "Francophonie as Culture."

44. Cooper, *Citizenship Between Empire and Nation*, 224.

45. See Rabemananjara, "Europe and Us"; and Diop, "Opening Discourse," *Présence Africaine*.

46. Initially published in *Présence Africaine*, June–November 1956, 51–65, the piece later reappears with minor modifications as "Negro-African Aesthetic" in *Liberté 1*. For an analysis of the lecture, see M'Baye, "Richard Wright and African Francophone Intellectuals"; Bonner, "Alioune Diop," 1–18; and Masse, "Diasporic Encounter."

47. Senghor, "Debate," 215.

48. Senghor, "Debate" 216. Frantz Fanon similarly contends that the "Black soul is a White man's construction" and postcolonial "history has already noted the fact that most 'Negroes' have ceased to exist." See Fanon, *Black Skin, White Masks*, xv. While Fanon critiques the notion of a uniform Black culture and admonishes Senghor for trying to establish "Black self-consciousness," he does not fundamentally oppose Senghor's idealized hope. See Fanon, *Wretched of the Earth*, 188, 234.

49. Senghor, "Socialism and Culture," in *Liberté 2*, 184–96, originally presented as the Report on Method for the Eighth Congress of the BDS, May 19–21, 1956.

50. Senghor, "Socialism and Culture," 202. Senghor emphasizes the absence of institutional resources to foster indigenous scientific research or economic infrastructures that could, long-term, eliminate the dependency on French investments.

51. Senghor, "Socialism and Culture," 202.

52. Corresponding with poet and editor Armand Guibert on September 14, 1948, Senghor mentions working on a "compendium titled *Éthiopiques*." See *Fonds Emmanuel Roblès–Patrimoine méditerranéen*. For further study, see Lambert, *"Éthiopiques" de Senghor*; and Senghor, *Poésie complète*.

53. The postface is marked September 24, 1954, Strasburg, most likely because of Senghor's work for the Council of Europe. See Senghor, *Éthiopiques*.

54. Daniel Delas has shown how Senghor's adoption—and alteration—of musical terminology in the postface provides him with a way to indefinitely postpone a theorization of a "Negro poetics" that eventually proves unsuccessful. See Delas, "Rythme, culture et poésie," 104.

55. Senghor, "Man and the Beast," in *Collected Poetry*; translation modified, 75.

56. See the introduction to *Éthiopiques* in Senghor, *Poésie complète*, 209–24.

57. Senghor, "Implementing the Decrees of the Loi-Cadre," in *L'unité africaine*, March 1957, reprinted in *Liberté 2*, 212.

58. Senghor, "Decolonization as a Condition for the Franco-African Community," in *Le Monde*, September 1957, reprinted in *Liberté 2*, 216.

59. Senghor published several responses given during debates at the French National Assembly in *Liberté 2*—albeit with questionable omissions. For further insights on the topic of decolonization, see Táíwò, *Against Decolonisation*.

60. For an extensive comparative study examining the various attitudes and subsequent decisions regarding the constitutional referendum across French West Africa, see Schmidt, "Anticolonial Nationalism."

61. In May 1958, Senghor adopted the novel term *palestiniser* (to "Palestinize") to broaden the metaphor beyond Europe's borders. See, for instance, Senghor, "National Independence and Confederation," in *Liberté 2*, 222.

62. Schmidt suggests that by the time of the referendum, the potential to establish a federation or confederation within the political structure of the French Community had already been quashed. In a September meeting in Normandy, Dia and Senghor concurred that the transition from autonomy to independence would take no more than five years. See Dia, *Mémoires d'un militant du tiers-monde*, 91; see also Colin, *Sénégal notre pirogue*, 102.

63. In one instance, a peasant remarked to Senghor, "If you had asked us to vote no, we would have done so." In another context, Senghor noted, "Had de Gaulle not offered the opportunity to form primary federations, Lamine Guèye and I would have likely voted no." See Senghor, "Referendum in Black Africa," in *Les cahiers de la république*, October 1958, reprinted in *Liberté 2*, 225–31.

64. Senghor, "Constitutive Elements of a Negro-African Inspired Civilization," in *Liberté 1*, 260.

65. For an in-depth account of the events leading up to the activation of Article 86 of the constitution and the early phases of the Mali Federation in the summer of 1960, see Cooper, *Citizenship Between Empire and Nation*, 398–413. For a focus on Senegal, see Langellier, *Léopold Sédar Senghor*, ch. 31.

66. Senghor, *La poésie de l'action*, 125.

67. Senghor, "Socialisme, unité africaine, construction nationale," in *Liberté 4*, 85; translation mine. The idea of the "United States of Africa" can be traced back to Marcus Garvey's 1924 poem, "Hail, United States of Africa," while W. E. B. Du Bois imagined its political framework at the fifth Pan-African Congress in Manchester, 1945. See Asi, *1945 Manchester Pan-African Congress*; see also Ayittey, "United States of Africa"; and Senghor, "Culture, développement, coopération" in *Éducation et Culture*.

68. See Boone, *Political Topographies of the African State*, 85–87; see also Gellar, "Circulaire 32 Revisited," 65–81.

69. For insights on the episode widely known as Mamadou Dia's coup in December 1962, see Colin, *Sénégal notre pirogue*, 300–323.

70. The special issue is titled "French: Living Language." For a more comprehensive examination, see Puccini, "Le fonctionnement du mot 'francophonie.'"

71. Senghor, "L'unité africaine," in *Liberté 4*, 108; translation mine.

72. Senghor, "L'unité africaine," 110.

73. Senghor, "Décoloniser pour créer," in *Liberté 4*, 115.

74. Senghor, "Une seule politique efficace: Celle du développement," in *Liberté 4*, 177.

75. Senghor, "Décoloniser pour créer," in *Liberté 4*, 152.

76. Senghor, "Décoloniser pour créer," 156. The resonance with Marx's eleventh thesis of Feuerbach is conspicuous, and Senghor indeed quoted it in the Fifth Congress of the UPS, in January 1966. See Senghor, "L'exécution du deuxième plan quadriennal de développement économique et social," in *Liberté 4*, 206.

77. Senghor, "Décoloniser pour créer," 157.

78. Gray Cowan, the founder and director of Columbia's Institute for African Studies, was also a professor of political science. More can be found in "African Institute Named National Resource Center." The related telegram is housed in the Archives Nationales du Sénégal (ANS, st928/FMAN/Pl).

79. See Ripert, "Decolonizing Diplomacy."

80. For an exploration of the intertwining of civil rights, jazz, and the Cold War, see Monson, *Freedom Sounds*; and Eschen, *Satchmo Blows Up the World*.

81. Ellington, *Music Is My Mistress*, 338.

82. Mercer Cook, US ambassador to Senegal, facilitated the planning behind the jazz performances of American artists. Ellington was the only musician to perform in the newly built national stadium, in contrast to gospel sensation Marion Williams, whose performances took place in Dakar's cathedral, limiting her audience to mostly white Christians. See "Festival Mondial des Arts Nègres," folder 22, Archives Nationales du Sénégal. Ambassador Cook hosted a noteworthy performance at his residence on April 8, 1966. See Cohen, *Duke Ellington's America*, 503.

83. While Ellington's renown partially stems from his extensive repertoire of popular songs, his virtuosic pianistic technique, and his mastery of rhythmic displacement, none of the recognizable traits emerge in the opening bars of *La Plus Belle Africaine*. Much like some compositions from his later period ("The Clothed Woman," "Summertime," etc.), the piece composed for the Dakar Festival breaks away from conventions. The piano has shifted backstage, backing the drummers and bassists, accompanying them with a gentle ostinato. Moreover, the instrument is more percussive than vocal and melodic—a trend that continues in other Africa-themed compositions ("Springtime in Africa").

84. For an examination of the 1968 student revolt and general strike in Senegal, see Blum, "Sénégal 1968."

85. Elizabeth Harney discusses the festival's elitism in her book *In Senghor's Shadow*, 75–76.

86. To understand Senghor's preventive measures against potential disruptions, including closing Cheikh Anta Diop University, see a transcribed interview with Frederick O'Neal from October 1966, archived in the United States Committee for the First World

Festival of Negro Arts, press agent's files, SC MG 220, box 2, folder 2, Schomburg Center for Research in Black Culture, New York Public Library.

87. See Lloyd Garrison, "Real Bursts Through the Unreal at Dakar Festival; Vitality and Diversity Last of U.S. Winners," *New York Times*, April 26, 1966.

88. Edwards argues that diaspora is less a historical condition and more a practice. See Edwards, *Practice of Diaspora*. Additionally, Jaji, *Africa in Stereo*, delves into transatlantic musical encounters and their role in the ongoing performance of Pan-Africanism, with a specific focus on the 1966 festival in chapter 3. For an insightful exploration of the challenges presented by the Dakar festival's performances, see Murphy, *First World Festival*.

89. Diagne, "La leçon de musique," 246.

90. Noting the cost disparities, one square meter of Senegalese tapestry ranges from 500,000 to one million CFA francs (equivalent to 762 and 1,524 euros) in a context where the minimum wage stands at 35,000 FCFA (53 euros). See "Les tapisseries de Thiès, des fresques du Sénégal aux quatre coins du monde," *Jeune Afrique*, September 19, 2012.

91. Subsequent decrees, notably Decree No. 76-1021 from October 14, 1976, delineate the objectives for a cultural policy, which the Senegalese government was obligated to execute through its established cultural institutions. For insights on Senghor's cultural patronage, see Abdou Sylla, "Le mécénat de Léopold Sédar Senghor," *Éthiopiques*, no. 59 (1997). Further readings include Delas, "Regard sur la politique culturelle"; Sylla, *Arts plastiques et État*; Snipe, *Arts and Politics in Senegal*; and Cochrane, "Growth of Artistic Nationalism."

92. In his semi-autobiographical work, Samir Amin critiques what he terms the "ideology of development," tracing its epistemological roots back to the first Afro-Asian conference in Bandung in 1955 and its economic foundation to the oil crises of 1975. See Amin, *Re-Reading the Postwar Period*. Mamadou Diouf offers a critical examination of Senegal's developmental strategies in that decade in his essay, "Senegalese Development."

93. Senghor, "Economic Community as Framework for Development," in *Liberté 4*, 561.

94. Senghor, *Letters in the Season of Hivernage*, 166–67; translation modified.

95. Mamadou Diouf observes that the marginalization of the masses from technocratic decision-making inadvertently led to the reemergence of networks among demographic groups. These networks aimed to counterbalance the overarching dominance of political and administrative power. See Diouf, "Senegalese Development," 308.

96. *Dialogue on Francophone Poetry* was first published in 1979 as an addendum to Senghor's *Major Elegies* collection. See Senghor, *Œuvre poétique*. In the 1990 edition of the compendium, twenty-six "Lost Poems" are inserted between the six elegies, including a new elegy to commemorate the passing of Senghor's son, Philippe-Maguilen, in 1981, and the essay whose title is now pluralized ("Dialogues . . ."). In subsequent publications of *Œuvre poétique*, the singular prevails.

97. For a personal recollection earlier in the same year where Senghor confided his plans of stepping down, refer to Diouf, *Mémoires*, 187.

98. Senghor, *Ce que je crois*, 201.

99. See Senghor, "Defending, Inventing, and Creating the French Language," 185. The letter is published in *Éducation et culture*, released in 2014 and prefaced by Felwine Sarr

with a postface by Souleymane Bachir Diagne, published by Senghor's eponymous foundation. It can arguably be viewed as the sixth installment in the *Liberté* series.

100. See the reference to Article 24 of the statutes in Académie Française, "Les missions," accessed January 8, 2025, https://www.academie-francaise.fr/linstitution/les -missions.

101. In that sense, this introduction paves the way for my forthcoming work, *Sustainable Independence*, which questions how pivotal moments, akin to dress rehearsals, can serve as preliminary steps toward the continuous practice of freedom—the latter theorized as an evolving practice shaped as much by imaginative epistemologies as strategic policymaking.

I

The Problem of Culture in French West Africa

SPEECH GIVEN IN DAKAR,
SEPTEMBER 10, 1937

Reprinted in *Liberté 1* (Paris: Seuil, 1964), 11–21

Shall I confess it to you, should it disappoint you? The presence of the press and distinguished ladies and gentlemen in the audience reminds me that I had intended to speak to you this evening as a simple peasant from Sine.

I had imagined an informal colloquy—and indeed, it will be a colloquy—among members of the Foyer and a few close friends. I had even imagined a dialectical exchange, a series of questions and answers, à la Socrates and our wise Koyte Barma. My intention is not to sway you to my views but rather to invite you to correctly formulate the cultural problem in French West Africa, arguably the most pressing problem of our time that the Foyer has undertaken, and to find an urgently needed solution. My intention is to invite you to join me to free yourself and give birth to the spirit of truth that you already hold within you, or better yet, to break free from embarrassing shackles—be they biases, interests, or passions.

First, we will attempt to scrutinize the word *culture*, to unearth its substantial meaning. Then, once the essence and objective of culture is defined, we will enlighten its racial and contextual aspects. Finally, we will need only to deduce the guiding principle that should inform any cultural policy in French West Africa and consider some applications relevant to various stages of educational policy. In doing so, I trust that we will not lose sight of the drama.

The time for seduction is over. It is high time we hang the seducers.

"*Culture*, such a great word," Samba Sène once told me.

To which I replied, "Sène, I believe it is a greater concept than it is a word, seeing as you also cultivate your field and feed your family from it."

Allow me now to attempt a definition of the word in relation to education and civilization. Culture is to education what the artist is to the craftsman. It is imagination, activity of the mind, for the word itself carries the idea of creative dynamism. I offer the following definition: *a racial reaction of Man on his milieu, striving toward an intellectual and moral equilibrium between both Man and milieu.* Since the milieu is no more immutable than race, culture becomes an ongoing effort toward a perfect, divine equilibrium. Education is the craftsman of culture and its instrument. For children, it consists in the acquisition of the accumulative experience of past generations, in the form of concepts, ideas, methods, and techniques. The collection of a people's concepts and techniques at a given moment in its history forms its civilization—also known as the collection of a people's successive civilizations.

Simply put, *culture* uses *education*, which is the study of the civilizations of a given people, to achieve its ideals. Thus, if educational curricula in France have increasingly focused on the study of foreign civilizations, singularly social and economic facts, it is because our idea of Man has changed alongside the expansion of international relations and socioeconomic sciences.

I will then say to my interlocutors, "What should we do with the Black Man of tomorrow, specifically the West African man?"

"A Frenchman," says Demba N'Diaye.

"N'Diaye, did you go to the Olympics in Berlin?"

"To get lynched? . . . I'd rather read the reports."

"I doubt Hitler would have considered you significant enough to have you lynched. Tell me, in which sports did the Negro excel?"

"In races and competitions requiring suppleness, lightness, limberness."

"Exactly."

He continued, "In fact, they did well to abstain from competing in other sports. They would have been defeated and ridiculed."

"Not quite. You should say that in other sports, they had already been defeated in America. You see, one should not misunderstand and force one's gift, even and especially in areas of the soul and the mind. Do you truly believe that, exceptional men aside, we could ever defeat the Europeans in mathematics, without proving that we are not an abstract race? 'Wanting to leave is not what allows one to leave; it is being able to leave that allows one to leave'":

Bega dèm tahoul
A dèm, men
A dèm a
Di tah a dèm

Race is a reality; racial purity is not. There are differences, but they mean neither inferiority nor antagonism. "We reveled in the sweetness of being whole and different," writes Delavignette.[1] Should you label me a reactionary, I will dissent. By distinguishing politics from culture, I suggest, "Let us work together to turn the West African man, from a political perspective, into a French citizen. But what about from a cultural standpoint?"

A second interlocutor told me, "We will give him a job: He will be a farmer, worker, civil servant." I worry that my friend was confusing a means with an end. One is not born a lawyer or street cleaner; one does not have a job just to earn a living.

A job, even considered as a goal of education, is only an accessory—so long as it does not serve a social function. It cannot be the ultimate end of education—let alone of culture. Otherwise, why would an aspiring engineer study Spanish literature or a future governor practice dance? And are there not students who might have made excellent professors of ancient Greek, yet whose test scores sealed their fate?[2] They would, in the name of scientific equality, which I am sure you'd agree is a cultural principle.

Silmang Faye, my village neighbor, told me, "We will shape the West African man into an honorable man."

"Faye, Kor Yandé, the sentiment of honor is noble. But I vividly recall a time when one of our servants threw himself into the river—fortunately, we fished him out—because the 'boss' had wrongfully accused him of being a liar, yet he, a servant, had a clean conscience. What does this say about a sentiment that takes the best of us from society?"

It is not enough that our man be a man of honor. He must also be well educated and open-minded. In a word, that he must be a Man in the full sense of the word, a Samba-Linguer, as Wolof N'Diaye would say. This is how we connect with the Greek *kalos-kagathos*, the Latin *vir bonus*, and the seventeenth-century French *honnête homme*.

If you will indulge me in considering the Samba-Linguer, our West African ideal of manhood—and I know how subjective such a concept might sound—two observations warrant attention. First, this ideal corresponds to specific qualities: a sense of honor, refined manners, a nimble rather than scholastic mind. Second, this ideal seems increasingly antiquated. It is tainted with a certain disdain for novelty, economics, and the exact sciences—to name but three flaws. Flaws that appear to be more serious each day, as our connection to the five parts of the world is far stronger than the cables that connect us—especially with France.

We share a common destiny and therefore we partake in unforgiving economic struggles as well as political rivalries. *Survival* necessitates adaptation—indeed, *assimilation*. We cannot evade it. Our milieu is no longer just West African, it is also French, it is international. In short, it is Afro-French.

Now, we can establish the guiding principle that the study of West Africa and France must form the two sides of education in West Africa, and this *bicephalism* will permeate all stages. As we move forward, the African side will lose its gravitational pull to the French side. We need to start from the milieu, the Negro-African civilizations where children are raised. They must learn to know and express the elements in their mother tongue, first, and then in French. Little by little, they will grow the circle of the universe around them, where they will act, tomorrow, as men. With their race, they will require a richer and more nuanced knowledge of French. Indeed, bicephalism demands bilingualism. Our guiding principle exhibits versatility in its application to the various stages of education.

If elementary education, primary education, aims at a cultural goal, you will agree that it cannot be uniform: It must adapt to the region, the milieu, a people's level of development. The curriculum will necessarily have to be flexible, somewhat independent from textbooks; teachers will need a greater spirit of initiative.

Let me offer a few examples to illustrate our guiding principle and definition of *culture*. The latest—cultural—direction of education in French West Africa brought several innovations: notably, the proscription of metropolitan textbooks in primary education, and the inclusion of hands-on and agrarian working hours in rural schools. The initial plan was, in effect, to implement bilingualism. I urge you to reflect on these measures and their nonuniform application.

Many see bilingualism as theoretically appealing but dismiss it due to the practical challenges, arguing it could compromise overall—and specifically French—education. Some sophisticated thinkers, however, take the opposite view. They believe practical considerations argue for bilingualism, a principle of culture. Black children, at the outset of their education, must juggle three distinct challenges that scatter their attention: learning to read, learning French, and absorbing basic scientific concepts. Instruction in the mother tongue, or vernacular education, could remedy the system's disadvantages. It would engage the students as early as five, not eight or even ten years old. For one, two, or three years, they would study basic geography, history, science, or native ethics in their own language. By the age of six or eight years old, with a soul fed with our rejuvenated old ideal, with a mind trained and already filled, children would embark on a more fruitful primary education. They would only need five or six years to finish, so long as classes and divisions are not multiplied as in urban areas where average students require seven, eight, or more years to graduate.

My viewpoint remains unchanged. The length and structure of a vernacular education may not be consistent across all areas. Perhaps, it might even be unnecessary in certain cities or neighborhoods, where Black children converse in French with their families. This does not mean, however, that natives have anything to gain culturally by disregarding their mother tongue—quite the contrary, as we will see.

The question of hands-on and agrarian working hours in rural and regional schools creates further divisions. Some have asked whether Médina was a city or a suburb, and if Black farmers possess farming skills. The more pertinent question would be whether Black farmers are indeed farmers, and whether those living in Médina share the mindset and professions of city dwellers.

We are not aiming to train exemplary farmers or qualified laborers—for training comes with experience. We want *agri-culture* to lead to culture—and jobs. It is about an integrative conception of culture and character training. The morality or the *évolué*, which should not be conflated with Anglo-Saxon puritanism or petit-bourgeois moralism, is dwindling daily. This decline is due to our forefathers abandoning their moral traditions. Even worse, the evolution of mores has outpaced the evolution of minds, with the latter failing to guide the former. Yet, the work we once deemed menial, and which now bestows dignity upon most men, not only hones their manual skills but also their self-discipline and a persevering desire to strive. Even savings are promoted, as students learn to handle their own educational form of social security.

Shall I discuss the importance of agrarian work, of this mystical sense of the Earth—which was once the hallmark of our farmers? Shall I make you realize that the most robust and healthy societies are those that hold the strongest sense of the Earth?

I know how little this work would succeed in the cities. I am no longer taken aback by the hostility of the petite bourgeoisie. It is as natural as it is universal and, from our cultural perspective, not overly damaging. Physical education, sports, or scouting have the same moral outcome as manual labor. Furthermore, team sports develop a desire to emulate, a sense of community, and the spirit of sacrifice for the collective good.

I will not delve deeply into textbooks, nor will I expend much effort in asserting that they must align with our bicephalism principle and adapt to the diversity of milieus. It would be quite easy to prove, as some rural schoolteachers have, that the famous *Mamadou and Bineta* works wonders in the bush. But it would not work with the students of Dakar, for it does not speak to the countless things that are familiar to city dwellers. I dream of a textbook tailored to each school and, reminiscent of Telemachus, even for each student. I am eagerly anticipating—and no longer merely dreaming of—the *Mamadou and Bineta* of the citizen, and a fifth-grade textbook that will compile the best pieces from colonial—Black and White—and metropolitan writers, complementing and illuminating each other.

Here, I will draw a distinction between degree of culture and degree of education. The former, a certain degree of engagement and intellectual finesse, would enable students to lucidly assess people and events and to live in harmony with their regional milieu. The latter, the degree of education, would be a certain body of knowledge certified by a diploma. Ideally, the degree of culture would continually escalate while the degree of education would remain stable. The latter naturally tends to be higher in the cities than the countryside, but this is inconsequential. The minds of the students in my village will be flexible enough that, should they make it to junior high or high school, they will adapt swiftly. Ultimately, it is the degree of culture that matters.[3]

I have always felt uneasy about junior high. I think of it as a sort of incomplete mix with a contradiction in its very name. Until recently, it purported to equip students for the workforce while providing unbiased education. One harms the other. Hence the last reform of education. An attempt has been made to assimilate junior high into high school, with a primacy on culture. I find it surprising that this moment was chosen to introduce, at Dakar High School, a junior high education in its most traditional and ambiguous form. I hear that my compatriots demanded it. It is not reason enough for me to follow their reasoning.

I deem it more logical to transform junior high in other parts of French West Africa into a professional path culminating with a terminal degree. Indeed, and not paradoxically, junior high schools should aim at the necessary cultural training to prepare students for eligibility for teachers' colleges.[4] This very training is found in the first-year curriculum at École Ponty where future teachers, doctors, and administrators study together.

Let us not undermine the cultural significance of the Maison des Artisans! Our objective is not to train workers to execute a plan, but rather to foster inspired craftsmen who draw inspiration from ancestral Black crafts and make them fruitful through the study of European crafts.

Among all professional schools, I focus on those with a cultural interest: junior high, teachers' colleges, Maison des Artisans. In line with our guiding principle, the general education curriculum at these schools should strive for a harmonious balance between primary and secondary education, not merely a compromise. Many students will become teachers, but even those who do not will educate and lead by example. Their chief quality will be to be African, through knowledge of Africa, especially through the sense of Africa. Some argue that these students are not lacking in this quality. I cannot stress enough the importance of acquiring it and, because one thing leads to another, so does the study and practice of a native language.

Knowing, however, is not enough. Educators must assess, and to assess, they must compare. This would be enough to require a deeper teaching of French history and literature. We reacted against "Our Ancestors the Gauls"; that is common sense. But the nature of a reaction is to be hectic. It might be time to react against the reaction. It is a question of pedagogy. We shall no longer amuse ourselves with the tales of the Vase of Soissons or the grandiose Napoleonic sagas; instead, we shall explain how a people rose to light and liberty, from their ancestors the Gauls and dark forests, through a series of falls and fumbles. How else can we explain colonial humanism: the work of a Faidherbe, the spirit of a Van Vollenhoven?

At first glance, the organization of secondary education in French West Africa appears impeccable. I can deny neither the caliber of teachers, especially my former ones, nor the remarkable results they achieve. Some might argue that France's curricular programs and regulations are pervasive. This is a matter of debate. They should and should not be enforced.

Our definition of culture, as you may recall, requires that the students be advised in accordance with their abilities, which are both inherited and determined by the milieu. I have heard that such advice was given in our high schools in a matter of minutes, with confidence, but with neither advisor nor advising, neither appeal nor revision, unless mandated from the top—a situation that calls for reflection. There is no familiarity with the students, no sense of their daily reaction to a poem, a problem, a tool. Their talents are assessed not based on their appetites and abilities but on their age! This is how children are placed on paths not suited for them. One who could have become a rich poet of the land is instead turned into an agricultural engineer bored to tears. To be precise, I am under the impression that French West African natives, *exceptis excipiendis*, have more gifts for the humanities than the hard sciences. I worry that we do not make it easy to pursue an education in the humanities, though we must also cherish, with particular affection, our far too few scientists. We forget the legacy of antiquity. The Romans, and especially the ancient Greeks, were more scholarly than skillful. Cato the Elder would not have felt like a stranger in the Sine, and I sometimes wonder whether the wily Odysseus, on his long peregrinations, left descendants in the Baol. We can only hope that advisers, if there is indeed advising, give advice with an abundance of caution and that signaling errors be easily correctable, as is the case in France where selection drives advising, which drives liberty. Such is the letter and spirit of the Jean Zay reform, democratic and cultural in its goals.

Following the principle of advising is that of bilingualism. General education, which students receive during their high school years, does not exclude the knowledge of one's country; it is based on it. Whence the predominance of French in secondary education. For us, Afro-French, it implies teaching French together with a native language, which will serve as a secondary language, as seen in Indochina and Madagascar. What language to choose from the multiplicity of languages and dialects? There are mother tongues and dynamic languages, languages that prey on others: Mandinka, Hausa, Yoruba, Fulani, Wolof. And I mean, along with their grammar, history, geography, folklore, also the civilization of their people.

In such an education, there is primarily a social interest. The elite is called to be both exemplary and intermediary. What is to be gained if they are detached from the roots of their race? What expertise can they possess if they are unaware of their people?

The cultural interest is even more substantial. The mission of intellectuals is to restore Black values in their truth and excellence, to awaken their people to the appetite for bread and mind games that make them men. In the humanities especially. There is no civilization without a literature that expresses and illustrates their values, like the Crown's jeweler. And without a written literature, a civilization cannot be more than a simple ethnographic curiosity.[a] Yet, how can we conceive a native literature that is not written in a native language? A Black literature in French seems feasible, that is true. Haiti did it, and other Black literatures also emerged after borrowing from a European language: Negro-American, Negro-Spanish, Negro-Portuguese. If I am being honest, I would deem it a bit premature. Our people, generally, are not ready to savor all the delicacies of the French language, and yet our writers would need to recognize and use all its resources. Last, such literature could not fully express our soul. There is a certain Black flavor, scent, accent, and timbre that European instruments cannot capture. The creators of *jazz-hot* understood this and used a muted trumpet and other instruments foreign to ordinary people.

Bilingualism, precisely, would enable an integral expression of the New Negro—I use the word deliberately; its dignity must be restored. Scientific works, among others, would be written in French. Literary forms that express the racial spirit—poetry, theater, folklore—would be written in one's native language.[b]

Some may argue that native languages are neither rich enough nor beautiful enough. I could answer that it does not matter, that these languages only need to be cultivated and shaped by skilled writers. Today, Malagasy is a literary language. Yesterday, it did not have a written grammar. Figures like Paul Laurence Dunbar, Claude McKay, Langston Hughes, Sterling Brown have transformed the Negro-American dialect, a mere babbling of unrooted slaves, into a thing of beauty.[5] But I refer you to the griot of erstwhile princely courts, or to the farmers of Cayor. I have always admired their language and how they turned a simple barter over a kola nut into a literary masterpiece, filled with subtlety and humor. Linguists often remark on the astonishing verbal inventiveness of languages like Mandinka. No, tools are not what is missing; I am merely awaiting the talented individuals we will have cultivated.

I hear whispers. Some colleagues might have wished for me to take a stance on practical matters, such as age limits or scholarships. That was not exactly my topic, and it does not really matter there. I have merely sought to analyze the problem with you and see how its parts all connect. Agreement on execution and details will come naturally: *Wah tio nydyèlbèn, moudy ga rafèt.*[6] I know that my opinions are open to debate. Whenever I consider the applications of our principles to education, I venture beyond those very principles. Therefore, feel free to debate them; you will be right to do so. I will be content if I have instilled some doubt, especially in the younger ones, if I have given you an idea

a Since then, I have changed my mind on this too shallow judgment (1963).
b I have also changed my mind on this judgment (1963).

of the complexity of the problem and the need for thoughtful, clear-headed solutions—not hard-fast ones.

Perhaps doubt is not enough. It is something concrete you seek to take away, some viaticum in line with our Yobel customs. Allow me then, as counterpoint, to share an example you might use against me: the case of the old colonies, where degrees are plentiful, yet education is a mere replica of the metropole.

I shall ask the Antillo-French of my generation: Aliker, a medical intern in Paris; Césaire, a student at the École Normale Supérieure; Monnerot, an essayist and literary critic; Sauphanor, a state-certified professor of physics.[7] What do they tell us? That in the French Antilles, there are many graduates but little culture, despite their keen intellect; that literature exists but is only the photographic negative, the pale copy of the metropole; that they come empty-handed to the gathering of peoples, the "rendezvous of giving and receiving" as Césaire called it, for the education they receive does not teach them the history or civilizations of their African ancestors. Listen to Léon Damas, the young poet from Guyana who defines himself a "Negro poet," and who sings, in an instinctively rediscovered tom-tom rhythm, his spiritual nudity in a postexile asceticism:

They came that night when the tom
tom
rolled
from
rhythm
to
rhythm
frenzy of the eyes
frenzy of the hands, frenzy of the feet
of statues
Since
how many of I
how many of I, how many of I, I, I
have died
since that night when the
tom
tom
rolled
from rhythm
to rhythm

frenzy of the eyes
frenzy of the hands, frenzy of the feet
of statues.

It is getting late, and you must be on your way. Let me accompany you far on the road. Take this viaticum, young men and young girls, my comrades. Reflect on these words by Claude McKay, the Negro-American poet and novelist born in Jamaica. He tells us in *Banjo*, in the words of Ray: "'Getting down to the roots of our race and building up from our profound foundation is not a return to savagery: it is culture itself.'"[8]

TRANSLATOR'S NOTES

1. Delavignette, *Soudan-Paris-Bourgogne*, 25.

2. In France, students take the Baccalauréat national exam, which officially sanctions the end of high school studies and opens access to university education. Since its creation by Napoléon, it has been a staple of French education.

3. Senghor refers to the Enseignement Primaire Supérieur or EPS, a now-defunct education system that existed in France between 1833 and 1941. Students entered the EPS after primary school, but the curriculum was still part of elementary education—not secondary education. It was replaced by the *collège moderne*.

4. Senghor refers to an establishment that was created in 1903 in Saint-Louis (Senghor's birth town), the École normale d'instituteurs William Ponty, renamed École fédérale in 1907, transferred to Gorée in 1913, and merged with the École Faidherbe that trained future administrators in 1921. For a comprehensive history of teaching education in French West Africa, see Barthélémy, "La formation des institutrices africaines en A.O.F."

5. In English in the original.

6. The proverb translates as "A wise beginning makes for a beautiful end."

7. The *agrégation* is a highly competitive state certification in the French public education system for civil service positions, which usually leads to a career as a professor in high schools and universities.

8. McKay, *Banjo*, 200; translation modified.

2

What the Black Man Brings

FIRST PUBLISHED IN *L'HOMME DE COULEUR* (PARIS: PLON, 1939)

Reprinted in *Liberté 1* (Paris: Seuil, 1964), 22–38

Wisdom lies not in reason but in love.
—André Gide, *Later Fruits*

They (Negroes) shatter the mechanical rhythm of America, we must be
grateful for that; we forgot men can indeed live without bank accounts, or bathtubs.
—Paul Morand, *New York*

The present deployment of African troops in Europe does not prove that Negroes are involved in shaping the new world; it merely confirms their role in tearing down the old, antiquated order. To be sure, Negroes reveal their true presence in some remarkable works by contemporary writers and artists; also in other works by Black men, less polished perhaps, yet still moving. But it is not this manifest presence alone I wish to speak of here. Rather, and above all, I want to delve into the latent presence that the study of Negroes allows us to glimpse.

I adopt the term as others have before me—it is convenient. Are there Negroes? Pure Negroes? Black Negroes? Science says no. I know there are. There has been a Negro culture whose reach is spread across Sudan, Guinea, and Congo in the classical meaning of those words. Let us listen to the German ethnographer: "The Sudan, too, is made of a vibrant indigenous civilization. It is a fact that the exploration of Equatorial Africa has uncovered nothing but vigorous and fresh ancient civilizations everywhere the preponderance of Arabs, Hamite blood, or European civilization has not removed the dust from the once-beautiful wings of the black moths. Everywhere!"[a] A unique and unifying culture[b]: "I know of no northern people that can compare to these primitives about civilizational unity." By civilization, I mean a culture born of the interplay of race, tradition, and milieu, one that, having emigrated to America, remained stylistically whole—save for some ergology.[1] Civilization may have disappeared, been forgotten; culture did not die. And slavery, precisely, substituted for the milieu and the disintegrative action of *métissage*.

I do wish to discuss this culture, but not quite as an ethnographer. I want to explore these new branches of humanity, the new palms grafted onto the old human roots. Partially, I admit. The flaws of the Blacks are well known; I need not revisit them, especially one that is particularly inexcusable: to not self-assimilate their profound personality. I am not saying to not let their style be assimilated. What interests me here, what is interesting, are the fruitful elements that their culture, elements of the Negro style, brings. Does it mean that the style remains so long as the Negro soul remains vibrant, dare I say, eternal?

First, we will study the Negro soul, briefly; then its conception of the world from where social life and religious life ensue; and finally, the arts, that depend on both. At which point, I will only need to gather into a single bouquet the treasures gleaned from this study in a humanist spirit.

A good number of books have been published on the Negro soul. Yet they remain like a mysterious forest seen from high above. Father Libermann would tell his missionaries, "Be Negroes among the Negroes so that you may win them over to Jesus Christ." Rationalist conception and mechanical-materialist explanations fall short here. Here, more than anywhere else. Many lost to the Minotaur might have found their way out had Ariadne, Emotion-Femininity, been complicit. To explain Negroes through utilitarianism when they are prac-

a Frobenius, *Histoire de la civilisation africaine*.
b By *culture*, I mean the spirit of civilization; by *civilization*, the works and achievements of culture. I take the meanings of those two words quite differently from Daniel-Rops, *Ce qui meurt et ce qui naît*. But in the end, this is only a difference of terminology.

tical, or through materialism when they are sensual, is a recipe for rationalist confusion.

Do we wish to understand their soul? Let us become as sensitive as they are: without literature between subject and object, without imagination in the common sense of the word, without subject or object. Let colors lose none of their intensity, the forms none of their weight or volume, the sounds none of their carnal singularity. . . . The Negro body and soul are permeable to all of the world's invitations, including the most imperceptible rhythms, apparently. Not only to the cosmos. Moral sensibility, too. It is a well-known fact that Negroes are sensitive to words and ideas, even more so to the sensory (shall I say sensual?) qualities of words, to the spiritual (rather than intellectual) qualities of ideas. Eloquence seduces them, and the communist theoretician, and the hero, and the saint, at once. Of Father Dahin, people said, "His voice moved men."[c] This might suggest that Negroes can easily be assimilated when in fact it is they who assimilate. Hence, the enthusiasm for Latin, and missionaries in particular who believe they can easily "convert" or "civilize" Negroes. Hence, often, their sudden disillusionment with some of the Negroes' typical and irrational revelations. "We do not know them . . . we cannot know them," confessed the same Father Dahin on his deathbed after fifty years of Africa.

Emotional sensitivity. *Emotion is Negro, as reason Hellenic.* Water wrinkled by every breath? "Souls of the Outdoors?"[d] Wind-rippled water or unripe fruit buffeted by the wind? In a sense, yes. Today, Negroes are richer in gifts than with work. But the tree sends its roots deep into the earth and the river flows deep to carry precious flecks. So sings the Afro-American poet:

I've known rivers
Ancient, dusky rivers
My soul has grown deep like the rivers.[e]

Let us close the parenthesis. The very nature of emotion, of the sensibility of Negroes, explains their attitude toward an object, which is perceived with such an essential violence. It is a surrender that becomes a need, an active attitude of communion; even of identification, should the action—I was going to say the personality of the object—be potent enough. A rhythmic attitude. Let us hold onto that word.

c Sauvage, *Les secrets de l'Afrique noire.*
d Hardy, *L'art nègre: L'art animiste des noirs d'Afrique,* 80.
e Hughes, "The Negro Speaks of Rivers," in *Collected Works of Langston Hughes,* 36.

Because Negroes are emotional beings, however, the object is perceived in both its morphological characters and its essence. Some speak of the realism of sentimental individuals, their lack of imagination. A Negro realism which, in dehumanizing situations, can be a human reaction leading to humor. For now, I will suggest that Negroes cannot imagine an object that differs from them in essence. They endow it with sensibility, a will, a human soul—but a Black one. As it has been observed, this is not anthropomorphism. The Jinn, for instance, do not always take human form. Some speak of their animism; I say their anthropopsychism. This does not necessarily mean, as we will see, Negrocentrism.

Thus, all of Nature is imbued with a human presence. It humanizes itself in the literal and etymological sense of the word. Not only do animals and natural phenomena—rain, wind, thunder, mountain, river—become humans, but so do trees and pebbles. They become humans who retain their original physical attributes as tools and signs of their personal souls. Indeed, this is the most profound, the eternal trait of the Negro soul. That which, in America, managed to resist all the attempts at economic slavery and "moral liberation." "He's probably raising taxes, grumbled Mrs. Cow, who hurriedly powdered her face and put on her canary-yellow satin shoes and her sky-blue muslin dress with embroidered flounces. Though sweaty and breathless, she was glad for the chance to show off her earrings and her French gold necklace, and she set out for the village on her mule."[f] Like a Negress—and like a cow. Even the flowers in *The Green Pastures* acquiesce, with a Negro accent and in a very Negro way, to the will of the Lord: "OK, Lord!"[2]

Such is the Negro soul, if one can even define it. It might be a daughter of the milieu, perhaps, and Africa could indeed be the "Dark Continent." Here, the action of the milieu is particularly palpable. From the primitively pure light of the savannah and the forest frontier where civilizations sprouted; a bare light that lays bare, that enhances the essential, the very essence of things; to this climate whose violence both exalts and tames. Why not, if it fosters a better explanation? In any case, this soul explains, in turn, religion and society.

It is said again and again that Negroes do not bring anything new in matters of religion. Neither dogma nor morals; just a certain religiosity. But if we think about it, isn't what matters not found in this dismissive word but rather in the thing itself? I want to examine the dogma and the morals of Negroes without being deceived.

f Cabrera, *Afro-Cuban Tales*, 51. The French edition includes a very interesting preface by Francis de Miomandre.

First, these distinctions do not hold. "Be Negroes with the Negroes"; and they know neither how to divide, count, nor discern.

"I believe in one God, the Father Almighty, maker of Heaven and Earth." The beginning of the Creed is no surprise to Negroes. Negroes are monotheistic indeed, as far back as their history can be traced, everywhere. There is only one God, who created it all, who is all power and all will. All the powers, all the wills of the Jinn and the Ancestors are but His emanation.

But this God, we are told by some well-intentioned people, has nebulous attributes; he takes no interest in humans. He is evidently not worshipped, not offered sacrifices. True. He is love: no need to escape his wrath. He is powerful and content: He neither eats nor needs libations. But this is not a "wooden God," some sort of joist. I recall my Serer grandmothers turning to Him in times of great distress. They would dress as men, with all the bells and whistles, fire shots and throw arrows to the sky. They would go so far as to curse . . . in French. And God, amused, answered.

Worshipping was reserved for Jinn and Ancestors. It should be noted, as Maurice Delafosse, the greatest and most attentive Africanist in France, does, that Ancestor worship seems more primal, therefore more Negro. It is spread across Black Africa. Sacrifices are not contractual obligations, not a "two-way street." Neither are utilitarian-driven magical practices, as seen in secret societies; those came later, and I would personally regard them as superstitious distortions, all too human; this is clear in the development of those magical practices in the degenerate Negro societies of America. I see sacrifices as having a threefold goal: to partake in the power of superior spirits, including Ancestors; to commune with them until a sort of identification arises; finally, to be charitable to the Ancestors. For the dead, no matter how powerful, do not live, and cannot secure the "fruits of the earth" that make life so intensely sweet.

No, neither fear nor material concerns dominate the religion of the Negroes, even though those are not absent, though Negroes too feel human anxiety. But love—and charity, which is love—drives the action. As a Tukulor proverb states, "What the laborer sees when he straightens himself is the village. It is not the desire to eat that is in question, it is the entire past that draws him to this side."[3] A similar feeling moves the son who works for his father, the man who labors for the community. The feeling of family communion travels through time, backward, within the transcendent world, to the Ancestors, to the Jinn, to God. Logic of love.

So, should we disregard ethics simply because there aren't any tangible repercussions? Not so. There is an inherent morality in this world, upheld by the communal conscience and its constituents. The feeling of dignity among

Black individuals is well documented. Morality lies in sustaining the communion between the living, the dead, the Jinn, and God, through acts of charity. And he who severs this mystical bond promptly experiences the punishment of isolation.

Let us revisit that word, *religiosity*. What Negroes bring is the faculty to perceive the supernatural within the natural, the sense of the transcendent and active surrender to love that accompanies it. This is as fundamental to their ethnic personality as animism. The study of Negro-Americans attests to this. Even among "radical" poets, the communizing poets, the religious feeling erupts to the sky, suddenly, from the depths of their Negritude. *Father Divine*, which the "Paris-Soir" crowds subjected to ridicule, would not have stirred up passion among Negro crowds had it not promised or given its "angels" the more intoxicating joys of the soul beyond mere feasting. Negro Hysteria? "Nervous postulation," to quote Baudelaire, who prevents the New World from quietly worshipping the Golden Calf.[4]

This leads us to the crux of the humanist problem: "What is the purpose of man?" Must he find the answer within himself alone, as Guéhenno, following Michelet and Gorki, proposes?[g] Or is Man only truly man when he transcends himself to find fulfilment beyond his self, and even beyond man himself? It does matter, as Maritain writes following Scheler, to "concentrate the world in man" and "dilate man to the world."[5] To this, Negroes respond by negrifying God, by making man—whom they do not deify—partake in the supernatural world.

> Lord, I fashion dark gods, too,
> Daring even to give You
> Dark despairing features[h]

Afro-American poets prefer to speak to Christ, to the Man-God.

Now, let us consider the natural aspect of the unitary order of the world: the *Negro society*.

For the Negroes, as for others, the family is not only the social cell, but society is also formed through ever larger concentric circles staggered upon one another, entangled with one another, based on the family model. Several families sharing the same dialect and feeling a shared origin form a tribe; several tribes sharing a same language and homeland may constitute a kingdom; several kingdoms can, in turn, enter a federation or an empire. Hence the importance of

g See Guéhenno, *Jeunesse de la France*, 139–42.
h Cullen, *Collected Poems*.

studying the *family*. We need only identify the elements that allow the Negro family to remain fruitful and enable it to fit in and enrich the new humanism. Indeed, as Westermann writes, "If the Africans succeed in preserving it intact during the transition period, in purifying it from unhealthy elements, and in saving it from degeneracy, there need be no anxiety about their future."[i]

Unity of the family. An economic unity since family assets are held collectively and indivisibly. Moral unity: The family's ultimate purpose is to beget children, who perpetuate the tradition, maintaining and multiplying the spark of life in their bodies and souls, piously.

But this unity does not ignore individuality, even though it expects them to subordinate to the group unity. Women as well as children have, next to the common goods, their private goods, which they can increase and use at their discretion. Children receive an education that is liberal yet strict at the time of initiation. They are not to be beaten and, within their age groups, they are responsible for their own maturation. And contrary to widely held belief, women are equal to men. Neither the prospective groom nor the bride is consulted more than the other; but they accept and live out their acceptance, which matters more than the semblance of choice.[j] Women are not bought; rather, their families are compensated financially. In fact, when the wife is offended by her husband, she retreats to her parents, and it is he who must shamefully come and make amends. Such is the custom, at least among the Serer. For women are also mothers, the custodian of life, the guardian of tradition. Some shallow minds have likened them to workhorses. The truth is, in the division of labor—for there is indeed division, not hierarchization—their task is often heavier; but consequently, their responsibility, their dignity, rises. Paradoxically, Black women who become "French citizens" lose some liberty, some dignity.

The family, thus defined, is not an autonomous unit: It lives in the clan family's "square" in the sense of a *gens*. This is the true Negro-African family. It encompasses all descendants of a common ancestor, male or female. The unitary aspect of the family, foundation and prefiguration of Black society, is most apparent here. The clan's Ancestor, a demigod and a Jinn himself, serves as connecting link between the divine and human realms. As such, he ignited a spark of life and continues to fuel it, to animate it like an eternal flame. He obtained the usufruct of a portion of the land, from the local Jinn of the earth, for his descendants, as a common and inalienable good. The head of the family, firstborn of the living, is in turn the connecting link between the living and the dead An-

---

i Westermann, *Noirs et blancs en Afrique*, 114; Westermann, *African Today*, 133.
j See Rougemont, *L'Amour et l'Occident*, 302–5; Rougemont, *Passion and Society*, 303–4.

cestors. Closer to them, partaking in their science and power, conversing with them familiarly, he is more a priest, a mediator, than a leader. Priest, for in this community, no one can act just for oneself—especially not those with power. Everyone is mutually charitable, and each life is deepened and multiplied in this family communion of the living and the dead.

In examining tribes or, more precisely, kingdoms, we can clearly discern the solutions that Negroes have implemented to address political and social problems. These solutions seem to have preemptively embraced the ideal of today's humanists, those genuinely committed to the cause: "pluralist unity."

Central to societal issues are the twin pillars of *property* and *labor*. For every individual, it matters to earn a living from labor understood as an essential source of property; above all, freed indeed by and from labor, it matters to find within it a source of joy and dignity. Far from self-alienation, labor must make us discover and fructify our spiritual riches.

The vice of capitalist society is not the existence of property, a necessary condition for individual growth; it is that property is not primarily founded on labor. In Negro societies, however, "labor, or more specifically, the product of labor, is the real source of property, but the right to property can only be vested in the object it produced."[k]

But as critics of capitalism have pointed out, property can only be theoretical if natural resources and the means of production remain in the hands of a select few. Here too, Negroes resolved the problem in a humanistic way. Land—with its rivers, forests, and wildlife—is a shared good among all families, with some members having temporary or usufructuary ownership. Meanwhile, the means of production generally, the instruments of labor, are the common property of family units or corporations.

Thus, since labor is a collective endeavor, the property resulting from farming or craftsmanship is also collective. This collective approach ensures everyone receives, materially, a "vital minimum" according to their needs. As a Wolof proverb goes, "When the harvest is ripe, everyone partakes." Additionally, and no less important from a personal standpoint, personal luxuries and necessities are attainable through labor since individual property is regulated but not eradicated.

While it is true that Negroes neglected the individual, they did not enslave the persona as people readily believe. The persona, to me, may lie less in the need for singularity championed by modern individualism, the relentless pursuit of uniqueness, and more in the depth and intensity of one's spiritual

k Delafosse, *Les Nègres*, 44; Delafosse, *African Art*, 139 [translation modified].

life. Negroes do not talk much about the persona—we know they seldom talk and debate; but they have nurtured personal life within the collective form of property.

"For a collective form of property to be an effective aid to the individual, it must not have as its aim depersonalized possession."[1] For Negroes, customs and traditions connect man to property juridically. Mystically, too. Here, each group—family, corporation, age band—has a distinct personality that each member profoundly feels. Family members feel a shared blood, a shared flame. Corporations are like clan families, only with ownership of a "craft." It is the relation to property that makes man feels himself—maybe as a part of a collective. Certain properties, especially natural landmarks like plains, rivers, and forests, are often felt as though they are personified beings. As previously noted, by occupying the land, Ancestors forged a timeless connection with their family name. And the Earth is a feminine Jinn; and we "solemnly" celebrate the mystical bond of the group and Mother Earth.

Thus, ownership of the means of production is not just a theoretical, transient, illusory concept. Workers are not just cogs in a machine; they see themselves as valuable individuals. They know their intelligence and their arms labor freely over something they truly own. Even corporate men, whose profession is viewed as lesser than agrarian labor, understand their unique and irreplaceable roles. Thus, the primordial human needs for true freedom, responsivity, and dignity, are met: the needs of the persona.

Work is not just a chore but a source of joy, enabling a being's realization and fulfillment. In many Negro societies, working the land is the most noble work. The agrarian spirit of the Negro soul persists. Look at the United States, for instance: Negro workers of the North, active voters, harbor a nostalgia for the plantations of the South where their brothers remain bound in serfdom. And their poets sing:

Fruit-trees laden by low-singing rills,
And dewy dawns, and mystical skies.
In benediction over nun-like hills.[m]

Tilling the land allows the reconciliation of Man with "creation," the core of the humanist problem. It aligns with the rhythm of the world: a not-quite mechanical rhythm, which is free and alive; rhythm of the day and the night,

1 Maritain, *Integral Humanism*, 40; Maritain, *Humanisme intégral*, 53.
m McKay, *Complete Poems*, 154. See also the poetic work of Jean Toomer: *Cane*. This is how a Caribbean student at the École Normale Supérieure, A. Césaire, was able to defend his master's thesis, titled "The South in Negro-American Literature," at the Sorbonne.

of Africa's twin seasons, of a plant's growth and death. Feeling in unison with the universe, Negroes rhythm their labor with song and tom-tom. Negro labor, Negro rhythm, Negro joy that frees itself by and from labor.

The political, naturally, intertwines with the social. The latter is to the former what artists' hands are to their minds. It matters to organize, to maintain, and to perfect the City: to govern and to legislate. Governing requires authority, legislation needs wisdom. Both must return to their source, the good of communities and individuals, of the City. But in many of today's Western democracies, these principles are unknown. Often, legislators owe their positions to political parties—a mesh of material interests; they create laws influenced by and for a financial oligarchy. Such legislation is tainted and lacks genuine human touch. Governments, even with expanding police forces, struggle to assert true authority. Authentic authority draws from spiritual leadership and keen policymaking, not from the political puppetry of politicians.

Traditional Negro kingdoms, like the Serer kingdom of Sine, offer a contrasting narrative. Their legislative chambers comprise esteemed clan leaders, dignitaries, whose wisdom emanates from deep-rooted traditions, lived experiences, and an innate sense of responsibility. What matters is to reconcile tradition and progress. Indeed, what some often denounce as a Negro spirit's resistance to progress is nothing more than the limits of its geographical conditions. The authority of the King is of a spiritual order.[n] He symbolizes the kingdom's unity. Originally, he is the direct descendant of the people's Leader; and he represents them just as he represents the people. The authority of the King—because the people honor themselves "through the person of the King himself and through their past."[o] Because the King is chosen by the people through the mediation of principal family heads. Because the people, electors themselves, can suspend or depose him. The effectiveness of power—because it rests upon the authority of and is exercised through numerous ministers whom he, the sovereign, can neither choose nor dismiss.

Juxtaposed against the "Negro tyrannulet," such a Pollyannaish harmonious community might seem idealized. Yet, it is a "pluralist unity," a city, modeled on these natural communities and resting upon them. Even corporations and associations wield influence.

Now, one might question, where does the individual fit? People often overlook individuals, mistakenly thinking they are driven by self-interest and a warped sense of freedom. When you consider the persona, it is a whole different

n Daniel-Rops, *Ce qui meurt et ce qui naît*, 37f.
o Westermann, *African Today*, 163; Westermann, *Noirs et blancs en Afrique*, 136.

matter. To be honest, Negro societies have not placed much emphasis on reason. And that is a significant oversight. For the persona had every chance to grow and make their mark within associations, corporations, and deliberative, *palavering* assemblies. The significance of discussion, *palaver* as we call it, has not been emphasized enough. There, everyone is treated as equals, with a profound sense of human dignity. This feeling moved even servants, even captives. I have known people who committed suicide—the free man's act—just because they were accused of lying or stealing.

What the modern world has overlooked is that the flourishing of the persona, a key factor in our current civilizational crisis, demands moving beyond mere individualism. It only occurs in the realms of ancestral legacies, grounded in the familial and communal atmospheres. The desire for brotherly communion is more deeply human than the desire to turn inward, and it is just as profound as our longing for the supernatural. Some said that pity was foreign to the Negro soul. Pity, maybe, but not charity or hospitality. Every community had its "square" or space for outsiders. Custom compels us to welcome passersby to share a meal at our table. The first Whites to arrive were received as if they were celestial hosts. In Wolof, the highest praise is *Bega mbok, bega nit*, meaning "Those who cherish their family cherish all." Even in the face of destruction of their civilization, even when confronted by slave traders and lynch mobs, Afro-American poets have consistently answered with words of peace:

> I return it loveliness,
> Having made it so;
> For I wore the bitterness
> From it long ago.[p]

That is not just empty rhetoric. This "humanity" within the Negro soul, this inability to sustainably hate, played a pivotal role in resolving racial issues in both Latin and North America. I am convinced what the Negro brings to societal and political realms will not stop here. It would be appropriate to speak about the humanist role of ethnology. In shaping a more human world, ethnology should enable each people to demand the best from within itself. And the Black peoples will not come empty-handed to the rendezvous of the social and the political, especially in a world torn between democratic individualism and totalitarian gregariousness.

p Alexander, *Poetry of the Negro 1746–1949*, 85.

Up to now, what the Negro has brought to the world of the twentieth century has manifested primarily in literature and the arts. While delving into African literature and burgeoning Afro-American works would be a worthy endeavor, it would divert our focus. Instead, I will briefly discuss music and the visual arts. They are distinguished from one another mostly for convenience; the same elements weave through both African and Afro-American works, regardless of expert opinions. The crucible of the American experience has, in many ways, allowed the removal of all that was transient and not human.

However, what was brought has been fruitful only for a handful of artists. Broadly speaking, many have resorted to fragmentary borrowings, sapped of vigor and spirit. I am wary that even surrealists might not have always viewed Negro artistry with the nuanced appreciation it deserves. In a world beholden to matter and reason, where reason is sidelined to proclaim the primacy of matter, what other outcomes could we expect? There lies the cause of artistic decadence in the nineteenth century; it is telling that the manifesto "For a French Art" in *Les Beaux-Arts* emerged then. Realism and impressionism share a core misjudgment. Reverence for reality can lead to photographic art. At best, the creative process gets reduced to mere reconfigurations of the real, resulting in nuanced, yet reality-bound depictions. A natural consequence of Théophile Gautier's attitude: "My rebellious body will not recognize the supremacy of the soul, and my flesh does not admit that it should be mortified. . . . Three things please me: gold, marble and purple: splendor, solidity, color."[q] Tastes might differ; the ethos—or its absence—may not. Hence Baudelaire's critique of the "Pagan School" and, later, the critique of Cézanne and Gauguin, whose disciples will gravitate toward Negro art until they find it.

For the merit of Negro art is neither mere play nor pure aesthetic indulgence: It is to *signify*.

To illustrate, I shall focus on one of the most typical visual art forms: sculpture. Even the decorative nuances on the humblest tools or household items, far from being mere embellishments, accentuate their core function. Practical art, not utilitarian. Classic, to the letter. *Spiritual art* indeed—that some mislabel as idealistic or cerebral—because of its religious undertones. At its core, the sculptor's task is to embody the departed Ancestors and Jinn, crafting effigies that serve both as symbols and sanctuaries. So that we can capture, we can feel their personal souls as efficient will, allowing for a gateway to the surreal.

By way of human representation; particularly when depicting the most genuine glint of the soul, the human figure. A remarkable observation: An-

q Gautier, *Mademoiselle de Maupin* (1866), 193; Gautier, *Mademoiselle de Maupin* (1930), 185.

thropomorphic statues—and notably, masks—predominate. Perennial focus of the Middle Man.

Such spirituality is manifested through the most tangible elements of reality. Negro artists tend more toward sculpting than painting, more toward architecture than design. With their very hands, they mold three-dimensional matter, akin to the Creator. Their material of choice is often the most concrete: not bronze, ivory, or gold, but rather wood, readily available and malleable to both coarse treatments and delicate nuances. They use colors sparingly—always vibrant and pure to saturation: white, black, red, the colors of Africa. More so, they emphasize lines, surfaces, and volumes: the most material properties.

However, precisely because this art strives for the *essential* expression of its object, it stands in stark contrast to subjective realism. Artists organize details according to a spiritual and consequently technical hierarchy. What many misinterpret as mere clumsiness or a failure to accurately depict reality is, in fact, a deliberate or conscious order, or more aptly, a subordination. I already spoke about the emphasis artists place on the human visage.

Rhythm is the organizing force of the Negro style.[1] It is both the most sensitive and least material thing. It is the vital element par excellence, the first condition and sign of art, as is life breathing; a breath that might hasten or slacken, find a rhythm or stutter, driven by the intensity of being and the quality of emotion. It consists of a central theme—a sculptural shape—that interplays with a brotherly theme, much like the rhythm of inhalation and exhalation. Symmetry is not what leads to monotony. Such rhythm is alive, free. For reprise is neither reiteration nor repetition. The theme is reprised in another plane, another level, combination, variation; and it finds new intonation, timbre, accent, thus enriching the overall effect with subtle shades. Thus, rhythm acts upon what is least intellectual within us, despotically, so that we can penetrate the *spirituality of the object*. Our own attitude of abandon is itself rhythmic.

This is classical art in the most human sense of the word, a "dominated romanticism," because artists, dominating their rich emotions, harness and direct our motion to the Idea using straightforward, unequivocal means. Everything converges toward that intent. Here, no anecdote, no ornament, no flower. Nothing disrupts. Instead of luring us in, artists captivate us. This is classical art as Maritain conceived it: "Such a subordination of the matter to the light of form . . . that no material element issuing from things or from the subject is

[1] Guillaume and Munro, *La sculpture nègre primitive*, 84–87; Guillaume and Munro, *Primitive Negro Sculpture*, 58–59.

admitted into the work which is not strictly required as support for or vehicle of this light, and that would dull or 'debauch' the eye, ear, or spirit."[s]

The music of the fading nineteenth century was not devoid of ideas or genuine spirituality—just consider talents like César Franck and Gabriel Fauré in France. Yet, it yearned for new sap, new means. To scholars, both God and the spirit remain elusive. There was an urge to transcend stale, traditional norms, leading figures like Claude Debussy, Darius Milhaud, and Igor Stravinsky to venture into uncharted territories and "invisible germs."

Negro music, only recently garnering serious attention in Europe, addresses these needs. While we resonate with its effect, our understanding of its technicalities remains limited. Neither sculpture nor music in Negro-African societies exists as self-sufficient art. It accompanies, primitively, ritual dances and songs. Secularized, it does not become independent: It finds its natural place in the collective performance of theater, agrarian work, and gymnastic competition. Even in the daily evening tom-toms, its performance is not purely aesthetic. It fosters a deeper sense of communion among its parishioners, in line with the rhythmic dance of the community and the world at large. Among the Westernized or Americanized Negroes, much has survived. For it is instinctively that they dance their music, *they dance their life.*

This is to say that Negro music, like sculpture, like dance, is deeply rooted in the fertile land, imbued with the rhythms, sounds, and resonances of the earth. This is not to say that music is merely descriptive or impressionistic; it certainly conveys feelings. But it is not in any way sentimental. It infuses much-needed vitality into an impoverished Western music, which has been constrained by and perpetuated through arbitrary and overly restrictive rules.

I will not dwell on what melodies bring; that's a well-trodden path. However, the situation with musical modes is different. Their richness is still underappreciated. In part, this is because certain "specialists" have denied even the existence of Negro harmony. Other musical scholars, like Ballanta, disagree.[t] Negroes, they note, often sing in chorus; while many other popular songs from different peoples are sung in unison, choirs in Negritie frequently have multiple parts. I personally recall how challenging it was for our good Father who led our Black children's choir to have us sing in unison, without any harmonies or variations. Speaking of Negro choirs, Delafosse notes that "their harmony is impeccable."[6] Gide, on the other hand, noted that "their rhythmical and melodic invention is prodigious (and apparently naive) . . . but their harmonics

s Maritain, *Art et scholastique*, 97; Maritain, *Art and Scholasticism*, 57.
t Ballanta, preface to *St. Helena Spirituals*, cited in Locke, *Negro and His Music*, 137–38.

are what is truly astonishing. I was expecting their songs to be monophonic. This is the reputation that precedes them, there are no 'songs in thirds or sixths.' The polyphony, in its broadening and compression of sound, is so unfamiliar to our Northern ears that I question if our notation methods can capture it."[u] Disconcerting indeed, impossible to capture, the rhythmic and melodic profiles—including intervals—are extraordinarily subtle. Gide had noted earlier that compared to these, "Our popular songs seem poor, laughably simple, rudimentary." Alluvial lands, which only wait for patient and hardy pioneers.

What the Negro brings most brilliantly, and unmistakably, is *rhythm*. Throughout this analysis, it has become evident that Negroes are rhythmic beings. They embody rhythm. Music is the lens that reveals this truth. Look at the emphasis on percussion instruments. Often, songs are accompanied solely by the tom-tom or perhaps just hand claps. Sometimes, percussion sets the fundamental chord from which melodies spontaneously burst forth. I would like to revisit what I mentioned earlier about the rhythm in sculpture. It is crucial to note that this rhythm propels even melodies and lyrics. The Americans term it the "swing." Distinctly syncopated, it is far from being rigid. It is a blend of consistency and novelty, tyranny and whimsy, anticipation and revelation. This might explain why Negroes can indulge in the same musical phrase for hours. Because it is never quite the same.

Beyond the dominant musical elements, Negroes have demonstrated what could be brought out of instruments hitherto ignored, arbitrarily despised, and set in a subaltern role. This was true for percussion instruments, like the xylophone, and for wind instruments, such as the saxophone, trumpet, and trombone. Owing to the purity, vigor, and nobility of their tones, these instruments were perfect vessels for the Negro style. And they were further elevated by the finesse and mysterious qualities that the finest "Hot-ist" performers drew out.[7]

The Negro influence is not limited to musical composition; it also touches upon musical interpretation. Perhaps here, Afro-Americans have remained closest to their roots. This is fundamentally a matter of style, a matter of soul.

Hugues Panassié illuminated the nuances that Negroes introduced to hot jazz, whose fundamental character is in its interpretation.[v] But this influence is destined to permeate classical music, perhaps more through vocalists than orchestras. The value of interpretation lies in intonation, which Panassié defines as follows: "Not only how the note is articulated, but how to sustain it, mold it, in short, make it expressive." "All is in its expression," he adds, "the accent

u Gide, *Le retour du Tchad*, 41; Gide, *Travels in the Congo*, 234 [translation modified].
v Panassié, *Le Jazz Hot*; Panassié, *Hot Jazz* [translation modified].

the performer imparts to each note, where his entire persona is laid bare."[8] No matter how "faithful" the interpretations of great artists like Roland Hayes or Marian Anderson are, there is always an intrinsic touch of Negro interpretation. It is this particular way to envelop the note, the sound, with an aura of flesh and blood, this "naive" way to translate, with the most carnal voice, even the most covert spiritual nuances into tangible experiences, that creates a misty, a mystical experience. Gide writes, "The soloist has an admirable voice, so distinct from what is expected at the Conservatoire, that seems sometimes choked by tears, bordering on a sob rather than a song, punctuated by abrupt, rough tones, as if out of tune. Then, suddenly, a sequence of incredibly soft, disarmingly sweet notes ensues."[w]

Whatever the extent, what the Negro has brought has profoundly reshaped contemporary music. It has become more rich and more bare, more muscular and more supple, more dynamic, generous, human because more natural. The ancient myth of Antaeus has not lost its truthfulness.

I would like to end with this Greek myth. The encounter between the Greek and the Negro is not an oddity. I am apprehensive that many who profess a Greek heritage today betray the essence of the Greeks. It is a betrayal by the modern world which has dissected man, enshrining him solely as a "reasonable animal," or rather, consecrating him "God of reason." The Negro's gift has been to restore, together with other peoples, the lost unity between Man and the World; to bridge flesh to mind, man to his neighbor, pebble to God. In other words, it tethers the real to the surreal—through Man not as center, but as crossroads, navel of the world.

TRANSLATOR'S NOTES

Epigraphs: Gide, *Fruits of the Earth*, 149. Morand, *New York*, page 270. The epigraphs have been modified from their source translations.

1. *Ergologique* comes from *ergologie*, an admitedly rare and specialized term referring to the study of human work, tools, and material culture. In France, it is a subsection of anthropology, which examines how people make and use objects, so it is not quite ergonomics. Here, *ergology* perhaps means that African "culture" as a whole remained the same when it landed in America—but of course, some things (human labor, tools, objects) changed . . . and those changes did not fundamentally alter that culture.

2. *The Green Pastures* is a controversial Pulitzer Prize–winning 1929 musical play by Marc Connelly and a 1936 Warner Brothers film.

3. Delafosse, *Les nègres*, 80; Delafosse, *African Art*, 203.

w Gide, *Le retour du Tchad*, 41; Gide, *Travels in the Congo*, 233 [translation modified].

4. Baudelaire, "Notes nouvelles sur Edgar Poe," 347; Baudelaire, *Baudelaire on Poe*, 140; translation modified.

5. Maritain, *Integral Humanism*, 188; Maritain, *Humanisme intégral*, 202.

6. Delafosse, *Les Nègres*, 64; Delafosse, *African Art*, 216.

7. Senghor references jazz musicians, as named by Hugues Panassié and Charles Delaunay in the French quarterly jazz magazine *Jazz Hot*, founded in Paris in March 1935. See also Panassié, *Le Jazz Hot*.

8. The exact passage can be found in Panassié, *Le Jazz Hot*, 79; Panassié, *Hot Jazz*, 46; translation modified.

3

Marxism and Humanism

LA REVUE SOCIALISTE, MARCH 1948

Reprinted in *Liberté 2* (Paris: Seuil, 1971), 29–44

Nearly everyone discussing humanism today laments its overuse for the past three decades. Yet, this very overuse might be auspicious. The sheer passion surrounding the term, the fervor with which it is wielded, suggests it touches on something fundamental. It is a sign of our times that the prank of a graduate from the elite École Normale Supérieure, more powerful than any oracle, can keep a nation awake with the forewarning of the world's end.[1] Thus, mankind— what I refer to as "nature"—is under threat. It is about time the term be no longer monopolized by clerics and dilettantes alone. Philosophers had already laid claim to it at the dawn of the last century, infusing it with fresh sap. Between the two world wars, however, it colored the hope of the proletarian masses.

It is indeed no longer literary history or mere speculation, though history does illuminate our present dilemma. It is indeed a question of saving the concrete world, with the concrete man, continually at the mercy of unhinged dictators and the looming menace of atomic warfare.

Do not assume that I have reached my conclusion before even defining humanism. This is where Maritain meets André Ulmann.[2] "The problem is that we erect humanism as a doctrine whereas, perhaps, more humbly and more effectively, it is an attitude or a method," writes the latter.[a] Maritain, on his part, introduces us to "practical philosophy."[b] I am inclined to adopt his encompassing definition of humanism that can unite thinkers of the twentieth century, but the essential dialogue is between Christians and Marxists: "To leave the whole discussion open, let us say that humanism (and such a definition can itself be developed along very divergent lines) tends essentially to render man more truly human ... by having him participate in all that which can enrich him in nature and in history (by 'concentrating the world in man,' as Scheler said approximately, and by 'dilating man to the world'); it at once demands that man develop the virtualities contained within him, his creative forces and the life of reason, and work to make the forces of the physical world instruments of his freedom."[c]

From Maritain's definition, I have only excluded this phrase: "to manifest his original greatness." Here, the Catholic philosopher introduces an element of transcendence, a metaphysical notion that feels not so much alien as it is nonessential to the question at hand.

Historically, Renaissance humanism was a reaction against the metaphysics of the Middle Ages, especially theocentrism. It was, in essence, a spirit of free inquiry and practical application. Even Maritain acknowledges this, noting: "Since the dawn of the Renaissance, the Western world has passed progressively from a regime of Christian sacral heroism to a humanistic regime."[d] He goes further, championing the "autonomy of the temporal," and asserting that "political good is a good worthy in itself of being an 'end' of Human Action (*Bonum Honestum*)."[e] Montaigne and Molina, aligning in thought, laid the groundwork for an anthropocentric humanism, the only one worthy of the name. For to speak of "theocentric humanism" is to introduce a contradiction in the words and ideas, to set up a problem that can be solved neither with reason nor in practice, to frame the problem incorrectly.[f]

a Ulmann, *Humanisme du XXe siècle*, 8; Ulmann, *Humanism of the Twentieth Century* [translation mine].
b Maritain, *Integral Humanism*, x; Maritain, *Humanisme intégral*, 6.
c Maritain, *Integral Humanism*, 2; Maritain, *Humanisme intégral*, 10–11.
d Maritain, *Integral Humanism*, 4; Maritain, *Humanisme intégral*, 13.
e Maritain, *Integral Humanism*, 176, 216; *Humanisme intégral*, 189, 230.
f I had, then, lost my faith [author's note].

Sources of Marx's Humanism

If the meaning of humanism has been consistent over three centuries—it only deepened with the establishment of capitalism—the conditions for its application have never stopped changing. So much so that many intellectuals question today whether Marx's message might not be outdated. Truth be told, the question of Marx's humanism has only gained traction in recent years, since the publication of some of his early works. It's been pointed out, and not without reason, that Marx had consigned these writings "to the gnawing criticism of mice."[3] It is because he perceived them merely as stepping stones to free himself from the Hegelian method, or, as he put it, to "put it back on its feet."[4] What mattered to him were the concrete solutions—political and economic—laid bare in post-1851 works.

But for us, men of 1947, men of the aftermath of the two wars who narrowly escaped the bloody contempt of past dictators only to face the looming shadows of new dictatorships, what profit could we gain of those early works? They house the principles of ethics of Marx, wherein he envisions the total liberation of man as the object of our practical activity. Let us cite here:

1844: *On the Jewish Question* (with Engels)
1845: *The Holy Family or Critique of Critical Criticism*
1847: *Theses on Feuerbach*
1844: *Economic and Philosophical Manuscripts (1844)*—a work we must compare with the manuscripts unveiled in the *Revue Socialiste* (February 1947), under the titles *Estranged Labor* and *The German Ideology* (1845–46, with Engels)

Marx's Philosophy

No self-respecting Marxist would suggest that the discourse on humanism can be divorced from its philosophical roots. Yet, when Maritain argues that "the Communist social solutions, concerned with the organization of work here below and in the temporal community, cannot be disjoined from atheism, which is a religious and metaphysical position," we must call him out for what seems like a deliberate obfuscation.[g] While Soviet communism may pledge allegiance to Marx's teachings, it is not the sole flag bearer of his ideas. To critique Marx by exclusively spotlighting the USSR, irrespective of the revolutionary nature of the Soviet uprising, is unsustainable. Moreover, while it is accurate

---

g Maritain, *Integral Humanism*, 36; Maritain, *Humanisme intégral*, 44 [translation modified].

to label Marx an "atheist" and a "materialist," it is a disservice to peg him as a "metaphysician"—especially when its meaning clashes with his own.

We will therefore start with the philosophy of Marx, which not only serves to debunk the critiques hitherto directed against the socialist thinker, but also to define the principles of his humanism.

It is essential to remember—and reiterate—that Marx's philosophy was both inspired by and reacting against the Hegelian system. The fundamental question of all philosophy is, as Engels writes, to know "whether objective truth is an attribute of human thought."[h5]

Idealists and materialists answer this question affirmatively. Idealists affirm "the precedence of mind over nature."[6] Hegel pushes this concept to its limit. For him, nature is a product—an exteriorization—of the absolute idea, that is to say, of thought as the only reality.[i]

While Marx does profess materialism and trusts in man's ability to "reach objective truth," here, we must be cautious about oversimplifying his stance. We have reflected deeply enough on his often-quoted phrase, "Life is not determined by consciousness but consciousness by life."[j] Let us say outright that life, history, and nature are one and the same, as are consciousness, thought, and mind. Two main observations arise.

First, anteriority. Engels emphasizes it. Marx simply underlines man's dependence on the mind, for man is an "in-carnated" being, to speak like Maritain. The question of primacy does not interest Marx; rather, to him, it is irrelevant. "Circumstances make men just as much as men make circumstances."[k]

Second, the very words *matter* and *materialism*. They recur in Marx's writings. Lenin aptly points out, "The *sole* 'property' of matter with whose recognition philosophical materialism is bound up is the property of *being an objective reality*, of existing outside our mind."[l] The socialist philosopher only defined a few properties of matter. Marx did not attempt to detail every attribute of matter, and his materialism is not crass or mechanical: "The element of thought itself, the element of the vital expression of thought—*language*—is sensuous nature."[m]

Marx's primary contention with idealism is that it is a philosophy of abstraction, therefore, of what is only probable. Thus, a purely idealist thesis is unverifiable because it is built upon something abstract, because another thesis,

h Engels, *Ludwig Feuerbach*, 82; Engels, *Ludwig Feuerbach et la fin*, 51 [translation modified].
i Engels, *Ludwig Feuerbach*, 21–22; Engels, *Ludwig Feuerbach et la fin*, 15.
j Marx and Engels, *German Ideology*, 15; Marx and Engels, *L'idéologie allemande*, 159.
k Marx and Engels, *German Ideology*, 29; Marx and Engels, *L'idéologie allemande*, 185.
l Lenin, *Materialism and Empirio-Criticism*, 267; Lenin, *Materialisme et Empirio-Criticism*, 242.
m Marx, *Economic and Philosophical Manuscripts*, 356; Marx, *Economie politique et philosophie*, 37.

just as valid from a theoretical point of view, can easily counter it. Empirical, scientific evidence alone commands unanimous consent. And it is less the mechanical, static evidence of precision tools than the dynamic truth given by life itself. What interests Marx is a "material, empirically verifiable act, an act the proof of which every individual furnishes as he comes and goes, eats, drinks and clothes himself."[n]

Marx delves deeper. He poses as an opponent of philosophy when it ventures into pure speculation, advocating instead for the only science: the science of man. Debating with him about the subjective nature of science due to its phenomenalist foundation would be missing the point. Marx is not attempting to grasp the surreal beneath phenomena. His contention is with how the question itself is framed: "Whether objective truth is an attribute of human thought is not a theoretical question but a *practical* one. Man must prove the truth—its reality, power, 'this-sidedness'—of his thinking in practice. The debate about the reality or nonreality of thought, when isolated from practice, is purely *scholastic*."[o] It is essential to remember Marx as a moralist, a man of practice, a revolutionary: "The philosophers have only *interpreted* the world in various ways; the point, however, is to *change* it."[p]

Despite the astuteness of Soviet communism's approach, to align with Maritain in viewing Marx's atheism as the metaphysical foundation of a "system of doctrine and life" would be misguided.[q] Marx himself scoffs at metaphysical atheism, confronts it with communism. "The philanthropy of atheism is therefore at first nothing more than an abstract *philosophical* philanthropy, while that of communism is at once *real* and directly bent toward action."[r] It is still the case of the revolutionary who adopts atheism because capitalism co-opted religion, making it its tool and turning it into "a palpable lie."[s] Most Catholic newspapers of the day provide ample evidence of this. Worth noting are these lines from *The Universe*: "A part of society lives in misery. It is a law of God to which one must submit. Society needs slaves. It is the price to pay for its subsistence. It is necessary that there be men who work a lot and who live Christianly."[t] In truth, Marx does not lean on atheism; he even rejects its "mediation."[u]

n Marx and Engels, *German Ideology*, 39; Marx and Engels, *L'idéologie allemande*, 181.
o Marx and Engels, *German Ideology*, 197; Marx and Engels, *L'idéologie allemande*, 142 [translation modified].
p Marx and Engels, *German Ideology*, 199; Marx and Engels, *L'idéologie allemande*, 144.
q Maritain, *Integral Humanism*, 36; Maritain, *Humanisme intégral*, 44 [translation modified].
r Marx, *Economic and Philosophical Manuscripts*, 349; Marx, *Economie politique et philosophie*, 25.
s Marx and Engels, *German Ideology*, 57; Marx and Engels, *L'idéologie allemande*, 218.
t Quote from Madeleine Rousseaux in *La république moderne*, July 1, 1947.
u Marx, *Economic and Philosophical Manuscripts*, 357; Marx, *Economie politique et philosophie*, 40.

Marx's strong rejection of the mediation of metaphysical atheism stems from the understanding that metaphysics is less about doctrine and more about method. Or, more precisely, the two are intricately intertwined. "To the metaphysician," Engels writes in *Anti-Dühring*, "things and their mental reflexes, ideas, are isolated, are to be considered one after the other and apart from each other, are objects of investigation fixed, rigid, given once and for all. He thinks in absolutely irreconcilable antitheses. 'His communication is yea, yea; nay, nay; for whatsoever is more than these cometh of evil.' For him, a thing either exists or does not exist; a thing cannot at the same time be itself and something else. Positive and negative absolutely exclude one another; cause and effect stand in a rigid antithesis one to the other."ᵛ While introducing this concept, Engels also defines the method, classical logic, grounded in the principles of identity, noncontradiction, and the excluded middle.

However, these principles, still taught in philosophy courses, were challenged just over a hundred years ago by advancements in science, notably in biology. Darwin's evolutionary theory comes to mind. With the abandonment of *fixism*, numerous discoveries have established, through the interconnectedness of various scientific disciplines and the interrelation between minerals, plants, and animals, the truth, or rather virtue: the efficacy of the principles of contradiction, reciprocal action, and change.[7] These tenets underpin the dialectical method, which Heraclitus articulated nearly two millennia ago.

Hegel is credited with developing this method. His error, after borrowing the principles of dialectics from the sciences, was to misconstrue their origin and subsequently apply them to the mind, which he posited as preceding matter.

Marx and Engels identified and called out this contradiction between conception and method, a lapse that led Hegel to pen "what is rational is real" and "what is real is rational."[8] And so, dialectic, daughter of the sciences, stands as the negation of the rational-logical but not of reason. And Marx could rightly write, in a letter to Arnold Ruge in September 1843, "Reason has always existed, only not always in a reasonable form."ʷ In fact, we now know there is a Hindu reason, a Chinese reason, a Negro reason, none of which are "logical." Marx's greatest merit was to return to the source of the dialectic, to its object, matter, to "put it back on its feet" when Hegel made it "stan[d] on its head."ˣ This corrective allowed Engels to articulate the dialectic, which is fundamentally materialist, in more precise terms than Hegel. Engels writes in *Anti-Dühring*,

v Engels, *Socialism, Utopian and Scientific*, 406; Engels, *Socialisme utopique et socialisme scientifique*, 12.
w Marx, "For a Ruthless Criticism," 14; Marx, *Œuvres philosophiques*, vol. 5, 206.
x Marx, "Postface to the Second Edition," 103; Marx, *Le capital*, 351.

"True, so long as we consider things as at rest and lifeless, each one by itself, alongside and after each other, we do not run up against any contradictions in them. We find certain qualities which are partly common to, partly different from, and even contradictory to each other, but which in the last-mentioned case are distributed among different objects and therefore contain no contradiction within. Inside the limits of this sphere of observation we can get along on the basis of the usual, metaphysical mode of thought."[y]

Thus, Marx and Engels substituted dialectical materialism or materialist dialectic with Hegel's dialectical idealism or idealist dialectic, ad libitum, depending on whether one emphasizes method or concept. Historical materialism is nothing more than dialectical materialism applied to history: the study of the evolution of human societies.

Historical Materialism

Prior to the nineteenth century, historical studies primarily centered around diplomatic and military events—my schoolbooks echoed this sentiment. It was assumed that human will, especially the will of "the great men," shaped the fate of the peoples, that the arc of history reflected autonomous development of the human mind. In other words, it was assumed that the social and the economic were products of the political, itself a pure creation of the conscious activity of the mind. This is still reminiscent of Hegel's idealist conception of history.

As we saw, Marx turns this equation around. "In direct contrast to German philosophy which descends from heaven to earth, here we ascend from earth to heaven."[z] True, early-century French historians had indeed shown the way. Marx and Engels's task was to hone this methodology, giving it philosophical—or rather scientific—foundations. For them, history was less about isolated individuals (no matter how great), classes, or castes, and more about individuals assembled in societies. It was not the history of abstract men created by the absolute *Idée* once and for all, but concrete men living in determined material conditions. Therefore, life was but to "make history." "But life involves before everything else eating and drinking, a habitation, clothing, and many other things. The first historical act is thus the production of the means to satisfy these needs, the production of material life itself. And indeed, this is an historical act, a fundamental condition of all history."[aa]

y Engels, *Anti-Dühring*, 73; Engels, *M. E. Dühring bouleverse la science*, 181.
z Marx and Engels, *German Ideology*, 14; Marx and Engels, *L'idéologie allemande*, 157.
aa Marx and Engels, *German Ideology*, 16; Marx and Engels, *L'idéologie allemande*, 158.

At the core of history lies the *infrastructure*: the productive forces whose nature conditions the mode of production and repartition, of exchange. The latter is not insignificant. Commerce, though crucial in the development of universal history, thus of communism, depends "not upon individual consumption but upon production."[bb]

The *superstructure* of social and political organization arises from these "real vital functions," subsequently producing "ideological echoes." "Morality, religion, metaphysics, all the rest of ideology and their corresponding forms of consciousness, thus no longer retain the semblance of independence. They have no history, no development; but men, developing their material production and their material intercourse, alter, along with their real existence, their thinking, and the products of their thinking."[cc]

It is common for critics to focus on atheism and accuse Marx of placing material causality in a "significant and primary determining role."[dd] Primary determining role indeed, and it is difficult to deny that life precedes consciousness, in prehistory and biology—as can be observed in children.

But nowhere did Marx infer anteriority from primacy. Nor is it correct to say that he rejected "the value of the immaterial in general."[ee] And Lenin is right to assert, "The statement that the scientific explanation of the world can find a firm foundation 'only in materialism' is nothing but a fiction, and what is more, an absurd fiction."[ff][9] Causality, which in Marx plays a capital role, is no more material than it is spiritual. It is not a linear causality, but an equivocal and spiral one. In a word: dialectical. As is often quoted, "Circumstances make men just as much as men make circumstances."[gg] This underscores the interplay and mutual influence between infrastructure and superstructure, between nature and man.

Marx's Humanism

The role of consciousness—the ability for man to act upon productive forces— sets us apart from animals and explains and justifies revolutionary action. It constitutes the very foundation of Marx's humanism, which is essentially

bb Marx, *Poverty of Philosophy*, 45; Marx, *Misère de la philosophie*, 33.
cc Marx and Engels, *German Ideology*, 14–15; Marx and Engels, *L'idéologie allemande*, 158.
dd Maritain, *Integral Humanism*, 48; Maritain, *Humanisme intégral*, 54.
ee Maritain, *Integral Humanism*, 43; Maritain, *Humanisme intégral*, 52.
ff Lenin, *Materialism and Empirio-Criticism*, 265; Lenin, *Materialisme et Empirio-Criticism*, 242.
gg Marx and Engels, *German Ideology*, 59; Marx and Engels, *L'idéologie allemande*, 185.

"acting."[hh][10] "The animal is immediately one with its life activity. It is not distinct from that activity; it *is* that activity. Man makes his life activity itself an object of his will and consciousness. He has conscious life activity."[ii] How far we are from the primacy of material causality, aren't we!

Recalling our earlier discussions on humanism, the core challenge is reintegrating man within nature, which he is a part of, reconciling him with nature and, in so doing, with himself.

Marx posits that nature is first given to us as an inorganic external world: "a direct means of life."[jj] In this respect, we are no different from animals. This is why Marx condemns such egalitarian communism, sharing-ish, that solely targets the fulfillment of basic, animalistic needs—eating, sheltering, reproducing—"negating the personality of man," "culture," and "civilization."[kk] In reality, this communal communism mutilates nature, treating it as an alien force, while simultaneously devaluing man. Rather than recognizing life as a harmonious creation with nature, it reduces it to merely a means of subsisting in poverty.

For man, however, nature is primarily "the matter, the object, and the tool of his life activity."[ll] While it is almost cliché to say that man is the historical and geographical product of nature, nature is also sculpted by man. It is this latter point we wish to highlight.

Our senses allow us to humanize the sensitive qualities of the external world. As generations pass, these senses refine, in turn refining their objects. Thus, nature becomes "a part of human consciousness"—a truth made clear when one delves into the natural sciences.

The tangible impact of these sciences is most apparent in our practical endeavors, particularly within industry. Here, man truly becomes a demiurge—a creator of nature. It is not necessary to distinguish art from industry. Industry's purely utilitarian nature emerged with the mutilation, the alienation of man. For

[animals] produce only when immediate physical need compels them to do so, while man produces even when he is free from physical need and truly produces only in freedom from such need; they produce only

hh See Somerhausen, *L'humanisme agissant de Karl Marx*.
ii Marx, *Economic and Philosophical Manuscripts*, 328; Marx, "Le travail aliéné," 161.
jj Marx, *Economic and Philosophical Manuscripts*, 328; Marx, "Le travail aliéné," 161.
kk Marx, *Economic and Philosophical Manuscripts*, 346; Marx, *Economie et philosophie politique*, 20–21.
ll Marx, *Economic and Philosophical Manuscripts*, 328; Marx, "Le travail aliéné," 161.

themselves, while man reproduces the whole of nature; their products belong immediately to their physical bodies, while man freely confronts his own product. Animals produce only according to the standards and needs of the species to which they belong, while man is capable of producing according to the standards of every species and of applying to each object its inherent standard; hence man also produces in accordance with the laws of beauty.[mm]

The circle is now closed. Man realizes his true nature by connecting with the natural world, and he is truly at one with himself only when he is aligned with nature, of which he is a part.

It seems misplaced to draw a distinction between man's generic being and his personal being, or to set society against the individual. After all, individuals arise not merely from their ancestry, but from the cumulative influence of society and past generations.

Their minds and bodies flourish within the framework of society. Consider the pivotal roles of physical training and language. Furthermore, their actions attain a human significance, distinct from the animal realm, when they emerge as creative, generative endeavors. "But even if I am active in the field of science, etc.—an activity which I am seldom able to perform in direct association with other men—I am still *socially* active because I am active as a *man*."[nn] Hence, an individual's personal life only realizes within the societal fabric, a collective endeavor of individuals; Man's being realizes itself within the nature fabric, which, in turn, is shaped by man. Put simply, Marx highlights the "consubstantiality" between an individual and society, and between man and nature.

Marx drew these conclusions from his objective study of the social man as an intelligent producer. Yet, he observed that the prevailing economic system, capitalism, disrupts this harmony and alienates man twice: from the fruits of his labor and the very act of laboring. In other words, capitalism alienates, at once, man from nature and man from himself.

Nature provides us with the matter for our activity. With her, our labor finds its realization in useful or artistic objects. In the capitalist system, however, objective labor—the product of labor—no longer belongs to the worker. Instead, it increases capital and becomes a foreign and hostile power that dominates the worker and deprives him of his means of subsistence. "So much does the realization of labor appear as loss of reality that the worker loses his reality to the point of dying of starvation. So much does objectification appear as loss

mm Marx, *Economic and Philosophical Manuscripts*, 329; Marx, "Le travail aliéné," 162–63.
nn Marx, *Economic and Philosophical Manuscripts*, 350; Marx, *Economie et philosophie politique*, 27.

of the object that the worker is robbed of the objects he needs most not only for life but also for work."[oo]

Alienation is not only visible in the product but also in the very act of production. We saw earlier that the generative activity of man is free, creative. In the capitalist system, labor becomes an external imposition upon the worker. "It is *forced labor*."[pp] "It is therefore not the satisfaction of a need but a mere means to satisfy needs outside itself."[qq] This is why man, fleeing work, feels like a man only when he caters to his animalistic needs. This leads to a devaluation, an authentic "derealization" of the worker. "The worker's *own* physical and mental energy, his personal life—for what is life but activity?—as an activity directed against himself, which is independent of him and does not belong to him. *Self-estrangement*, as compared with the estrangement of the *object* [*Sache*] mentioned above."[rr]

Due to self-estrangement, man becomes a stranger to himself, and by extension, to other men. When dominated by the product of his labor, he is simultaneously dominated by the alien power that claims ownership of that product. "Only man himself can be this alien power over men."[ss] Yet, this very man, who is a wolf to man, betrays his generative being. Twice. He becomes increasingly parasitic, relinquishing the role that was intended for him, creator, in favor of the role of technician. The technician, in turn, alienates the worker from the fruits of his labor, and thus breaks the circle; he breaks the natural harmony essential for his personality to thrive. The capitalist world thus becomes an unbreathable world for all because all that is in it is dehumanized. Because, as Marx writes in *The Holy Family*, "The propertied class and the class of the proletariat present the same human self-alienation."[11]

Marx, as we have seen, identifies the cause of this alienation in the capitalist system. Here, we should outline the history of the formation of modern capitalism through the lens of historical materialism. Engels does exactly that in some illuminating pages from *Socialism, Utopian and Scientific*, where he also makes references to Marx's *Capital*. Already, a profound vision of the genesis of these ideas can be found in *The German Ideology*.

At the heart of all historical discourse is the foundation of human existence, which is, fundamentally, man's conscious activity through labor. This involves appropriating and transforming nature's productive forces. These very forces

oo Marx, *Economic and Philosophical Manuscripts*, 324; Marx, "Le travail aliéné," 157.
pp Marx, *Economic and Philosophical Manuscripts*, 326; Marx, "Le travail aliéné," 160.
qq Marx, *Economic and Philosophical Manuscripts*, 326; Marx, "Le travail aliéné," 160.
rr Marx, *Economic and Philosophical Manuscripts*, 327; Marx, "Le travail alienė," 162.
ss Marx, *Economic and Philosophical Manuscripts*, 331; Marx, "Le travail aliéné," 164.

determine the modes of production and exchange which, in turn, determine class formation and social superstructure. As previously emphasized, this determination is primary but not unilateral; there is always reciprocal action.[tt]

In the era predating modern capitalism—specifically during the Middle Ages—the productive forces were weak. "The instruments of labor—land, agricultural implements, the workshop, the tool—were the instruments of labor of single individuals, adapted for the use of one worker, and, therefore, of necessity, small, dwarfish, circumscribed. But, for this very reason they belonged, as a rule, to the producer himself."[uu] The dynamics of labor began shifting due to a dual transformation. On one front, "simple cooperation" started replacing isolated or familial endeavors. Concurrently, technological advancements like steam power and mechanized tools began overshadowing rudimentary instruments like spinning wheels and blacksmith's hammers. This transition saw corner shops yield to small-scale workshops, soon overshadowed by expansive factories. With the birth of the city came the rise of the affluent bourgeois, displacing the feudal lord. With the alteration of class relations came the intensification of class conflict.

"But this revolution only affects production; it only affects the old forms of exchange."[vv][12] The means of labor had achieved unprecedented power, and collective labor had supplanted individual work; yet private property endured. This implied a disjunction: The mode of exchange no longer mirrored the mode of production. "But the bourgeoisie . . . could not transform these puny means of production into mighty productive forces without transforming them, at the same time, from means of production of the individual into *social* means of production only workable by a collectivity of men."[ww] This intrinsic tension births the law of capitalist competition—so commonly defined there is no need to dwell on it. Industry leaders, in their self-centered pursuit of the "for-itself," amalgamate their capital—the contradiction is superficial—to expand their factories and refine their machinery. Eager to amplify their production, they vie for dominance in both national and global markets. But the development of machinism brings unemployment, and therefore, underconsumption. Hence, cyclical crises endemic to the capitalist organization (or rather, capitalist disorganization) emerge "because the capitalist form of production prevents the productive forces from working and the products from circulating, unless they are first turned into capital—which their very super-

tt Marx and Engels, *The German Ideology*, 19–20; Marx and Engels, *L'idéologie allemande*, 163.

uu Engels, *Socialism, Utopian and Scientific*, 412; Engels, *Socialisme utopique et socialisme scientifique*, 18.

vv Engels, *Socialism, Utopian and Scientific*, 412; Engels, *Socialisme utopique et socialisme scientifique*, 18.

ww Engels, *Socialism, Utopian and Scientific*, 413; Engels, *Socialisme utopique et socialisme scientifique*, 19.

abundance prevents."[xx] This imbalance, contravening natural—and by extension, human—laws, alienates man, particularly the worker, exacerbates class antagonisms, and calls for a revolutionary solution. "In reality for the practical materialist, i.e., the communist, it is a question of revolutionizing the existing world, of practically attacking and changing existing things."[yy]

The keystone of this imbalance is private ownership. Its eradication is imperative to restore products and production forces to a natural stewardship, which, in contemporary times, can only be societal. This "communist" revolution will have a twofold advantage. Man, instead of being dominated by nature and its own products, will dominate them. "Anarchy in social production is replaced by systematic, definite organization."[zz] Thus, all products will benefit all men as objects of existence and enjoyment for each one of them. Marx fearlessly reiterates this capital idea. If I could, I would cite pages 65 and 66 of *The German Ideology* from top to bottom. A few lines will do. "This appropriation is first determined by the object to be appropriated, the productive forces, which have been developed to a totality and which only exist within a universal intercourse. . . . The appropriation of these forces is itself nothing more than the development of the individual capacities corresponding to the material instruments of production. The appropriation of a totality of instruments of production is, for this very reason, the development of a totality of capacities in the individuals themselves."[aaa] Indeed, the "communist" revolution will champion liberty.

A contemporary ethicist—be it Mounier or perhaps Sartre—somehow parallels the problem of humanism with that of liberty, and he is right. Marx, however, preempted this parallel by a century. We must be clear. For the practical revolutionary man, this is not about the abstract freedom that metaphysicians debate, nor is it about liberty in the liberal sense outlined in the constitution of 1793. For bourgeois liberty essentially hinges on the right to private property. It is the liberty of anarchy, "liberty of capital to crush the worker," liberty to secede from other men, in a word, liberty to estrange man.[bbb]

Indeed, individual freedom presupposes the elimination of external constraints—and those imposed by capital are undeniably the most external to man; however, the term lacks real meaning if it does not also encompass the potential to develop individual faculties. We have observed that one's personality

xx Engels, *Socialism, Utopian and Scientific*, 427; Engels, *Socialisme utopique et socialisme scientifique*, 30.
yy Marx and Engels, *German Ideology*, 34; Marx and Engels, *L'idéologie allemande*, 160.
zz Engels, *Socialism, Utopian and Scientific*, 426; Engels, *Socialisme utopique et socialisme scientifique*, 29.
aaa Marx and Engels, *German Ideology*, 66; Marx and Engels, *L'idéologie allemande*, 241–42.
bbb Marx, *Free Trade*, 40 [translation modified].

can only flourish through economic liberation, the goal of the "communist" revolution. "Only in community with others, each individual has the means to cultivate his faculties in all directions; only in the community, therefore, is personal freedom possible."[ccc]

Marx, in his characteristic fashion, brings his argument full circle by dispelling theoretical divides. But the solution he has discerned through factual reasoning will only be realized, as he consistently emphasizes, by the transformation of the world. "It can be seen how subjectivism and objectivism, spiritualism and materialism, activity and passivity, lose their antithetical character, and hence their existence as antitheses, only in the social condition; it can be seen how the resolution of the theoretical antitheses themselves is possible only in a practical way, only through the practical energy of man."[ddd]

The Message of Marx Is Still Relevant

The publication of Marx's philosophical works has rejuvenated Marxist studies. To say the least, this revival has placed the question of socialist humanism— that has been simmering for quite a while—at the forefront. Such a resurgence underscores the relevance of Marx's message, even a century on. The fact that a figure like Maritain refrains from directly confronting Marx, opting instead to challenge the interpretations of Marx's disciples—interpretations that are indeed up for scrutiny—testifies to the inherent value of Marx's message. Since the release of *Integral Humanism* in 1936, an ever-growing number of Catholics have engaged in a dialogue with Marx. Among them are voices like Mounier, who ardently defends Marx against the reductive views of "social Christians" and "liberal socialists," who bypass Marxism and pretend to surpass it. The founder figure of personalism reasonably underlines the legitimacy of a materialist foundation, underscores its methodological character, and denounces the idealist deviations of "historical Christianness" he sees as a threat to Christianity itself. In an article published in *Le Populaire*, Mounier pays a distinctive tribute to Marx, not as the mere theoretician of the mutilation of man, but the staunch militant of "integral humanism." He does not quote Maritain. He does better and adeptly cites seminal lines from the *Economic and Philosophical Manuscripts*: "Here we see how consistent naturalism or humanism differs both from idealism and materialism and is at the same time their unifying truth."[eee]

ccc Marx and Engels, *German Ideology*, 74; Marx and Engels, *L'idéologie allemande*, 226.
ddd Marx, *Economic and Philosophical Manuscripts*, 354; Marx, *Economie et philosophie politique*, 33.
eee Marx, *Economic and Philosophical Manuscripts*, 389; Marx, *Economie et philosophie politique*, 76.

We must conclude. Our conclusion will be that Marx does not conclude. For in the end, he offers neither a doctrine nor a system but, again, a method of action at the service of the total man—a method that repudiates both totalitarianism and fixism because man is forever to be realized. Marxism is not a catechism—a fact forgotten by many of its critics; it prompts an incessant transcendence—not just of its method but of its outcome. Marxism is dialectic. It moves with time, with the progress of human knowledge and the accumulation of human facts. It calls upon us for an ongoing, renewed commitment—both individually and collectively—to consciously will to resolve the contradictions inherent to any given state. Truth be told, there is no definitive state: Everything is movement, struggle, change. The "communist" revolution itself, for Marx, is but the solution of a given state at a given time. The socialist state, in turn, also presents contradictions demanding their eventual reconciliation. "*Communism* is the necessary form and the dynamic principle of the immediate future, but communism is not as such the goal of human development—the form of human society.[fff]

TRANSLATOR'S NOTES

1. A student at the French École Normale Supérieure, an elite public higher education institution where Senghor studied from 1934 to 1939.

2. Jacques Maritain (1882–1973), a renowned French Catholic philosopher of the interwar period, specializing in Thomas Aquinas, is a recurring reference in Senghor's works.

3. Senghor does not provide any reference, but the quote is from Marx, *A Contribution to the Critique of Political Economy*, 4.

4. Similarly, the quote is from Marx's postface to the second edition of *Capital*.

5. The quote is from the "Thesis on Feuerbach," penned by Marx in 1845. Engels discovered it forty years later in an unfinished state and prepared it for publication. See Marx and Engels, *German Ideology*, 197.

6. Senghor quotes from Le Houx, *L'esprit et la paix*, 17. Le Houx was the pen name of businessman François-Joseph Troubat.

7. "Fixism" refers to a defunct hypothesis stipulating that no mineral, animal, or plant life has changed since its creation. See Grimoult, "Créationnisme continuiste," 73–96. The "fixists" were opposed to the "continuists," equivalent to modern-day creationists. See Laplanche, *La bible en France*.

8. Senghor does not reference Hegel's original text. The quote is found in Friedrich Engels, *Ludwig Feuerbach*, 10. The original passage is in the preface to Hegel, *Philosophy of Right*, 10; translation modified.

fff Marx, *Economic and Philosophical Manuscripts*, 358; Marx, *Economie et philosophie politique*, 41.

9. Lenin is quoting a Russian scientist named Valentinov, *Philosophical Constructions of Marxism*, 67.

10. The word in the original French is *agissant*, mirroring the title of Somerhausen's book referred to in Senghor's footnote.

11. Marx and Engels, *Holy Family*, 51.

12. The paragraph containing this sentence does not appear in any of the English translations of Engels's essay.

4

Negro-American Poetry

LECTURE, 1950

Reprinted in *Liberté 1* (Paris: Seuil, 1964), 104–21

It will come as no surprise to you that the art of a people never emerges ex nihilo. When artists—be they poets, painters, or musicians—create forms previously unseen or unheard, they do so by expressing distinct ideas, employing specific techniques that constitute the common heritage of their people, a heritage shaped by their history, their geography, their ethnicity.

The Negroes of the United States of America are no exception to this law. Their poetry can only be understood, tasted, by keeping three essential facts in mind: They are descendants of Negro-Africans; their ancestors, deported to America, were enslaved for centuries; and even a century after the abolition of slavery, Negroes remain and feel themselves an ethnic minority. It is worth noting that the prejudice against this Black minority remains, perhaps even more deeply entrenched than during the era of slavery. While slaves were despised, the dynamism of emancipated Negroes is met with apprehension.

Initially, the prejudice came with the practice of segregation. In the South and sometimes in the North, Negroes still live at the margins of communal life. They have their own neighborhoods, schools, theaters, churches—or other services—designated sections on trains—quite simply, their little corner. "Untouchables." Whether it is Alain Locke or Marian Anderson, the service entrance remains the Negro entrance.

Discrimination, equally degrading and even more prejudicial, doubles the impact of segregation. A Negro is employed only when no one else is available and often for the most menial and demeaning chores. They are no more favored by the police or the court than by management. Arrested at the slightest accusation or suspicion, their word has no value. If allowed to, they may argue their case or offer a defense. Naturally, they face the harshest penalties, if they are not handed over to mobs for lynching. American citizens? Some states have craftily introduced legislative amendments effectively stripping them of their voting rights. And there exist even less legal, more effective methods of suppression.

Folk Poetry

The historical conditions that paved the way for a Negro-American literature came relatively late. Paul Laurence Dunbar, the first notable Negro poet, released *Oak and Ivy* in 1893. By this time, a rich and diverse folklore had already taken root.

Although Black slaves had largely forgotten African languages and, to a smaller extent, African folklore, they retained its essence: an unparalleled receptiveness to the currents of the external world, a heightened sense of cosmic forces. This sensibility, this *animism*, fertilized folklore even as some deep-rooted connections tethered it to their ancestral traditions.

The earliest manifestations of Negro-American folklore can be found in Negro spirituals: religious songs derived from Protestant canticles and African melopoeia. Indeed, slaves were quick to convert. Naturally. Their earthly existence was a "vale of tears."[1] How could they not believe in a Heaven where "the last will be first."?[2] But the spirituals, lest we forget, are Negro before they are Christian. Jesus symbolizes Negro suffering. He has curly hair and a black face, much like Mary, His mother: *Nigra sum sed formosa.*[3] Heaven is not abstract. There, we sing, dance, eat, and look "sharp":

I've got a robe, you've got a robe,
All of God's children got a robe.
When I get to heaven, gonna put on my robe,
Gonna shout all over God's heaven.
Heaven! Heaven!
Everybody talking about heaven ain't going there.[4]

I said the spirituals are deep-rooted Negro songs: The old man remained true to his roots. Over time, the spiritual wellspring has dried. Besides Sunday services, he no longer sings Christ's pain or heavenly delights, but his own sorrows and the "Fruits of the Earth."[5]

As ancient as the spirituals and even more prolific, the secular vein has birthed what are known as *folk ballads*—as they are fittingly termed.[6] These age-old secular folk songs have, without a doubt, absorbed influences from the ballads sung by the early colonizers. These melodies reflect the daily lives of a people physically constrained, yet spiritually unshackled.

The many themes and forms of folk ballads have gotten more refined over time, leading to the emergence of two primary genres: work songs and the blues.

Emerging from the rhythm of daily labor, work songs not only embody but also complement that rhythm. Much like in Africa, where virtually every human activity is rhythmed by songs and tom-toms. Sung in a choir, these work songs are composed of a short, assonant, free verse, often punctuated by pauses for hammer strokes and so on. Their rhythm, arguably more potent than that of the blues, is irresistibly infectious. From ordinary laborers to inmates, everyone sings while working. They sing about the freight train that brings you back home, the anticipated communal feast; they sing the beauty of labor, they sing the hate of the White owner—maliciously:

Small bees draw nectar,
Large bees savor honey.
The Black man reaps wheat and cotton,
The White man reaps money.

The blues, a later development, is synonymous with paleness, and sadness, "down in the dumps." There is a perpetual shadow in the eyes and voices of the Negro, but also a spark of sunlight.... Could it be because they are atavistic migrants? Exile and slavery have deepened this sense of nostalgia—less cerebrally morbid than the Nordic "spleen." Blues thus are sorrow songs: romance and melodies in a minor mode. Classic blues follows a three-line verse, followed by an unexpected epigraph-like ending. The three lines finish with the same assonance:

Sweet child, gonna leave, the time ain't far,
Indeed, the time ain't far.
If you don't believe I'm gonna leave, count the days since you left.

The Poetry of the New Negro

Despite its richness and savor, this folk poetry was ignored and even scorned by Negro intellectuals and the earliest published poets before the Civil War. The scars of slavery tainted and ostracized anything labeled "Negro," fostering a deep-seated inferiority complex within the bourgeoisie of color. It was only after Whites took an interest that Negroes began to embrace their own folklore.

Whites, including musicians and writers, began to take notice shortly after the [American Civil] War of 1861. They aspired for America to make a distinct artistic contribution. They looked deep into the roots of the people, and the Negroes stood, indeed, as a part of the "people." This commendation of Black values was consecrated by renowned figures: musically by [Antonín] Dvořák—and later by French composers like Darius Milhaud and Debussy; poetically by Vachel Lindsay and the Jazz School; dramatically by Eugene O'Neill; and in literature, by Carl Van Wechten.

Around the same time, Europe was discovering Negro-African art and civilizations. In France, pioneers like Maurice Delafosse led the exploration into civilization, while Paul Guillaume and Guillaume Apollinaire championed the artistic discovery, creating ripples that touched American shores. Among the celebrated artists that paid some attention to Negro art, I shall mention Picasso, Vlaminck, Derain, Braque, Matisse, to name a few.

Despite their deep-seated inferiority complex, or perhaps precisely because of it, intellectuals maintained an acute awareness of everything pertaining to the "racial question." It is remarkable to observe that Negro-American scholars often had a deeper grasp of the latest Africanist research than us Africans. This insight led them to reevaluate perspectives on racial questions and cultivate a new value system. Here lies the origin of the New Negro movement.

Every cultural movement often starts by seeking patronage—which the New Negro movement found, naturally, in Negro-African civilizations. Their magnificence and authenticity presaged its impending success. What was the aspiration of the movement's pioneers? A Negro Renaissance. The question shifted from one of inferiority, superiority, or antagonism, to its fruitful difference. The Negro personality has asserted itself in its past. It was further deepened by the experience of slavery. In the present, what matters is to express this personality with beauty, to define one of the most human facets of the human condition. Listen to Langston Hughes:

> We younger Negro artists who create now intend to express our individual dark-skinned selves without fear or shame. If White people are pleased, we are glad. If they are not, it does not matter. We know we are beautiful. And ugly too. The tom-tom cries and the tom-tom laughs. If colored people are pleased, we are glad. If they are not, their displeasure does not matter either. We build our temples for tomorrow, strong as we know how, and we stand on top of the mountain, free within ourselves.[7]

I now come to my central focus: written poetry—or rather, meticulously crafted poetry. My intention is not to embrace all poems penned by Blacks. Many encompass universal themes rendered in European style. My lens is on *Negro* poetry, the one that brings a "new thrill."

The Dialect School

First, the Dialect School. Its poets, driven by folklore, seek to express the Negro-American soul. But the School has long borne the mark of its origins—like a mark of infamy. The root cause? Its precursors were minstrels, more buffoons than troubadours. Black or White, their primary duty was to entertain a predominantly White audience by portraying a somewhat childlike, caricatured, and ridiculed Black model. The show was not performed but counterfeited, conventional.

The later entrants to the Dialect School vehemently resisted this tradition of buffoonery. They aspired to unearth the true values of Negro-American spirituality, aiming not just for *authenticity*, but a genuine expression resonant with the voice of the people—an expression steeped in artistry.

There are two trends here, as we saw with folklore. On one side, the epic trend, which is mystical. On the other, the elegiac, which is sentimental—with a touch of humor.

It was said repeatedly that, so long as the Latin elements ruled, "The French do not do epic."[8] The ideas being that for the French, intoxication was mild, for intelligence always curbed instinct and imagination. Negro-Americans do epic. James Weldon Johnson's *God's Trombones*, especially its *Seven Negro Sermons in Verse*, stands as a testament to this genre. Resonating with the Negro spirituals, these poems eschew dogma, opting instead for an assimilated mysticism, a yearning for transcendence, for communion with heroism: with the divine.

Negro imagination unfolds there. This does not mean it gets free rein. The poet might sing "God's waving," the almighty Yahweh, as in "The Last Judgment":

> But God will stop his ears.
> Too late, sinner! Too late!
> Good-bye, sinner! Good-bye!
> In hell, sinner! In hell!
> Beyond the reach of the love of God.
> And I hear a voice, crying, crying:
> Time shall be no more!
> Time shall be no more!
> Time shall be no more!
> And the sun will go out like a candle in the wind,
> The moon will turn to dripping blood,
> The stars will fall like cinders,
> And the sea will burn like tar;
> And the earth shall melt away and be dissolved,
> And the sky will roll up like a scroll.
> With a wave of his hand God will blot out time,
> And start the wheel of eternity.[9]

But this God is a human god. He resembles an old Negro fellow in so many ways, assuredly powerful and fair, yet patriarchal and good, much like in "The Green Pastures." He has his ways, his allure, his voice:

> Then God sat down—
> On the side of a hill where he could think;
> By a deep, wide river he sat down;
> With his head in his hands,
> God thought and thought,
> Till he thought: I'll make me a man!
>
> Up from the bed of the river
> God scooped the clay;
> And by the bank of the river
> He kneeled him down;
> And there the great
> God Almighty
> Who lit the sun and fixed it in the sky,

Who flung the stars to the most far corner of the night,
Who rounded the earth in the middle of his hand;
This great God,
Like a mammy bending over her baby,
Kneeled down in the dust
Toiling over a lump of clay
Till he shaped it in his own image;
Then into it he blew the breath of life,
And man became a living soul.
Amen. Amen.[10]

Somewhere, Gide writes, "The blooming of art is only possible at those corners of our world where the sky touches the earth, I mean when gods become men and men gods."[11] That is the case here. What lends beauty to this epic poetry is the magnanimity of the characters, their historical significance and, as in the heroic deeds, the simultaneous humanity of feelings and character. And then, of course, there is the style!

Let us delve into the *style* of our poets for a moment, which, though it varies based on temperament and schools, carries certain unmistakable characteristics: Negro traits. To clarify, I do not assert that such characteristics cannot be—or are not—found in other ethnic poetry. But the unique blend, the specific illumination in which these traits are found, enables the revelation of their Negritude.

One often speaks of "the imagination of the Negroes." It is a mistake. Though Negroes are both Semitic and Kamitic métis, they are not oriental. Their imagery does not stand out for sheer abundance or fantasy. What sets them apart is the potency and simplicity of these images; their strength of conviction arises from their fairness. Negroes are "emotional," and it is true that emotion is at the source of representation. Yet, Negroes do not invent; instead they make use of an astute observational eye that knows how to see the external world. Recall the two quotes from *God's Trombones*. Take, for instance, the conclusion of "Cabaret," by Frank Marshall Davis. Often, the poet relies more on direct imagery than metaphors:

Weave for me a strange garment, O Maker of All
Make me a jacket of silver stolen from the cornet's high c
Take the violin's tremolo and make me a shimmering golden waistcoat
Of black, O Maker of All, the piano has plenty to spare
Just a little of its bass would make a long thick cloak
I'll die some day I hope

Death must be a winsome hermaphrodite
or men and women would leave those arms.
I'd like, O Maker of All, to wear the garments when I take my last dance
    with Death.[12]

This quality of the imagination explains why Negro poets do not upheave the
laws of language. Their idiom adheres to a pure and sculptural line—they are
sculptors more than they are draftsmen or painters.

But the essential feature of the Negro poetic style is its *rhythm*—melody
occupies a secondary place; I am not saying it is insignificant. More frequent
than rhyme, there are assonance and alliteration, the latter utilized very freely.

Returning to rhythm, it is indeed the most vital element of language: It is
its sign and primary condition. Just as the rhythms of life's breath, inhales and
exhales can become steady or spasmodic, modulated by the degree and depth
of our emotions, the tensions within our being. This is rhythm in its rawest
form, in its purity, in the finest and among our most Negro poets. For instance,
James Weldon Johnson:

Jesus, my lamb-like Jesus,
Shivering as the nails go through his hands;
Jesus, my lamb-like Jesus,
Shivering as the nails go through his feet.
Jesus, my darling Jesus,
Groaning as the Roman spear plunged in his side;
Jesus, my darling Jesus,
Groaning as the blood came spurting from his wound.
Oh, look how they done my Jesus.[13]

This rhythm explains why most poems are crafted for recitation or singing. Paul
Laurence Dunbar was fond of reciting his verses with his beautiful baritone
voice. And this leads me, in fact, to other reasons: Many have drawn inspiration
from folk songs; moreover, Negro voices have always harbored a talent for diction and melody. It is no wonder that several poets inscribe musical directions
within their works.

You feel it; nothing about this rhythm is codified, rigid: It is free as a verse.
Its only law: that accompaniment be to emotion as drums are to jazz. The ongoing reprises might project a semblance of monotony, but a reprise is no more
reiteration than it is repetition. The word resumes with a variation, elsewhere, in
another group, carrying another accent, another intonation, another timbre.
The cumulative effect is amplified—nuanced. It evokes African songs wherein,

soon enough, the musical ear discovers a rare refinement and subtlety beneath an apparent simplicity and monotony. André Gide echoes this, extensively. But listen to Langston Hughes evoke Africa:

The low beating of the tom-toms,
The slow beating of the tom-toms,
Low . . . slow
Slow . . . low—
Stirs your blood.
Dance![14]

Even the most sophisticated poets, who stand apart from the Dialect School, retain the fundamental qualities of Negro rhythm—or rhythms, to be precise. The excesses of the Jazz School have frequently masked this reality. In the words of the discerning Negro critic Alain Locke, it is "vibration more than shock, sliding more than walking." Citing these two stanzas by Jean Toomer:

Pour O pour that parting soul in song,
O pour it in the sawdust glow of night,
Into the velvet pine-smoke air to-night,
And let the valley carry it along.
And let the valley carry it along.

O land and soil, red soil and sweet-gum tree,
So scant of grass, so profligate of pines,
Now just before an epoch's sun declines
Thy son, in time, I have returned to thee,
Thy son, I have in time returned to thee.[15]

And we are back to the Dialect School, more specifically to its secular and elegiac movement, although truth be told, neither term resonates with me. These poets often sing in a minor key. They occasionally exhibit cheerfulness, and sometimes a fervency akin to that of believers, yet their voices persist in being pure and simple. Their pursuit is twofold: to capture the authentic inspiration found in folk ballads and, simultaneously, to embrace the blues technique, a method that somewhat shatters the rigid structure of tercets. This movement has a long history, reaching back to the era of Joseph Cotter and Paul Lawrence Dunbar, of "Chrismus on the Plantation" and "When Malindy Sings."[16] Yet, newcomers, chiefly Langston Hughes and Sterling Brown, have elevated the authenticity and artistry of the folk poem to an unprecedented pinnacle of perfection.

Within it, we uncover the most sophisticated and spontaneous feelings and behaviors of American Negros. Hence the ill-fated love and longing for the forsaken home, the Deep South, Dixie soiled by the haunting memory and scars of slavery. Here is Langston Hughes's "Po' Boy Blues":

When I was home de
Sunshine seemed like gold.
When I was home de
Sunshine seemed like gold.
Since I come up North de
Whole damn world's turned cold.

. . . .

Weary, weary,
Weary early in de morn.
Weary, weary,
Early, early in de morn.
I's so weary
I wish I'd never been born.[17]

Sometimes, it manifests merely as a vague and ancestral instinct of a voyage to "somewhere." It is also a distinct Negro sentiment of friendship, more delicate than love, yet intertwined with it. Take a moment to listen to our dear Hughes once again:

I'm gonna walk to de graveyard
'Hind ma friend Miss Cora Lee.
Gonna walk to de graveyard
'Hind ma dear friend Cora Lee.
Cause when I'm dead some
Body'll have to walk behind me.[18]

You feel it, intertwined with this sentiment is the idea, the feeling of death. Not without familiarity, or humor—just a bit. This familiarity with Death, here again a lineage to Africa; there, no irreducible opposition between Life and Death, and the Ancestors remain active participants in the life of the living. But perhaps what should be seen here is nothing more than the familiarity with the pariah's plight, those who suffer frequently, and find death easily knocking at their doors, as hinted at in Sterling Brown's "Tornado Blues":

Black wind come a-speedin' down de river from de Kansas plains,
Black wind come a-speedin' down de river from de Kansas plains.
Black wind come a-roarin' like a flock of giant aeroplanes—

Destruction was a-drivin' it and close behind was Fear,
Destruction was a-drivin' it and close behind was Fear,
Grinnin' Death and skinny Sorrow was a-bringin' up de rear.

Newcomers dodge de mansions, and knocked on de po' folks' do',
Dodged most of the mansions, and knocked down de po' folks' do',
Never know us po' folks so popular befo'—
Foun' de moggidge unpaid, foun' de insurance long past due,
Moggidge unpaid, de insurance very long past due,
All de homes we wukked so hard for goes back to de Fay and Jew.[19]

Here, the classic technique of the blues is unmistakable. Yet, what becomes nearly impossible to convey is this amalgamation of gravity and bonhomie—one that teases and distills the very flavor of the style.

This brings us to *Negro humor*. In contrast to French wit, which epitomizes the recognition of an unforeseen yet subtle connection between two ideas or words, inviting a smile, an affirmation of intellectual superiority, Negro humor does not dabble in words or ideas. It reveals the perception of a discrepancy between two facts or situations—a human discrepancy. Yet, instead of protesting in the name of reason, asserting the primacy of the intellect with a smile, Negroes assert the primacy of life, with laughter. They react against inhumanity with a will to live:

Makin' a road
Through the palmetto thicket
For light and civilization
To travel on.
Makin' a road
For the rich old white men
To sweep over in their big cars
And leave me standin' here.

Sure,
A road helps all of us!
White folks ride—
And I get to see 'em ride.
I ain't never seen nobody

Ride so fine before.
Hey buddy! Look at me.
I'm makin' a road![20]

You recognize Langston Hughes.

Do you not agree that my reluctance to settle for the term *elegiac* to describe such poetry was justified? A "minor" poetry this certainly is not. And given the profound mystical instincts of Negroes, I maintain that labeling it as "secular" does not do it justice either. But this instinct, now less Christian than ever, no longer speaks in the Bible "bi' words" or even African "song of heroic deeds." It speaks in a subdued and muffled voice—a voice I am inclined to describe as secular. Listen to Sterling Brown's "Memphis Blues."

Scholarly Poetry

Alongside the Dialect School, a more scholarly form of poetry developed, aiming to be less a voice of the people and more a reflection of Black intellectuals. For a long time, this poetry was soiled with insincerity and artificiality, often conveying a petit-bourgeois inferiority complex.

As it happens in states that have recently thrown off the yoke of subjugation, this complex often manifested as a hypertrophied racial feeling exacerbated by scholarship, a need to vociferously assert oneself to gain reassurance. This resulted in an oratory and sentimental poetry, laden with expletives, apostrophes, and magnifications:

To be a Negro on a day like this.
Alas! Lord God, what evil have we done?[21]

Here too, at the dawn of the century, the same influences that rejuvenated the Dialect School began to take effect. Negritude must be accepted, claimed, cultivated with delight, not viewed as a sign of inferiority. Rightfully so, Claude McKay can be considered the true inventor of Negritude. I am not referring to the term itself. I am referring to the values of Negritude. The poet had already brought a significant contribution to the Dialect School with his *Songs of Jamaica*. If I did not mention this earlier, it is because these poems, written in the dialect of their land, are so thickly authentic that they deserve a separate discussion.

I know the dark delight of being strange,
The penalty of difference in the crowd,
The loneliness of wisdom among fools,
Yet never have I felt but very proud,

Though I have suffered agonies in hell
Of living in my own peculiar cell.[22]

Pride, when shattered, beckons hatred. Here, the hatred is hard as steel, pure as gold. A critic noted that it embodies a "proper, never low-grade or vicious" hatred, vital to the defense and rootedness of Negritude:

My being would be a skeleton, a shell,
If this dark Passion that fills my every mood,
And makes my heaven in the white world's hell,
Did not forever feed me vital blood.[23]

McKay's hatred is the hatred of evil: hatred of hating. This leads him to move beyond resentment, to eventually acknowledge the fruitful contributions of White civilization.

I believe that such a purity in the feeling and affirmation of Negritude has been unparalleled in Negro-American poetry. On such ground, to be Black, or even "Negro," is of course acceptable; there is an element of stoicism here. Observe Countee Cullen, the quintessential scholarly—and bourgeois—poet. Hence the drama in some of his poems:

So I lie, who find no peace
Night or day, no slight release
From the unremittent beat
Made by cruel padded feet
Walking through my body's street.
Up and down they go, and back,
Treading out a jungle track.
So I lie, who never quite
Safely sleep from rain at night—[24]

Hence, again, the common assimilation of Christ with the Negro:

At first I said, "I will not bear
His cross upon my back;
He only seeks to place it there
Because my skin is black."
But He was dying for a dream,
And He was very meek.[25]

But McKay's lesson was finally heard. The poets of today not only factually accept their race, they foster a deep-seated faith in it. They believe race, and its corresponding values, brings a fresh sap capable of rejuvenating American civilization. With reverence and passion, adoration and longing, they venerate the Black Woman symbolizing Negritude. For women, more than men, are attuned to the mystic rhythms of life and the cosmos, more receptive to joy and sorrow. I could recite the "Songs to the Dark Virgin" by Langston Hughes, who, like a few others, is as adept at writing in classical English as in dialects. Here is an excerpt from Gwendolyn Bennett, "To a Dark Girl":

> I love you for your brownness,
> And the rounded darkness of your breast,
> I love you for the breaking sadness in your voice
> And shadows where your wayward eyelids rest.[26]

Indeed, women stand as symbols. Much like in Black Africa, the aim is to express her spiritual richness beyond her physical beauty—a detail not overlooked by the poet. This is captured by Frank Marshall Davis in "To You":

> Your eyes—more beautiful than April rainbows
> Your lips—sweeter than old wine from Bordeaux
> Your touch—softer than the fall of snow upon a hillside
>
> Yet it is not for these things that I remember You
> I do not love You for just your body
> for bodies become old ... bent ... condemned.
> But I do say your soul is a golden chalice
> Into which I have poured the rich red wine of my own
>
> . . . .
>
> there comes and goes one Shining White Thing ...
> Very–Love![27]

And "The Black Child" is sung with a rhythm reminiscent of a lullaby. Like one would find in Africa. And our poets sing, with delight, the lesser-known elements of their Negritude: those facets which were least desired, yet most profoundly human. Singularly, they sing their life-colored *sensuality*—so much so that it morphs into something chaste. They sing the Negroes' warmth and vibrancy, a raw force simmering just beneath consciousness. Here is Countee Cullen:

> For there is ample room for bliss,
> In pride in clean, brown limbs,

And lips know better how to kiss
Than how to raise white hymns.[28]

At the end of this journey, the spirit of the race morphs into something barbaric, something monstrous, in the Dionysian sense of the word:

This is a song for the genius child.
Sing it softly, for the song is wild.
Sing it softly as ever you can—
Lest the song get out of hand.

. . . .

Nobody loves a genius child.
Kill him—and let his soul run wild.[29]

Langston Hughes is the singer here.

What stands out is the elevated sublimation at such an extreme juncture of racial sentiment. The most "Negro" poems are not necessarily those overtly proclaiming Negritude. Rather, Negritude resides more in the singular quality of *emotion* and *style* than in its explicit proclamation. Above all, "Negro" poems are those where the elements of wind and water are sung, where the fragrances of grasslands and forests, and notably, the land, are breathed in; poems where is expressed the peasant soul of Negroes who, there, in Africa, yearly commemorate the mystical union of Man and Earth. As in "Spring in New Hampshire" by Claude McKay, and in "The Negro Speaks of Rivers" by Langston Hughes—or his "Earth Song," here:

It's an earth song—
And I've been waiting long
For an earth song.
It's a spring song!
I've been waiting long
For a spring song:
Strong as the bursting of young buds,
Strong as the shoots of a new plant,
Strong as the coming of the first child
From its mother's womb—
An earth song!
A body song!
A spring song!
And I've been waiting long
For an earth song.[30]

As in the poems in *Cane* that gave Jean Toomer his fame:

> My ears are caked with dust of oat-fields at harvest-time.
> I am a deaf man who strains to hear the calls of other harvesters whose throats are also dry.

> It would be good to hear their songs . . . reapers of the sweet-stalked cane, cutters of the corn . . . even though their throats cracked, and the strangeness of their voices deafened me.[31]

The discourse surrounding Race inevitably intertwines with the discourse surrounding Africa. Claude McKay rarely and discreetly evokes Africa. He acknowledges her as the land of his ancestors, yet one marred by destitution and savagery, one his ancestors left for good reason.

With Cullen and Hughes, it is a different matter entirely. The African mystique preached by Marcus Garvey has been fruitful. Upon unearthing Negritude, it is nurtured and exalted, Africa is seen as akin to a rich inheritance. Of course, this Africa is adorned with attributes absent in the White industrial civilization: bravery, nobility, allure. The innocence of liberty, too. Hence, Africa emerges as a shelter of peace over against the harshness of the American world, a sea of primeval life over against the sophistication of White culture. Africa is an earthly Heaven. Here is the idyllic image crafted by Countee Cullen:

> No less, once in a land of scarlet suns
> And brooding winds, before the hurricane
> Bore down upon us, long before this pain,
> We found a place where quiet water runs;
> I held your hand this way upon a hill,
> And felt my heart forbear, my pulse grow still.[32]

A poet like Langston Hughes imagines Mother Earth in a similar romantic vein, yet without the struggle and anguish that pervade Cullen's renowned poem "Heritage." He is naturally more pagan:

> We should have a land of sun,
> Of gorgeous sun,
> And a land of fragrant water
> Where the twilight
> Is a soft bandanna handkerchief
> Of rose and gold,
> And not this land where life is cold.

We should have a land of trees,
Of tall thick trees
Bowed down with chattering parrots
Brilliant as the day,
And not this land where birds are grey.

Ah, we should have a land of joy
Of love and joy and wine and song,
And not this land where joy is wrong.[33]

In recent years, Negro-American poetry has endeavored to overcome the discourse surrounding race, through union with God—or the proletariat. Claude McKay and Langston Hughes are prominent figureheads of this new trend. Richard Wright also, though he is better known as a novelist:

I am black and I have seen black hands
Raised in fists of revolt, side by side with the white fists of white
    workers,
And some day—and it is only this which sustains me—
Some day there shall be millions and millions of them,
On some red day in a burst of fists on a new horizon![34]

Poems are beautiful, with an epic breath. Yet, despite their grandeur, the proletarian poems are not the most beautiful ones. Proletarian solidarity, perhaps because it is something we feel, is more asserted than lived. More fundamentally, it must be noted that the allure of Negro-American poetry emanates less from ideas and expressed feelings than from its expression: its Negritude. And this expression naturally reverts to its authenticity when it sings of Mother Earth. For it is so true: Negroes are the sons of the Earth!

TRANSLATOR'S NOTES

1. The Christian phrase, which alludes to the tribulations of life one leaves behind upon entering Heaven, is found in Psalm 84:6. The Latin Vulgate renders the phrase as "*valle lacrimarum*" in Psalm 84:7 (equivalent to Psalm 84:6 in English versions), while the King James Version (1611) refers to the "valley of Baca."

2. The phrase, "the first will be last and the last, first," is cited in several significant passages of the Bible: Matthew 19:30 and 20:16; Mark 10:31; and Luke 13:30 (King James Version).

3. Translated as "I am Black but Beautiful," this phrase hails from a composition by the sixteenth-century composer Giovanni Pierluigi da Palestrina.

4. The text is excerpted from a traditional Negro spiritual, "Going to Shout All over God's Heaven," first recorded by the Fisk Jubilee Singers. See John Wesley Work, Fisk

University Jubilee Singers, Alfred Garfield King, Noah Walker Ryder, and J. A Myers, *Little David, Play on Yo' Harp*, 1909, Audio. https://www.loc.gov/item/jukebox-128180/.

5. This quote alludes to André Gide's prose-poem that explores desires and the awakening of the senses, titled "Les nourritures terrestres," published in 1897.

6. The words *folk ballads* are in English in the original.

7. Langston Hughes, "The Negro Artist and the Racial Mountain," *The Nation*, June 23, 1926, as cited in Brawley, "Negro Genius," 368.

8. The line is drawn from Voltaire's "Essay on Epic Poetry," amalgamated with his poem titled *The Henriade: An Epic Poem*, published in 1732. To delve deeper into the line and its contextual significance, see Usher, *Epic Arts in Renaissance France*, 209.

9. Johnson, "The Judgment Day," in *God's Trombones*, 56.

10. Johnson, "The Creation," in *God's Trombones*, 20.

11. Gide, *De l'importance du public*, 37.

12. Davis, "Creator," in *Black Moods*, 24.

13. Johnson, "The Crucifixion," in *God's Trombones*, 41.

14. Hughes, *Collected Works*, 59.

15. Toomer, "Song of the Son," 26.

16. Dunbar, "Christmas on the Plantation," in *Collected Poetry*, 137; Dunbar, *When Malindy Sings*, 82.

17. Hughes, "Po' Boy Blues," in *Collected Works*, 78.

18. Hughes, "Young Gal's Blues," in *Collected Works*, 123.

19. Brown, "Tornado Blues," 68.

20. Hughes, "Florida Road Workers," in *Collected Works*, 124.

21. Corrothers, "At the Closed Gate," 14.

22. McKay, "My House," in *Complete Poems*, 214.

23. McKay, "The White City," in *Complete Poems*, 168.

24. Cullen, "Heritage," in *Collected Poems*, 26.

25. Cullen, "Heritage," in *Collected Poems*.

26. Bennett, "To a Dark Girl," 191.

27. Davis, "To You," in *Black Moods*, 42.

28. Senghor does not identify the author of "The Black Child." Cullen, "To a Brown Boy," in *Collected Poems*, 6.

29. Hughes, "Genius Child," in *Collected Works*, 138.

30. Hughes, "Earth Song," in *Collected Works*, 148.

31. Toomer, "Harvest Song," 91.

32. Cullen, "Brown Boy to Brown Girl," in *Collected Poems*, 8.

33. Hughes, "Our Land," in *Collected Works*, 56.

34. Wright, *Richard Wright Reader*, 245.

5

For a Federalist Solution

FIRST PUBLISHED IN *LA NEF*, SPECIAL
ISSUE, "WHERE IS THE FRENCH
UNION GOING?," JUNE 1955

Reprinted in *Liberté 2* (Paris: Seuil, 1969), 158–70

It is often said that "France is always one war behind." I, along with others, have adapted this phrase to assert that she has always been "one reform behind." Upon reflection, this critique seems unjust. In truth, France missed only the war—and the revolution—of 1870. This initiated the political stagnation of the Third Republic, a period that continues to this day, a stagnation that has permeated every sector except for the arts and letters. The revival incited by the Liberation was nothing more than a flash in the pan.

Let us set aside the military issue for now. 1870, or more precisely, 1875, was indeed the year of the missed opportunity. Had France, echoing the historic gestures of 16 Pluviôse, Year II, and April 27, 1848, granted "French citizenship" to the native peoples overseas, it might have sustained this enlightened momentum through its new conquests. This would have altered the complexion of the Empire, and the issue of the Union would not be confronting us today. However, even the Popular Front, held captive by the "system" or, even worse, by the bourgeois ethos of the Third Republic, missed another opportunity in 1936. Had she *assimilated* the Arab-Berber people of Algeria, as Ferhat Abba asked, we would not be facing demands for an "Algerian Republic" today, nor would the overseas representatives be pressing for a "French Federal Republic."

As it stands, the crucial matter is that the approach of assimilation has become obsolete as a solution, giving way to the current issue of forming a federation or, perhaps, a confederation. It is futile to bury our heads in the sand like an ostrich, or cover our eyes with our hands in a simian gesture of denial. How did we get here? It would make for an enthralling narrative if time allowed. Others have trodden this path before me. My intention here is merely to encapsulate, in a manner akin to an introduction, the saga of nationalism.

"Long live the Nation!" With this rallying cry, the French Army emerged victorious at the Battle of Valmy.[1] As Denis de Rougemont astutely points out, this chant is not synonymous with "Long live France!" For France is a fatherland: "A reality steeped in instincts and sentiments, a birth mark, as the term suggests, a local and seldom expandable geo-physical implant."[2] "Long live the Nation!" was an act of faith, the battle cry of the governing revolutionary faction. For the nation was, and still is, an ideal, not a reality; more precisely, it is an ideal that must continuously be realized, therefore, an ideal of conquest—I was about to say: a *colonial ideal.*

Have we not recently experienced this truth firsthand? Consequently, in the nineteenth century, we saw the resistance of Germany, Russia, and Italy. Subsequently, we saw the resistance of the Slavic, Hungarian, Romanic, Greek, and Irish fatherlands. This led to the birth of European movements for national liberation and the rebirth of local languages and cultures. This is because the Nation, albeit vaguely conscious of its vulnerabilities, constantly seeks to ground itself in the chthonic and vital realities of the fatherland.

The nationalist movement eventually radiated out from Europe to other continents in the twentieth century, initially engulfing Asia—a region more populous, more advanced, and more conscious of its own merits, thus growing increasingly restless under the oppressive yoke. This impatience intensified especially as Europe, in the aftermath of the self-destruction of her power and prestige following the fratricidal war of 1914, became ever more arrogant and severe. With the intervention of Russia and America, the war of 1939 precipitated the end of Europe because, in the interwar, Hitler heightened antagonisms and instilled in the peoples of the world their *racial* consciousness. We know what followed and how, successively, Syria, Lebanon, India, Pakistan,

Ceylon, Indonesia, among others, reclaimed their freedom. Today, a tidal wave of nationalism has swept across the entirety of Asia, transforming into a formidable hurricane battering the shores of Africa. Is there a need to delve into the situations in Egypt, Tunisia, Morocco, Sudan, or Kenya? It suffices to reflect upon the meaning of the Afro-Asian Conference in Bandung, where colonialism, and notably Europe, was squarely held to account.

These are the facts—and we, for one, will not press charges. And the evidence concerns, first and foremost, France: colonial power, world power, and especially African power. Again, her own territories have not been spared the wrath of the storm.

It is in the eye of the storm that, paradoxically, a French general managed to grasp the meaning of these "great events that change the world." Perhaps he leaned more toward being a patriot than a nationalist, more of an aristocrat than a Jacobin, interestingly, more revolutionary than bourgeois. Reportedly, he suggested to Governor Laurentie that "the future belongs to the métis." Undoubtedly a visionary and a prophet, he initiated the 1944 Brazzaville Conference by rejecting "the false prudence of yesterday," advocating for a federal blueprint for the French community. He urged, "Here, you will explore the moral, social, political, economic, and other conditions that, in your opinion, should be gradually implemented in each of our territories, allowing them, through their own development and the progress of their population, *to merge into the French community while preserving their individuality, their interests, their aspirations, and their prospective futures.*"[3] The emphasis is mine.

Alas! The majority of the delegates, many of whom were steeped in Jacobin philosophies, declined to tread the proposed path. Instead, they settled for a vaguely articulated compromise, reverting to "the false prudence of yesterday." This, despite the earlier stance of the Overseas Parliamentary Intergroup, who had advocated for a federalist solution. What remains is the proposal they presented to the Constitution Commission, from which I will only quote two articles:

Article 109: The progress that the peoples of the Union undertake with the people of France must usher them toward self-determination. Pertaining to those territories yet to attain the status of Free States, they shall, within a maximum not exceeding twenty years, select their own governmental structure.
Article 110: The territories constituting the French Union shall establish local assemblies responsible for drafting their individual constitutions.[4]

I admit that amid the euphoria of Liberation and their own political inexperience, the overseas parliamentarians—led by Lamine Guèye—perhaps overreached. Their agenda was fundamentally a rebuke against the "French of the Colonies," who, congregated in an "Estates General of French Colonization," sought to retain the Native Code under the guise of assimilation, in the name of French presence. Although the staunchest nationalists among them might not have represented the majority of the "Europeans" in the colonies—primarily settlers and merchants—they nonetheless constituted the most vital and aggressive faction: a sort of raw colonialism. When questioned, these parliamentarians hastily renounced any secessionist intentions. Typical French doctrinaires, they overlooked one vital aspect: delineating the federative connection. Yet they opposed the colonialism propagated by the Estates General of French colonization in the name of an antinationalist nationalism without much awareness of it, recognizing only their "local patriotism." As is well known, this is the shameful way nationalism operates. The compromise encapsulated in Title VIII of the Constitution emerged under these conditions.

The Constitution of 1946 and the Dynamism of History

We must now study this compromise. It was foreseeable, as early as 1946, that it would not hold up against the dynamism of history, the pressure of the "great events that change the world." The reluctance to confront these events head-on led to the refusal to discuss the new charter with the peoples from the overseas territories. The newly minted citizens of color were not even accorded the privilege of participating in the referendum.

The main pitfall of the 1946 compromise was the inherent contradictions it harbored, contradictions of various kinds. In this regard, I wish to begin with the French Union, where the significant contradiction lies between the Preamble and Title VIII. The Preamble unambiguously asserts the principle of federation, stating, "France shall constitute a Union with its overseas populations, grounded on *equal rights and responsibilities*, devoid of distinctions based on race or religion."[5] However, Article 62 imposes, unilaterally: "Members of the French Union shall consolidate all their resources to ensure the defense of the Union as a whole. The Government shall oversee the coordination of these resources and *execute the necessary policies* to ensure this defense."[6] This clause opened a gap in what was supposed to be a solid and harmonious system. Yielding to external pressures, three Associated States would ultimately undermine the fortress.

These pressures were: the isolation of the States in Indochina, situated thousands of miles away from the metropole—at a time when France was still a metropole; the burgeoning anti-European nationalism unfurling its influence across Asia; the permeation of English, or more accurately, American English, and the influx of the US dollar; and notably, the communist world's frantic advance toward the South China Sea and the Indian Ocean. The repercussions were profound: Indochina became a proxy battlefield in the conflict between the USA and USSR, with France sacrificing its finest in bloody battles where only honor was saved. Meanwhile, the three Associated States, prone to conflicting ideologies or even interests, eventually leaned toward Asian nationalism, seeking greater independence with each passing year. That is how we got to the treaty of October 22, 1953.

Article 2 of the Franco-Lao Treaty of Amity and Association is a useful illustration; it marks a decisive turn. It reads as follows:

> The Kingdom of Laos freely reaffirms its adherence to the French Union, an association of independent and sovereign peoples, free and equal in rights and duties, in which all the members pool their resources to guarantee the defense of the Union as a whole.
>
> It reaffirms its decision to serve on the High Council where the coordination of those means and the general conduct of the Union are implemented under the presidency of the President of the French Union.

This marks a substantial revision of Article 62. We shall soon see the ramifications.

External influence was equally decisive in the evolution of the political landscape in Morocco and particularly in Tunisia. But here, it was less the result of communism or the American dollar, and more the influence of the Arab League: a more unadulterated form of nationalism, more reasoned than mere pretext. Look at the Moroccan Workers' Union and the direction it lends to its actions. The signing of the Franco-Tunisian Agreement somewhat validated this Arab nationalism, albeit regrettably appearing as a fruit torn away by violence: A better solution might have been to wait until the fruit was ripe, until it became the fruitful product of a drawn-out Franco-Arab grafting. In North Africa, as in Indochina, that event calls for constructive conclusions.

I will dedicate more time to discussing the overseas territories, specifically those in Black Africa, with which the associated territories of Togo and Cameroon share a natural connection through ethnic, geographical, and development factors. The fact is that in Black Africa almost nothing has been done in terms of institutions, that everything can still be saved, and that finally, impatience employs the weapons of legality—but for how long? The case of Madagascar demonstrates that dismissing Black patience as mere impotence would be a gross miscalculation. Truth be told, are the most potent weapons not those of the law, as in a strike?

Thus, the 1946 compromise did not satisfy the Blacks any more than it did the Asians or the Arab-Berbers.[7] For it was merely a compromise that fell far short of indigenous demands, a compromise that was never fully realized. Let us recall how the problem of the status of overseas territories was shirked, how the law demanded that the government address it through a bill. Despite the law of February 6, 1952, only the bill concerning Togolese institutions has been enacted; all other proposals have been tabled.

Despite persistent affirmations of the "unity and indivisibility of the Republic" since 1946, true assimilation remains elusive. Forty-three million metropolitan citizens have 544 congressional representatives, while a nearly equal number of overseas citizens are granted only sixty-three seats. This disparity is starkly amplified within the governing councils. Indeed, the current Laniel administration has reached a new zenith of neglect, boasting thirty-nine ministers with not a single representative from the overseas territories.

Meanwhile, Congress indulges in frivolity. French intellectual prowess and creativity, revered as among the most vibrant in the world, have been reduced to a spectacle. Congressmen squander time orchestrating subtle strategies, sculpting the party's image or nurturing personal aspirations, always with an eye toward the impending government reshuffle or the forthcoming elections. Meanwhile, the critical organic laws, eagerly anticipated by the overseas peoples, languish and gather dust. As the wait stretches indefinitely, those peoples lose patience ... and dream. Increasingly, they dream of a status allowing them to "mind their own business," given the apparent incapacity of the "one and indivisible Republic." Even economic dilemmas remain unresolved, with the Colonial Pact persisting de facto. The signs are everywhere. The establishment of FIDES was initially hailed as a breakthrough, shifting from a "draft economy" to a "gift economy." Yet, as Professor Lecaillon notes, a substantial portion of the credit—85 percent—flows back to the metropole through various channels.[8] Indeed, the overseas territories continue to undervalue their exports to the metropole to the tune of 10 to 20 percent below world prices while simultaneously facing "French" imports inflated by 30 to 80 percent.

Out of these frustrations were born the proposals to amend Title VIII of the Constitution. It would be profoundly erroneous to associate the proposals solely with the legislators who ratified them. Truth be told, the discontent is pervasive, afflicting nearly all the representatives from the overseas territories, particularly those from Black Africa. This unease permeates even deeper layers, fueled not only by internal factors but also influenced by external developments such as the internal autonomy of British West African territories. It is an open secret that these regions are swiftly advancing toward *dominion* status, toward *Independence*. The time is ripe to address these issues decisively; as the saying goes, *domani troppo tardi!*[9]

Toward a "Union of French and Overseas Confederate States"

Regarding the French Union, it is widely acknowledged that the member states have grown disdainful of the epithet. Words bear a significant weight overseas compared to France. While certainly an issue of perception, it transcends mere imagery. The resistance is not against camaraderie or cherished French values, but against a term that has come to symbolize domination, betraying a quest for equality and, fundamentally, dignity. My suggestion for a new title is devoid of any authorial vanity; alternatives are welcome. The terminology, after all, is merely a marker. The primary concern is addressing the realities manifested in Title VIII, specifically the provisions of Article 62.

The necessity of incorporating a reference to the French Union in the 1946 French Constitution, or its successor, has been debated. The necessity is apparent as the Preamble concedes to "limitations upon its sovereignty necessary for the organization and preservation of peace" and references "Diplomatic Treaties" in Title IV. Consequently, the Constitution must provide for future agreements with the confederate states.

Yet another evidence is that we cannot turn back time. The Franco-Laos Treaty and the collateral agreements have set an irreversible movement. This was corroborated by the French Government's Declaration on July 4, 1953, to the Associated States of Indochina, and further solidified by subsequent agreements with these states. The principles outlined in paragraphs 16 and 17 of the Constitution's Preamble have now become tangible realities. The new Confederation must be founded upon those established principles.

We are moving beyond an era of unilaterally decreed "granted charters." The new title should simply delineate principles, foremost among which is allowing France to form a confederation with other "independent states," wherein all members willingly cede a level of sovereignty. Another principle would require that diplomatic treaties outline confederate organisms and set their appropriation. Those treaties would be ratified not only by the French Parliament but also by the competent authorities in the confederate states.

Predicting the nature of these organisms, today, is nothing but speculation. Two solutions present themselves. One draws inspiration from the ad hoc Assembly of Strasbourg, proposing the establishment of a Confederal Parliament and executive power. The alternative suggests retaining the existing High Council, augmenting its power. This latter proposition appears more prudent to me, likely preferred by the States of Indochina. It acknowledges the geographical, cultural, and ethnic diversities that mark these states.

The confederal approach offers another significant benefit—imparting a more resilient and thereby stronger juridical structure to the forthcoming Franco-Tunisian and Franco-Moroccan agreements.

Many have pondered it before me, and they cannot be considered revolutionaries. This is substantiated by the resolution proposed by M. Caillavet and M. Laforest, current Ministers of Associated States, who tend to make of Tunisia an Associated State. It would be futile to deny that the imminent Franco-Tunisian and Franco-Moroccan agreements are but a stepping stone toward independence. Bourguiba, unquestionably the most lucid and reasonable among Neo-Destour leaders, admitted as much in an interview with *Paris-Presse-l'Intransigeant* on March 18, 1955. "Independence has always been our goal, we never kept it a secret. Which, by the way, does not mean we want to live in isolation, away from the French orbit. *Independence can be accompanied by a limitation of sovereignty* toward a cooperation that recognizes and benefits our two peoples." We have been warned: With each review of the Franco-Tunisian agreements— planned biennially—the Tunisians will ask for a bit more independence. This stance inevitably fuels a revisionist movement fraught with skepticism, ready to escalate at the slightest provocation, and carrying the latent risk of eventual secession. This holds as true for Morocco as it does for Tunisia. Under these conditions, the merits of a confederal framework are evident. It would alleviate the apprehensions harbored by France's interlocutors. Assured of eventual independence, they would show greater forbearance, align more closely with the West, and possibly make more concessions regarding France's defense policy. We know the strategic value of Tunisia and Morocco.

Such is the meaning of Bourguiba's words. A Tunisian minister articulated it more plainly: "Amend Title VIII, establish a confederation, and grant us entry. We will not reject the offer."

In Favor of a "French Federal Republic"

Earlier, we noted how several overseas representatives, following their constituents, advocated for the transformation of France into a Federal Republic.

In this regard, we have no intentions of taking a step backward. Some believed the remedy lay in augmenting the representation of Algeria and overseas departments and territories in the Parliament. This would entail granting them over half of the seats, effectively turning the metropole into what President Herriot once called "a colony of colonies," a solution overseas citizens themselves would dismiss. They, too, would fear losing their personality. African nationalism is willing to forgo the nation, not the African fatherland. Hence, we must forge ahead and dare to imagine.

What should we imagine, you ask? My response is a "French Federal Republic." Let me be clear—because this is especially important for Black Africa and Madagascar—overseas representatives are well aware of the historical underdevelopment of their respective countries. They realize that forming a federation requires not merely a unity of language, religion, or culture, but some degree of similar evolution. They are patient. The resolution proposed by overseas Independents anticipates a fifteen-year delay to establish a French Federal Republic.

The move will occur in three phases. We are currently experiencing the first phase, delineated by the decree of October 23, 1946, lasting roughly a decade. The second phase, initiated by the law of April 16, 1955, concerning Togolese institutions, focuses on amplifying the powers of local assemblies and fostering the nucleus of an executive authority, composed equally of elected and appointed members. We must now prepare for the final phase, which will require amendments to various provisions of the October 27, 1946, Constitution.

As expected, this intricate and sensitive topic calls for a profound examination of relevant documents, a task that could be delegated to a dedicated commission operating under the purview of the President of the Council. This commission would include administrative officials from the relevant departments with experts well versed in the problem, like those who contributed to the special issue of *Politique étrangère* on the proposed modifications to Title VIII of the Constitution. Yet, we can already outline a direction.

Let us revisit the terms of the problem. In our final phase, we need to emulate the Canadian, Swiss, or West German models, and transform our centralized and centralizing unitary republic. Specifically, we must grant Algeria and the overseas departments and territories *internal autonomy*, make them into states that are not so much associated with but rather integrated into the French Republic.

This raises numerous questions. Nations and their sovereignty would fall squarely within the French Republic, which would not necessarily be the fatherland. A critical discussion would revolve around the allocation of resources between the federal state and the integrated states, an easily solvable dilemma. Foreign affairs, national security, treasury, and economic coordination—to name a few—would remain under the federal government and parliament's jurisdiction; all remaining matters not governed by the federal state would be delegated to local governments and legislatures. Another question is whether the integrated state operates as a territory or a part of a group of territories. I favor the latter, as a state, even an integrated one, is more viable when it is economically strong—by which I mean rich in manpower and resources. Indeed, nothing precludes the state-group-of-territories, under its current situation, from eventually becoming a federation.

With the foundational principle established, we can now speculate on which provisions in the Constitution might be subject to amendment. Within Article 1, France would retain her status as an "Indivisible Republic," yet the addition of a federal vocation would be warranted. Furthermore, Article 13 should also be amended to enable assemblies and, later, local parliaments, to cast votes on local laws as permanent delegations. Title VIII emerges as the section requiring the most substantial adjustments. However, in this endeavor, we shall remain cautious and adaptable, entrusting the phased progression to organic laws.

Once again, in this study, my intention is merely to delineate a trajectory, a preliminary outline. The responsibility of delving into the nuances and drafting a definitive plan will lie with the Special Commission.

To Choose or Not to Choose

"To govern is to plan," wise nations proclaim. Lately, the formula seems to have been replaced by "To govern is to choose." In reality, choosing depends on planning.

Planning for a changing world where, a decade hence, there will be no more "dependent people" seems a straightforward endeavor. The British, ever pragmatic, recognize this fact. While enforcing a ruthless repression in Kenya, they simultaneously initiate reforms across continents. This is aptly captured in Roy Lewis's piece in *Civilizations*, where he notes that "everywhere, the tendency is to give local communities a greater control of their own affairs, with autonomy and the *creation of new sovereign states* as final goal, in accordance with the British policy adopted to fit the political evolution of the Commonwealth. In conclusion, we see that if the current plan continues to develop normally, *in ten years*, the Gold Coast, Nigeria Federation, West Indies Federation, Malagasy Federation, and Central African Federation will doubtless share the same political status as India, Ceylon, and Australia."[10] The gathering of twenty-nine nations in Bandung exhibited even more magnanimity. In Chou En-Lai's words, they granted European powers a twenty-five-year timeline to give "freedom and independence" to dependent peoples. Like many Frenchmen, I am saddened by the injustice against France, which has been pegged as the scapegoat of the conference. A bourgeois nation perhaps, France never was racist; she is the least "colonial" of the colonial powers. Nevertheless, it would be perilously naive to dismiss the gravity of the threats and not plan accordingly. For "what matters"— as Robert Guillian writes in *Le Monde* on April 26, 1955—"are not the texts but something else: the conscious awakening of the men that are here; that is the event. The raised hopes, the powerful words." "It is up to Asia to help Africa," said Nehru in his final speech.[11] There are ideas that will leave Bandung and strongly resonate throughout Africa, like the tom-toms.

France must therefore plan—especially in light of parliamentary interest in revisiting Title VIII—and choose. But transcending the false choice— assimilation or total independence—offered by extremists on both sides is imperative. This dichotomy neither reflects the realities of the twentieth century nor the French genius.

I often find myself at odds with Denis de Rougemont, who, inspired by some sort of continental nationalism in contradiction with his own federalist stance, tends to idealize, even deify Western Europe. Yet, he accurately identifies the incongruity between nationalism and "the technical evolution and the news forms of scientific thought."[12] Not only do the "technological prowess of the century, electric then atomic energy, aviation, radio, and new weaponry fully escape national boundaries," he notes, so do the solutions to problems that are properly economic, such as credit, unemployment, emigration, and increase of living standard in underdeveloped countries. So far as scientific thought is concerned, it renounces the old Cartesianism, surpassing and replacing it with the principle of *complementarity*. This is true for wave mechanics as it is for quantum physics. Truth no longer appears as linear but as dialectical logic. It is no longer revealed through an autarkic monologue but conceived by dialogue: by colloquia.

This evolution of science and technology, together with the imperative for peace, has fostered the rise of federalism, a trend mirrored in international cooperation efforts. But technology, science, federal institutions are only the means to *culture*. The constituents of 1946 understood it well, who assigned as main goal to the French Union the development of the "respective civilizations" of the peoples of the Union. Yet, culture itself is colloquia. History teaches us that all great civilizations—Egyptian, Indian, ancient Greek—rose from *métissage*. So did French civilization, whose exotic contributions profoundly renewed the arts in the early twentieth century, whose succulence of her fruits, as Paul Valéry says in "Images de France," comes from a grafted tree.[13]

Therefore, we must choose to refuse to choose between the uniformity of assimilation and the stranglehold of total independence, two totalitarian worlds that, for better or worse, are one and the same: nationalism. The unitary republic is isolated: severed from the lifeblood of the land. Should the overseas territories secede, they would wither like branches severed from a tree. The mutual progress of both hinges on their collaboration. This sentiment was perfectly captured by the sociologist Lévi-Strauss in the controversy that opposed him to the Cartesian Roger Caillois: "If men are to progress, they must collaborate; and, in the course of their collaboration, the differences in their contributions will gradually be evened out, although collaboration was originally necessary and advantageous simply because of those differences."[14]

It is because France knows how to plan that she will choose the federalist solution, the sole viable response to the realities of the twentieth century.

TRANSLATOR'S NOTES

1. The Battle of Valmy, September 1792, marked the French forces' first significant victory during the revolutionary wars following the French Revolution.

2. Rougement, *Écrits sur l'Europe*, 227.

3. De Gaulle, *Mémoire de guerre*, 555–57.

4. *Séances de la Commission de la Constitution*, 195. Although the debates are accessible in the digital version at https://archives.assemblee-nationale.fr/, the textual representation is not available.

5. Preamble to the Constitution of October 27, 1946, Constitutional Council, https://www.conseil-constitutionnel.fr/en/preamble-to-the-constitution-of-october-27th-1946.

6. Constitution de 1946, IVe République, Conseil Constitutionnel, https://www.conseil-constitutionnel.fr/les-constitutions-dans-l-histoire/constitution-de-1946-ive-republique. While the Conseil Constitutionnel's official website offers an English translation of the preamble, the remainder of the constitution is available only in French. Translation mine.

7. Senghor originally used the term *les Jaunes*, which historically referred to East Asians. The term *Asians* is used here to reflect contemporary language yet still carries Senghor's essentialized overtone.

8. The Fonds d'Investissements pour le Développement Économique et Social (FIDES) was a French infrastructure initiative, established by law on April 30, 1946, to foster the economic and social development of the French Union's overseas territories.

9. The Italian translates as "Tomorrow is too late."

10. Lewis, "Commonwealth et Empire Britannique," 113.

11. Nehru, "Asia and Africa Awake," 195–210.

12. Rougemont, *Écrits sur l'Europe*, 230; translation mine.

13. Valéry, "Images de France," in *Regards sur le monde*.

14. Lévi-Strauss, *Race et histoire*, 117; Lévi-Strauss, *Race and History*, 132.

6

Like the Manatees Go Drink at the Source

FIRST PUBLISHED AS A POSTFACE
TO *ÉTHIOPIQUES*, 1956

Reprinted in *Liberté 1* (Paris: Seuil, 1966), 218–27

This is not a preface. I am not addressing the reader. The golden rule remains "to please," as Molière put it three centuries ago. If I pen these lines, it is at the behest of some critic friends of mine. To address their inquiries and to respond to the criticism from a few others who summon Negro poets, because they write in French, to also "feel" French—when they are not accusing them of imitating the great national poets. One criticized me for imitating Saint-John Perse, though I had not read his work before I composed *Shadow Songs* and *Black Hosts*. Another criticizes Césaire, claiming his tom-tom rhythm is tiring, as if a zebra could shed its zebraness. In truth, we are like the manatees who, as African mythology tells us, drink at the source, just as they did in days past when they were quadrupeds—or perhaps humans. I cannot tell which it is: myth or natural history.

But let us return to literary history. As I have mentioned elsewhere, the journey undertaken by the poets of the *Anthology* was not a literary pursuit, not even a diversion: It was a passion.[a] For the poet is akin to a woman in labor: There is an imperative to bring forth life. This is especially true for the Negro, who hails from a realm where words spontaneously metamorphose into rhythms the very moment man is moved, left to himself, to his authenticity. Yes, the spoken word morphs into poetry. Must I disclose it? Aimé Césaire's *Journal of a Homecoming* was a painful parturition. The mother was on death's doorstep, risking her life, by which I mean her reason. She is marked for life, like those seers whom Europe confines in asylum-prisons, but whom Africa continues to nurture and venerate, recognizing them as God's messengers.

Certainly, to use an unsavory term, the Negroes have *evolved*, especially since the decree of the 16th Pluviôse Year II; they have evolved dramatically: They have remained inherently themselves. Men who *feel*, rather than think. Always, beauty has struck them, straight-shooting, at the root of life—and disaster. For me, the *event* brings me to a point of sickness. My face turns dark. *She* says I am a comedian! Standing before the Ocean gate in Le Havre, before an autumn landscape in Île-de-France, a Florentine palace, a fresco by Giotto, at the sound of a famine in the Indies, a cyclone in the Antilles, an earthquake in Antananarivo, there they stand, the Negroes, *startled* to the core, struck by lightning. Like the griot before the prince, the maiden before the athlete, her Lion. They sing, but not of the vistas their eyes behold. Yes, they have evolved—the days of courtly love and athletic games are long past! No longer nourished by the rhythm of tom-toms and balafons, the voice of koras, or the incense of Amante. Here they stand, poets of the times, grayed by winter in a gray hotel room. How would they not muse over the Kingdom of Childhood, the Promised Land of the future amid the void of the present? How could they not sing "Negritude rising"? And since they were robbed of their instruments, let those be replaced with tobacco, coffee, and sheets of white graph paper. Here they stand, like the griots, with the same knots in their belly and throat, joy buried in anguish. I say: love and parturition. Here they stand, now, poets at the end of the road, lover-beloved, slobbery, gloppy, leaning not on sorrows but, ah! triumphant: light, mellow, and caressing the son, the poem, as did God at the end of the sixth day.

Why should I deny it? The poets of the *Anthology* have undergone influences, manifold influences, and they wear them as badges of honor. I will even admit—taking a cue from Aragon—that I have immersed myself in literature,

a Senghor, "Apport de la poésie nègre"; Senghor, *Anthologie*.

from the troubadours to Paul Claudel. I have imitated, too. I had to write *in French*, I will elaborate why shortly, in a language that was not inherently mine. I will also acknowledge that upon discovering Saint-John Perse, post-Liberation, I was just as blinded as Paul on the road to Damascus. The *Book of the Dead* too stirred within me a similar *rapture*. No surprise there! This poetry is not quite from Europe, and it is not without reason that Jean Guehénno asserts that the texts of the Dogon cosmogonies "bear resemblances to the poems of M. Claudel or of M. Alexis Léger (Saint-John Perse)."[b] But by that time, I already had the material for two collections in the back of a drawer. The truth is, I have predominantly read, or more accurately, listened to, transcribed, and annotated Negro-African poems.[c] And the Antilleans, who were oblivious to them—Césaire was an exception—would naturally rediscover this poetry by delving deep within themselves, swept away by the torrent, a thousand meters beneath the surface. If we are to find our masters, it would be wiser to seek them on African shores. Like the manatees go drink at the source in Simal.

Beyond our desire for a fraternal *message*, this would foster a better understanding of the style of the poets of the *Anthology*: their *Negritude*. Some critics have either lauded or rebuked us for our picturesqueness. Inadvertent picturesqueness, let them be convinced of it. I recall that during my elementary school years, everything about the French language seemed picturesque to me, down to the music of the words. And to the women in my village, who during periods of drought, in the cold season, adorned themselves—trousers, helmets, dark glasses—and conversed in French to amuse the gods and coax the rains, everything was picturesque. When we say *kora, balafon, tom-tom*, not harp, pianos, and drums, we are not picturesque: We simply call a spade a spade. We write primarily, and not exclusively, for the French of Africa, and, if the French of France find a hint of the picturesque in it, we might almost regret it. The imagery, the message, is not there; it is found in the mere act of naming things. It is what lends poetry to *The African Child*, the novel by Laye Camara, or the *Tales of Amadou Koumba* by Birago Diop. The power of the spoken word manifests itself already, and even better, as I have attempted to demonstrate elsewhere, in the Negro-African languages, where almost every word is descriptive, be it in terms of phonetics, morphology, or semantics.[d] The word is more than mere image, it is an analog image without even the need for metaphor. To name the thing is to unveil the meaning beneath the sign. For Negro-Africans, every-

b Guéhenno, *La France et les noirs*.
c Senghor, "Langage et poésie négro-africaine."
d Senghor, "Langage et poésie négro-africaine."

thing is sign and meaning, simultaneously; every being, every thing, but also matter, shape, hue, odor, and movement and rhythm and tone and timbre: the hue of the loincloth, the shape of the kora, the pattern of the bride's sandals, the steps and movements of the dancer, and the mask, what more can I say? I remember the reception bestowed upon me in Yamoussoukro, a grand honor from my friend Houphouët-Boigny. Adorned before me, in ceremonial order, the entire Baoulé nobility stood. Long gold necklaces and plates the size of my hand; flywhisks with handles shrouded in golden leaves; above all, diadems with gold-sculpted elephants, spiders, and cornucopia. This order, these regalia spoke to me in a language that was crystal clear. About that verbal image, the French language had developed a habit of emphasizing the analogy with a second word, one that was abstract, moralizing. It is no coincidence that, as André Rousseau recently observed, Paul Claudel felt the need to make the meanings of biblical images more palpable in his translations. Centuries of rationalism have transformed what once was a transparent veil into a wall. Surrealism deserves credit for revealing that two concrete words are sufficient, and that the image grows stronger as the "relations between the two juxtaposed realities" become more "distant."[e] But Negro-African poets, as I mentioned, often settle for a sign:

There are no more young people in the village.
Dyakhère, son of Moussa, hear me.
The sun at its zenith, and not a whisper!

Not a metaphor, yet beneath these simple words, we sense, with a meridian peace, the solemn presence of the spirits.

And since I must shed light on my poems, I further confess that nearly all the beings and things they evoke belong to my country: A few Serer villages nestle amid the *tanns*, the woods, the *bolongs*, and the fields.[f] Merely naming them brings the Kingdom of Childhood back to life—and I hope it brings the reader along with me—"through forests of symbols." I once lived there, mingling with shepherds and peasants. My father would often punish me, in the evening, chastising me for my wanderings; and to "discipline" me, he finally decided to send me to the White Man's School, much to the despair of my mother, who protested that at seven years of age, it was too soon. Thus, I dwelled in that kingdom, witnessed with my own eyes, heard with my own ears the fabulous beings

---

e Breton, *Premier manifeste du surréalisme*, 32; Breton, *Manifestos of Surrealism*, 20.
f See the lexicon for *Chants pour Naëtt*. Senghor, *Chants pour Naëtt*; later republished as "Chants pour signare" in *Nocturnes*.

beyond the things: the *kouss* in the tamarind trees, the crocodiles safeguarding the springs, the manatees singing in the river, the Dead of the village and the Ancestors who communicated to me, initiated me to the alternating truths of the night and of the light.[g] To prophesy the city of tomorrow, which will rise from the ashes of the old—fulfilling the poet's mission—I simply had to name the elements of my childlike universe.

But the power of analogical images only unleashes itself under the influence of rhythm. Only rhythm can ignite the poetic short-circuit that transmutes copper into gold, speech into verb. In the interwar period, many overly indulged in the "stunning image," even portraying it as the quintessence of poetry. It is fortunate that André Breton himself counteracted this overindulgence, emphasizing the sensitive—I would even say sensual—qualities of words in his "Golden Silence."[1] "Never as much as in surrealist writing have poets trusted to the tonal value of words. The negativist attitudes inspired by instrumental music do seem to find compensation in this fact. Regarding language, nothing has captivated, and still captivates, surrealist poets so much as this property words have to link together into singular chains and thus to shine forth at this very moment when one is least trying to find them."[2] A few lines down: "Great poets have been 'auditories,' not visionaries."

I aim to stay true to my words, refraining from passing value judgments. Negro poets, both those in the *Anthology* and those from the oral tradition, are primarily "auditories": bards. They are tyrannically subjected to the "inner music," primarily to rhythm. I recall the Gymnic poets from my village; the naivest among them could—did—only compose in the trance of the tom-toms, sustained, inspired, fueled by the rhythm of the tom-tom. It begins with an expression, a phrase, a verse whispered in my ear, like a leitmotif, and when I begin to write, I do not know what the poem will become. This situation of the Black poet is misunderstood by Henri Hell, who writes about Aimé Césaire:

> One loves the power of incantation, the obsessive rhythm in some of his poems like *Batouque*. Yet, such brilliance, such exaggeration, such provocative excess can be tiring. Is such an orgy of rare words (*ramphoriques, trémail, coalescences*, etc.) necessary? This constantly heightened lyricism generates monotony. *And the Dogs Were Silent* is no longer a tragedy but a long lyric outcry whose violence turns dull. The continual tumult of

g *Kouss* are Jinn that recall the first inhabitants of Black Africa, the Pygmies that were exterminated or exiled by the Great Negroes.

words deafens. The incessant flickering of images (however dazzling) blurs the vision. A poem that merely adds enumeration upon enumeration, cries upon cries, ceases to be a poem. Such a work, with no rhythm other than the regular repetition of a few incantatory words, eventually unweaves itself. The relentless and uncontrolled surge of images strips them of all effectiveness.[h]

Please forgive my extended citation of Henri Hell. He allows us to frame the problem by presenting a critic who refuses to understand, who denies himself the virtue of *sym-pathy*. Let us revisit the images. If the critic mentions the "unceasing and unrestrained surge of images" and their "gratuitous nature," it is because he has not fully grasped their meaning. His alibi is that he would have needed to embody the dual culture of the French and Negro poet. Worse, he failed to perceive that in Césaire's work, the images are more than ambivalent: They are multivalent, and doubly so. The same idea-feeling is portrayed through a series of images, where each image emanates a life of its own, radiating from all its facets of meaning, like a diamond. Worse even, Hell did not realize that the "incessant flickering of images" is merely one form, among others, of rhythm. Because rhythm remains the problem. Sartre grasped this well when he penned in "Black Orpheus,"

> As a result, one can speak here of *committed*, even *directed* automatic writing—not that reflection intervenes but because the words and images perpetually express the same torrid obsession. In the depths of himself, the white Surrealist finds release from tension; in the depths of himself, Césaire finds the relentless inflexibility of demand and resentment. Lero's words are organized flabbily, relaxedly, by a loosening of logical connections, around vague, broad themes. Césaire's words are pressed up against each other and cemented together by his furious passion. Between the most daring comparisons, the most distant terms, there runs a secret thread of hatred and hope.[3]

This is possible only because the New Negro is driven by lucid passion, because the alum of the École Normale Supérieure remains, in his delirium, the magnificent master of his language. I assert that rhythm remains the problem. Not only in the nuances of modern French, also in the repetition of words

h Hell, "Poètes de ce temps."

and grammatical categories, even in the—instinctive—use of certain figures of speech: alliterations, assonances, homoeoteleutons.[i]

> helmsman of the night populated with suns and rainbows
> helmsman of the sea and of death
> freedom of my gawky gal your legs sticky with fresh blood
> your cry of a surprised bird, of a fascine
> and of a shabeen in the depths of the water
> of an alburnum and of a trial and of a triumphant lychee
> and of a sacrilege
> crawl crawl
> my gawky one populated with horses and foliage
> and with risks and with acquaintances
> with heritage and with sources
> at the peak of your loves at the peak of your delays
> at the peak of your canticles
> of your lanterns
> on your insectlike and rootlike tips
> crawl great drunken spawn of bulldogs of mastiff of baby wild boards
> of lanceolate pit vipers and of fires
> in order to rout the scrofulous examples of poultices.[j]

At the poem's very navel, rhythm, birthed from emotion, in turn begets emotion. And humor, the flip side of Negritude. This underscores its multivalence—and the image's. As it appears in the works of Léon Damas:

> All to your need,
> all to your joy
> all to the illusion,
> all to this Côte-d'Azur
> all at last to yourself and alone
>
> but nothing
> but again nothing
> but again, always nothing
> and nothing in my hotel mailbox
> if not for

---

i See essays by André Spire and the phoneticians: Father Rousselot, Georges Lote, Robert de Souza, and Maurice Grammont.
j Césaire, "And the Dogs Were Silent," 37; Césaire, *Et si les chiens se taisaient*, 101.

the poor pendent
key that dangles
key that gives no dang.[k]

Our goal is not to pit the poets of the *Anthology* against the great national poets,
although some—Gaëtan Picon, Jean-Paul Sartre, André Breton—do not hesitate to elevate Césaire to that pinnacle. Our aspiration is humble: to pioneer,
to pave the way for an authentic Negro poetry that does not foreclose being
French. Just as those painters in Flanders, Holland, and Italy who are referred
to as "primitive" did. I must emphasize this study aims to highlight the disparate circumstances, asserting that although the essence of poetry remains the
same everywhere, the poet's temperaments and techniques are diverse. Criti-
cizing Césaire and his contemporaries for their rhythm, their "monotony," in
a word their style, is to reproach them for being born "Negroes," Antillean,
or African, and not "French" or even Christians; it is chastising them for being
unapologetically themselves, undeniably sincere. "Such exaggeration, such pro-
vocative excess" in Césaire's works can only be attributed to his Antillean origins, by centuries of slavery, the alienation from Africa and from himself. For
centuries, I assert, he was uprooted from *his* world order, thrown into the suf-
ferings of exile, the contradictions of *métissage* and capitalism. Is it so surprising
that he wields his pen as Louis Armstrong does his trumpet? Or better yet, like
Voodoo worshippers with their tom-tom? He needs to lose himself within the
dance of words, follow the tom-tom rhythm, to find himself anew in the Cosmos. Henri Hell writes about Jouve: "Since we are in the world for the capital
union with God, and if God is the universal Soul, poets, like mystics, must lose
the notion of their personality. They must shed the illusory individuality for a
superior 'I' located *beneath* personality. The 'I' consents to its own destruction so that it can grow toward the ultimate Reality." Emphasis is mine. Instead
of *toward*, perhaps one should read: *above*. I fully subscribe to this judgment.
Indeed, this is Césaire's approach, albeit with means that belong to his race and
his native island, the "snake-charming Martinique."

One more thing. My friend Clancier advises me, "Let us wish that Senghor
succeeds in crafting a discourse with a more diverse rhythm, where an image or
word will suddenly stand stark, around which the figure of the poem evolves;
only then will he truly usher us into his poetic universe, one that is original
and brimming with rich humanity." That was in 1945. Dear Clancier, I might
have succumbed to your counsel, now echoed by many. What a shame if I did

k Damas, *Graffiti* [translation mine].

so consciously. Can you not see that you invite me to sculpt the poem *à la française*, as a *drama*, when for us, it is a *symphony*, like a song, a tale, a play, a Negro mask? The monotony of tones, after all, is what distinguishes poetry from prose. It is the hallmark of Negritude, the incantation that grants access to the truth of essential things: the Cosmic Forces.

You will ask me: "Why, then, do you write in French?" Because we are cultural métis, because we feel like Negroes and express ourselves in French, because French is a language with a universal vocation, because our message is directed at the French of France and other men, because French is a "kind and honest language."[1] Some might say it is a drab and lifeless language, reserved for engineers and diplomats. Yes, I proclaimed the same for the purpose of my argument in my dissertation. I seek forgiveness. For having savored, gnawed, and disseminated it, I know its resources, as I know that it is the language of the gods. Listen to Corneille, Lautréamont, Rimbaud, Péguy, Claudel. Listen to the great Hugo. French is like the great church organ capable of evoking a limitless palette of sound and effects, from the softest tones to raging thunderstorms. It is flute, oboe, trumpet, tom-tom, even cannon, successively or simultaneously. Not to mention that French also graced us with abstract words—a rarity in our native languages—where tears crystallize into precious gems. In our languages, words naturally emanate an aura of sap and blood; French words shine brilliantly, like diamonds. Like flares that illuminate our darkness.

We have arrived at our last point: the *diction* of a poem. I deem it vital. The profound lesson I gleaned from Marôme, the village poetess, is that poetry is akin to a song, if not music itself—and this is far from being a literary cliché.[m] A poem is like a jazz score, where the performance holds equal weight to the text. This sentiment has deepened within me from one collection to the next; when I write instrumental directions in a poem heading, it is not a mere formulaic addition. The same poem can thus be recited—I do not mean spoken—chanted, or sung. Initially, one might recite the poem following the French tradition, accentuating the prominent inflection in each word group. I harbor hope that the expressive punctuation I have incorporated in this collection will facilitate this. Alternatively, the poem might also be recited with an instrumental accompaniment: tom-tom, *tama*,[n] kora,[o] *khalam*,[p] as Maurice

---

l Guéhenno, *La France et les noirs*.
m I discovered the gift of Marône doing fieldwork on Negro-African poetry's oral tradition. Author of some two thousand Gymnic songs, she was known to the far ends of the Kingdom of Sine (Senegal).
n Small talking drum mostly used by the griots.
o A kind of harp.
p Tetrachord guitar.

Sonar Senghor does. Here, the emphasis falls on accentuating the verse's concluding note and the crests of its lyrical waves, reminiscent of a town crier in Black villages. The poem may be psalmodized against a musical backdrop: with the same instruments, or, preferably, flutes, organs, or a jazz orchestra. Cinema offers a glimpse into this technique. Here, the tone is more monotone. Finally, the poem can truly be sung with a musical score. The music that Ms. Barat-Pepper, the composer of the *Messe des Piroguiers*, wrote for the *Chant de l'Initié*, on African themes, provides us with an excellent illustration.[q]

I remain convinced that the poem is achieved only if it melds song, word, and music. The current trend of so-called *expressive* diction celebrated in theaters or in the street is the *antipoem*. As if rhythm was not, beneath its variety, a monotony that exhibits the *substantial* movement of cosmic Forces, of the Everlasting! . . . It is time to halt the rampant disaggregation of the modern world, most urgently, of poetry. We must return poetry to its source when it was sung—and danced. As it was in ancient Greece, Israel, or the Egypt of the Pharaohs. Much like it is, today, in Black Africa. "A house divided against itself," and the arts will perish.[4] Poetry must not perish. For if it does, where then, would the World seek its beacon of hope?

TRANSLATOR'S NOTES

1. Breton, "Golden Silence," 70–75.
2. Breton, "Golden Silence," 73–74.
3. Sartre, "Black Orpheus," 33; translation modified.
4. Matthew 12:25 (King James Version).

q Senghor, *Chants pour Naëtt.*

7

Balkanization or Federation

FIRST PUBLISHED IN *AFRIQUE NOUVELLE*, 1956

Reprinted in *Liberté 2* (Paris: Seuil, 1971), 180–84

We do not regret tackling the problem of unity in French West Africa. We have addressed it for several years now. During the debates on the Loi-Cadre, we once again made our case, warning our African counterparts against a balkanization of overseas territories. We forcefully returned to the issue in the discussions held by the relevant committees of the National Assembly, which for several months have been deliberating on amending the Constitution, notably Title VIII.

We are glad to see that our position has sparked vibrant reactions, some supportive, others hostile. What matters is that the debate is now before the African public opinion and remains open-ended. It was *Afrique nouvelle* that, in its editorial on October 16, 1956, revisited the issue with striking clarity. This is an opportune moment to appreciate the constructive role this newspaper has played in fostering the discussion.

But what lies at the heart of this problem? The future political organization of overseas territories, of French West Africa especially, within the framework of a French Federal Republic and a Confederal Union. In French West Africa proper, there are three solutions. (1) Each territory, endowed with a status of internal autonomy, will be directly integrated within the republic, bound to the metropole in a practical way. (2) The eight territories of French West Africa merge into a unitary state with one government and one legislative assembly, and this state, under national law, is integrated in the republic. (3) Each of the eight territories of French West Africa retains a degree of autonomy yet forms a federal state still integrated into the republic.

Let us scrutinize these various solutions.

The first option amounts to *balkanization*, a position embraced by Mr. Apithy and most African congressmen. Mr. Apithy asked me, in *Afrique nouvelle*, for the meaning of the word *balkanization*. My response is that there is no need for extensive academic credentials . . . to understand the metaphor; it is enough to use the African sense of storytelling.

But let us explain ourselves, since it is what Mr. Apithy is asking for. So therefore, to balkanize French West Africa is to divide, artificially, its eight territories into political, economic, and cultural entities that do not ignore the metropole but do ignore each other. *Entities* without *reality*. Obviously, current territorial borders are nothing but the outcome of military musings and bureaucratic curiosities. They bear no relation to any reality, be it geographic, economic, ethnic, or linguistic. Even if we undertake a re-membering, as advocated by my friend Nazi Boni—his argument is not without merit—the problem remains unresolved. Disparities between rich territories and poor territories would persist; the Fula people would remain dispersed, and the Mande people, chiefly the Africans, would continue to be segmented.

If we focus solely on economic and cultural considerations, we must ask what influence could smaller entities like Senegal, or Côte d'Ivoire, with its population of two million—speaking only of the so-called rich territories—hope to exert when juxtaposed against a metropole of forty million, the wealthiest and most intellectually rich among Western European nations? And who would extend a helping hand to the impoverished territories when the writings of Mr. Raymond Cartier so deeply resonate with the metropolitan public opinion? Yet, assuming these issues are resolved, and that includes boundary disputes, how can we justify divisiveness at a time when France, in the name of *culture*, moves toward the path to European federation, signaling an inappropriate time for us to turn away from one another? At this historical juncture, it is only natural that we seek to fortify our traditional culture—though,

I readily concede, in the light of European reason. And how can we safeguard the human values of our Negritude if we do not begin by uniting and understanding one another, if we do not start by jointly taking stock of it? To accept the balkanization of Africa is to accept, with our misery, the alienation of our reasons for existence.

The second solution is that of a *unitary state*, subject to national law, integrated into a French Federal Republic. This implies that the eight territories of French West Africa would unite to form *a single entity of 25 million people*, pooling their resources and frameworks. This approach would offer numerous benefits. The collective will of 25 million citizens—exceeding half of the metropolitan population—would not be insignificantly influential in dialogues with the metropole. Pooling resources would enable a swifter economic and social development in the impoverished inland territories, generally stymied by their arid climate and remoteness from ports. Moreover, political unity—characterized by a single government and legislative assembly—would foster the self-consciousness of our collective personality and the building of an authentic culture founded upon Negro-African values, fertilized by the French spirit, and open to the contemporary world. To be clear, this unity would not preclude the establishment of provinces delineated by geographical and ethnic realities, thereby fulfilling the wish of Mr. Nazi Boni, endowed with congressional authority to deliberate on local affairs.

You have guessed it, this is the solution we favor. We recognize, however, that it is somewhat premature. If our educated youth ask for it, our laboring and farming masses are not yet sufficiently enlightened to tackle the problem, especially when most African parliamentarians take great care to not enlighten them. The opposition from these individuals poses the primary obstacle to political unity. They would rather come first in Cotonou, Ouagadougou, or Bamako, than second in Dakar.

These considerations have led us to opt for the third solution, for now. This does not change our current situation. The eight territories of French West Africa would remain largely unchanged, aside from a light re-membering if necessary. Each would be endowed with a ministerial council and a legislative assembly to address all territorial interests. However, superseding the local governments and parliaments, a federal government and a federal parliament would be established, addressing matters of common interest.

Let us be clear. Contrary to frequent, unfounded criticisms, we have no intention of maintaining the current overlaps and duplications. In Dakar or elsewhere—should another capital be chosen—only the directorates of common services would exist: security, transportation, telecommunications, customs,

higher education, justice, treasury and economic coordination, federal personnel. For territorial matters, only technical teams reporting to the government
and parliament of French West Africa would operate. Thus, the Departments
of Health, Primary and Secondary Education, Public Work, Agriculture, Farming, Territorial Personnel—the list is not exhaustive—would report to territorial authorities. The corresponding technical teams, as their name indicates,
would only provide technical guidance to the territories and facilitate some
degree of administrative harmonization across territorial governments.

The benefit of such a system is obvious. It accommodates desires for local
autonomy while preserving the main advantages of unity. From this perspective, indeed, it is the Federal State of French West Africa that would be integrated into the French Federal Republic. The Dahomeyans in Senegal have
perceived these benefits with clarity and articulated them lucidly in motions
submitted to the Dahomeyan Territorial Assembly. In doing so, they have
preserved Dahomeyan honor and rendered a significant service to the entire
French West Africa. It remains that the stance of my friend Zinsou, whose intervention I found as brilliant as ever, is not so different from theirs, or ours.
If balkanization prevails, we, Senegalese, will not hesitate to embrace all non-
Senegalese residing on our soil. We left behind the age of racial and tribal struggle long ago.

One final note. A certain party, proclaiming itself to be "the only African"
one, has made anti-Senegalism the cement of its unity. Its leaders loudly assert
that, if the elected representatives of Senegal advocate for the unity of French
West Africa, it is for selfish ends. Simple facts, backed by precise figures, contradict this theory. If balkanization were to fully prevail, it would result in a
substantial rise in the standard of living for the Senegalese masses. Do not take
my word for it, take Louis Delmas's, French Union advisor for Guinea. Senegal
sacrifices FCFA five billion annually on the altar of international solidarity. I
would add that, should there actually be a Ministerial Council of French West
Africa, its president would probably not be Senegalese. The truth, once again,
is that Senegal's long political experience has given her the clarity to rise above
the artificial oppositions born of geography, race, or language.

I confess, we have not yet succeeded in having our thesis adopted by the
National Assembly's Overseas Commission. We managed to avoid the worst:
the disaggregation of French West Africa. That is what matters most. Our hope
is that, through the efforts of our educated youth and the pressure from the
masses, the unity of French West Africa will eventually prevail—for the benefit
of all, and primarily, the impoverished territories.

8

The Fodéba Keita
African Ballet

FIRST PUBLISHED IN *L'UNITÉ
AFRICAINE*, 1959

Reprinted in *Liberté 1* (Paris: Seuil, 1964), 287–91

Every time I had the pleasure of attending the Fodéba Keita African Ballet, I would find myself experiencing a joy that went beyond mere enjoyment. Since the artist's "golden rule" is "to please," I inferred that, each time, the caliber of the ballet had heightened. This sentiment was especially strong during a memorable evening at the Théâtre du Palais in Dakar on June 28, 1959. Even more striking than the unanimous applause was the intensity of the clapping from the European spectators—and how many were there. It revealed a rare quality of the ballet: its ability to make Black and White peoples commune in a shared artistic emotion. "Excellent," murmured a European woman seated next to me, over and over again. Her remark was spot-on.

Let us begin with a tribute to the ballet master. For a Negro-African to assemble a show of such international caliber not only reflects an extraordinary stroke of method and organization but also a deep grasp of Negro-African art. But without further ado, let us get to the show.

More than anything else, these are ballet dances: Negro-African ones. Not too long ago, I encountered a critique stating something like "Mr. Fodéba Keita has betrayed Black Africa. We are miles away from Negro-African folklore where dances are danced on the town square, under moonlight, around a fire." To this, I mentally retorted, "Sir, you are confusing *art* and *folklore*." Popular dances, be they Spanish, Basque, Hungarian, Polish, or Russian, are as distinct from European ballets as Negro-African dances are from Fodéba Keita's ballets. The town square is not a theater stage. The latter demands a certain degree of perspective and stylization that captures the essence of folklore more so than its forms, its rhythm more so than its gestures. It is a separate realm, a different moment in time. The aim is not to replicate popular dances exactly, like a photograph, but rather to craft fresh works inspired by them while keeping their spirit alive. That is precisely what Keita achieved.

Dance, in its original form still pervasive in Black Africa today, is an all-encompassing language. It mobilizes the whole body, man as a whole: head and torso, arms and legs. The whole art corps: poetry, song, music, painting, sculpture, and of course, dance itself. The point is to express an idea or a feeling musically and plastically at once: through intimately tied visual and sonorous images.

Consider, for instance, part 2, number 7: "Lions and Panthers." Here, Man-Lion is opposed to Woman-Panther, noble Force to feline Grace. While it is undoubtedly a creation of Fodéba Keita, it is based on a *lived* experience of dance. The idea and writing, along with the transposition of dance to the strict staging and timing of theatrical production, come from the author. But the steps, the gestures, the rhythm, indeed the rhythms: They all come from eternal Africa. We have seen them, heard them elsewhere.

Now, rhythm. One of the African Ballet's greatest accomplishments is its preservation of this rhythm, the common denominator of Negro-African arts, essentially expressed by the drum, or rather, drums. Ladji Camara, such a wonderful drummer! His talent was on full display in an unforgettable performance of "Nanaba." But we truly begin to grasp Negro-African rhythm in part 1, number 1: "The Call of the Tam-Tam." Mamadou Touré and Aliou Sissoko drum the basic rhythm, imperiously, to support Ladji Camara, who, like Antaeus upon Mother Earth, builds upon it and lets his imagination soar. From this point on, all bets are off: from the dazzling flights to the sky to the most unexpected acrobatic eruptions of contretemps and syncopation. This Negro-African rhythm comes back to us through the masks, whether worn by the dancers or displayed in the background. I am not so sure these masks are authentic. I bet they rarely are. It does not matter; authenticity is a question of style, and the masks of the African Ballet are true to the style of Black Africa. Expressive, they are merely imbuing form and color with symbolic value.

Returning to rhythm, musical instruments like drums and koras are not ends but means to accompany dancing and singing. Dancing especially. From the moment the great explorers of the Renaissance made first contact with Black Africa, they beheld the regality of the tam-tam on the continent. To such an extent that, under the spell of the tam-tam, the Europeans overlooked all other musical instruments for a considerable period. Worse, they overlooked the existence of a rich and subtle Negro-African musical tradition. Remember, there is no music for its own sake. Here, musical instruments accompany singing and dancing; they support more than inspire them. Indeed, they support and inspire them concurrently. There is dialogue, mutual inspiration, a dialectic of drummers and singers, drummers and dancers.

Enough said about drummers. Let us speak about dancers. To reiterate, the ballets are primarily Negro-African dances just as the masks, songs, and music are a language-image. Negro-African dances remain close to the source. They express drama. For Negro-Africans, dancing is the most natural means for conveying ideas and emotions. Let the emotions—joy or sadness—take hold of them, they dance—a dance that greatly diverges from European ballets. This is not an intellectual exercise. There are no *pointe* techniques, straight lines, erudite arabesques, or *entrechats*. There are telluric dances, bare feet flat on the ground, drumming against the earth tirelessly and endlessly. Yet, these same Black bodies can produce prodigious feline-like leaps. They are slender, muscular, supple, and light. Their only secret is to wholly surrender their moldable selves to the rhythm, to allow themselves to be enfolded and driven by the archetype, to live—not to perform—their role with the true truth of emotion.

The Negro-African dancers in Fodéba Keita's troupe are more than dancers, they are actors. Casual actors who play their role to perfection because they live it: with their mouths (I will return to this later), their eyes, but especially with their feet, arms, and hands. These are dancers. Since they live the drama, our dancers do not merely perform a series of complex and elaborate movements but bring the archetype to life as expressed in naturally stylized gestures: embodying the Lion, the Panther, the Sorcerer, the Sower. No risk of falling into the academicism of stereotypes.

This imaged language, this *symbolic naturalism*, prevents the compartmentalization of the arts. Dancers wear masks and makeup in accordance with our purest tradition. They use the accompaniment of our drums and kora—and what a shame when they do not. And they sing. Fodéba Keita is correct. If our dancers were not actors, if they were not singers, they would not be *Negro* dancers. One can sense that they have not been trained in conservatories because their voices have not been distorted. I like them as they are: natural, rough yet pure, as they keep the earthy flavor of the land.

Let me say a few words about the set and costumes before concluding. Since Negro-African performances traditionally occur in village squares or forest clearings, there is no need for set or background. But a stage is not a village square. I did not like the early sets of the African Ballet; they seemed artificial and overly European. The Dakar set, on the other hand, was a lot different: only a few meaningful objects, discreetly hinting, nothing more. That was all. That was better. The actor-dancers' costumes also lost the ostentatious glamour they had at the Théâtre des Champs-Élysées. They can certainly be stylized, pure creation, as befits theater. So long as their form and color draw inspiration from true costumes in the symbolic style of Black Africa, they do not impede dancing but highlight the steps and movements of the dancers.

Fodéba Keita's African ballets are total works of art. Better: They are Negro-African works of art where dance assumes its full meaning and value through interaction with the complementary arts: painting, sculpture, singing, and music.

Here are a few friendly suggestions for the ballet master if he would kindly consider them.

First, he should refrain from replacing dancing with singing and acting. We are talking about ballet; therefore, dancing should permeate everything. Even singing and acting should themselves be danced. Dancing must be without rest or interruption, its rhythms leading and propelling the entire performance with an irresistible force from start to finish.

Second, the ballet master should ensure the performances are not overwhelmed by the European, and particularly American, spirit. He should steer clear of wit and anecdote. For there is a Negro humor, which is a response to life's hardships through laughter. He should use it generously. Above all, he should not fall for eroticism, which intellectualizes sensuality and verges on pornography. I hear those who object that "Younou Gambie" is a Wolof dance. Yes, but with an Americanized flavor of Arabo-Berber cuisine, which is not the Maghreb's best. Fodéba Keita should instead revert to the *sensuality* that embodies Negro-African spirituality.

These are minor flaws, and I believe, if pointed out to the ballet master, he will promptly rectify them.

Let me share with you one last thing. After Guinea gained her independence, I was concerned that she might sacrifice art in the name of industrialization and politics. I am pleased to note that this has not been the case. We cannot stress enough that true independence is *cultural independence*. Guinea is gaining it. So is Mali, with the creation of a Department of Arts and Letters and a plan to organize a "Dakar Season" annually. So is Senegal, where the secretary of state for youth and sports, Alioune Tall, shall overhaul cultural activities. So is Sudan, whose government returned to the roots by requesting the recovery of folk literature masterpieces. By fostering a Negro-African Renaissance, there is nothing to lose and everything to gain.

9

From Federation to the Civilization of the Universal

TOAST TO DOCTOR NNAMDI AZIKIWE,

GOVERNOR GENERAL OF NIGERIA,

LAGOS, FEBRUARY 8, 1961

Reprinted in *Liberté 4* (Paris: Seuil, 1983), 45–51

Esteemed Governor General, I am deeply honored and grateful to be here today in response to your fraternal and noble words.

Representing one-sixth of Africa's total population, the Federal Republic of Nigeria stands as the largest state on our continent. She is led by exceptional men like yourself, Sir, and Sir Tafawa Baléwa, who have been among the greatest architects of the African liberation movement. You have carefully thought through and methodically prepared and organized your independence. Indeed, for you, independence is neither an end nor a means for internal dictatorship or external imperialism. On the contrary, it is a driving force for human development and African cooperation.

The people of Senegal, whom I represent here today, share your reasoned method and your noble ideals. I come as a brother. It is therefore as a brother that I shall respond.

Independence and Federation, British Commonwealth and French Community

For both of us, national independence is not an end. It is not a shiny jewel to flaunt and impress our neighbors. Neither is it a distraction. In truth, it is both a negation and an affirmation, a tool for national liberation and nation-building.

The first step is to restore equality by restoring the freedom that was confiscated and alienated by the colonizers. I am not talking about social equality by way of a classless society, which is the goal of classical socialism. I am speaking of equality between colonizers and colonized: between two peoples, two races, two civilizations.

This freedom is initially an act of refusal, though: the refusal of foreign domination. At best, it is a freedom to choose between several ways and means, an uncharted territory we must survey. Indeed, it can also become the freedom to wallow in ignorance and sickness, the freedom to starve.

Independence is the collective affirmation of a people united in solidarity. Not just in words, but through concrete, methodically organized action. Decolonization is not achieved through the most anticolonial speeches—if only it were that simple!—but through rationally developed plans to overcome ignorance, sickness, and misery. Our goal is to raise both living and cultural standards by harmoniously developing the whole man and all men in the shortest possible time at the lowest possible cost—just as Professor Lebret suggested. Simply put, true independence is a relentless battle that must be continuously waged, a delicate balance that must be maintained, a victory not over the colonizer but over ourselves.

I spoke about the "collective affirmation of a people united in solidarity." Evidently, on their own, individuals cannot be independent; nor can nations that shield themselves behind their borders, especially when their population numbers only in the hundreds, or thousands, or even millions. Dwarf states are bound to stagnate in an era marked by the real interdependence of nations, despite the persistent reality of nationalism—or at least national sentiments. We must reconcile the apparent contradictions between—and demands of—autonomy and independence, independence and interdependence. You have wisely solved this issue, among others, thanks to the ongoing Federation of Nigeria and your sustained association with the Commonwealth.

I have often praised federalism. Today's most powerful nations are federal states: the United States of America, the Soviet Union, Canada, Brazil, India, the Federal Republic of Germany. Federalism certainly provides a dual advantage. It enables countries and their peoples, deeply rooted in their land, customs, language, and art, to thrive. It also allows nations to bring diverse people together into a dynamic whole by extracting fresh forces from the sap of their land to foster development. We are beginning to understand that population size and density are key factors of progress. In the case of Nigeria, they play a crucial role in bolstering its power.

You might ask me, "Why, then, did you dissolve the Federation of Mali?" Allow me to provide a straightforward answer. We Senegalese have always endorsed the federal idea. Back in 1956, when the enforcement decree of the Loi-Cadre was under debate in the French Parliament, we were almost alone in opposing the semiautonomy it granted to former French West Africa. We believed it would lead to balkanization and undermine the federation, which had been an efficient factor in fostering African unity. We persisted in our efforts before the Constitutional Consultative Committee in 1958, to no avail.

Undeterred, we revived the federal idea a year later, in 1959, resulting in the formation of the Federation of Mali. The initial plan was to include four states. Unfortunately, the governments of Dahomey and French Upper Volta reneged on their promises. Soon, only two states remained: Senegal and French Sudan.

Building a federation with just two states is challenging because there can be no majority and thus no mediator to resolve conflicts, as occurred in the case of Mali. Truth be told, personal squabbles did not play a significant role. The reasons for the breakup instead lie in ideological differences, revealing sociological differences despite ethnic similarities. If the Senegalese thwarted the coup, it was indeed to uphold the regional autonomy on which every federation is to be based.

There is also another reason, which is that we aimed too high too fast, and followed an abstract plan à la française instead of considering our territorial realities. As Sir Tafawa Baléwa wisely put it, "Abrupt changes upset people, gradual changes are better."

The failure did not deter us from our federalist spirit, however. The day after the dissolution of the Federation of Mali, we reached out to President Houphouët-Boigny and asked him to spearhead an initiative to regroup the former French West African states under the key principles of independence, equality, and cooperation. Since then, the initiative has taken shape. Neither Guinea nor Mali have joined us, but our family has grown. Today, the African and Malagasy Union consists of twelve states. It is not a "federation," not even a "confederation," but rather a highly flexible association, built up gradually with a grounded approach. The experience of the Federation of Mali has made us cautious.

Some, including you, were surprised that we did not reach out to Anglophone states. On this matter, too, we want to be realistic.

The union of Anglophone and Francophone countries faced—and continues to face—obstacles that are difficult to overcome. Those are facts we cannot deny. There are historical and cultural differences, there are differences in economic structures. These differences breed unavoidable dissensions that need to be understood before they can eventually be resolved.

Former British colonies and French colonies have different histories that intersected about sixty years ago. This may not seem to be a lot, but it is something. In Senegal, colonial history is three hundred years old—although we were under British occupation at the start of the previous century, and our elite continue to read English, though they speak it badly. Let us begin at the beginning, then: On our side, we need to teach English, which is already a part of our high school curriculum; on yours, you shall teach French. Progressively, we must also transform our economic structures to better integrate them. To that end, a rapprochement between the Inner Six and the Outer Seven, especially between the British Commonwealth and the French Community, could further enhance African cooperation.

You were right to remain in the Commonwealth. Why? Because going against the tide of history carries the risk of getting swept away by it. Like it or not, the British occupation forever altered your culture, politics, and economy. Just like other African states, you rely on foreign aid, particularly from Europe. Why, then, switch the current interlocutor when the former colonizer is today a faithful partner? In addition, switching partners is a surefire way to plunge Africa into the throes of a Cold War where she stands to gain nothing—quite the reverse. Just look at some of the newly independent states, like the Republic of Congo-Leopoldville.

I spoke about Nigeria's place within the Commonwealth; the same could be said for Senegal's position within the French Community. I know it has become trendy to rail against France, especially in some international circles. But the facts are clear, irrecusable. You can never argue with the facts. From 1945 to 1958, my friend, President Mamadou Dia, and I were among the fiercest critics of French colonialism, voicing our condemnations on the very floor of the French Parliament. Today, though, I must recognize a fact: In just two years, from 1958 to 1960, France granted independence to fifteen former territories and colonies. Among the major White powers quick to champion anticolonial rhetoric, tell me, which of them were never racist or colonialist, which of them willingly decolonized and combated racism? Aside from France and Great Britain, I know of none, though I readily admit it was the pressure from Afro-Asiatic nationalisms that set the process of decolonization in motion.

There remains the bloody Algerian tragedy. In Senegal, we did not wait until 1960 to call for peace in Algeria, specifically, for the self-determination of the Algerian people. Back in 1955, when I visited your country as a member of the French government, I called for a roundtable between the French government and the National Liberation Front (FLN). God willing, we can now hope for Algeria's independence in 1961. Following de Gaulle's lead, the French people recently voted overwhelmingly in favor of the self-determination of the Algerian people. Together with other peoples from the African and Malagasy Union, we Senegalese continue to apply gentle but firm pressure on both parties to reach a negotiated peace leading to independence, with no partition of the Algerian people.

The Fight for Africanity and Negritude Is a Fight for the Civilization of the Universal

Governor General, the goal is to achieve independence of all African peoples within a united Africa. Independence and unity are prerequisites for world peace. They will significantly contribute to the construction of the civilization of the universal. I shall return to this point.

There has been extensive discussion in recent years about a United States of Africa. I first spoke of it with M. Kwame Nkrumah at the All West African Congress, when he was still a student in London in 1946. A few years later, at the Consultative Assembly of the Council of Europe, I signed the draft resolution of Labor Party member R. W. G. Mackay toward a constitution for a United States of Africa with my compatriot M. Ousmane Socé Diop. A noble goal, was it not?

Yet again, we must be realistic and brave enough to recognize that a United States of Africa will not happen overnight. Here, too, the issue must be analyzed perceptively, setting aside sentimentality and eloquent demagoguery. Then the project must be thoroughly prepared. Finally, the latter must be executed step by step. A certain number of conditions must be met, without which the very idea of a United States of Africa is bound to remain a literary topic.

The first condition is to have faith in Africanity. To believe in Africanity means to believe there are certain values that are specifically African, shared by Black Africa and White Africa. In the words of Leo Frobenius, the German ethnographer, these values are expressed with a distinctly African style: "Bitter, strict, thoughtful, direct, and serious." Neither Christianity, Islam, nor any form of colonization has been able to eradicate it. It is the style of Augustine, the Amazigh, as it is the style of our eminent Muslim writers. Beyond this style, it is by returning to the source that we can retrieve and recover our original values, therein lies Africanity.

The second condition is the desire to restore those values through the independence of all African peoples, without exception. As I mentioned earlier: Colonization is more than just one individual or one people dominating another; it is the domination of a civilization by another: the destruction of original values by foreign ones. Fortunately for us and for the world, though colonization in various forms did erode many African values, it never lasted long enough to destroy them entirely. To be fair, I should add that it brought us alternate values that we need to preserve and grow.

Once those conditions are met, and as we wait for the dawn of independence for all of Africa, we must embark on an "intermediary action" of *African cooperation*. The African and Malagasy Union, in its regional form, is one facet and potentially a key component of this cooperation. Nothing prevents other independent states from joining it. But a cooperation that expands to all of Africa must be planned for, starting today. The president of the Republic of Côte d'Ivoire, Mr. Houphouët-Boigny, was tasked by the Brazzaville Conference of December 1960 to reach out to other independent states. The idea is to organize a Pan-African conference that would lay the groundwork for this "intermediary action," fostering an African cooperation across as many areas as possible.

To succeed, this cooperation must rest upon some fundamental principles. We sought to outline them in Brazzaville: *nonuse of violence* to regulate African issues, irrespective of motive; *noninterference in the internal affairs of another African state*, and, by extension, the respect of its territorial integrity; last, equality in cooperation.

This African cooperation first requires cooperation between states south of the Sahara—dare I say it, a Negro-African cooperation. The African and Malagasy Union is, in part, a response to this requirement.

Of course, in recent years, the Western or Eastern White world—whether conservative, liberal, or communist—has frequently derided the mysticism of Negritude, the "myth of Negritude," as if myths were not universal and enduring human necessities: their emotional self-realization—the only true one—of one's place in the world. I mean the place of any people.

Governor General, I say it is time we wake up, we have been misled, we are being betrayed. We have not overcome the problem of Negritude, not in the least. It is more relevant than ever, at a time when other races deride our "dark faces." And why? Because we refuse to choose between East and West, we rebel against blind conformity. "Neutralism"? It is time to reject neutralism, which is rarely neutral. The time has come for Negritude.

Governor General, did you not yourself call for Negritude, in 1934, in *Renascent Africa*, when you called for mental emancipation as a precondition for independence? Is it not true that the worst colonization is the colonization of the mind? Today, in the face of propaganda and ideological lies that hardly conceal antagonistic interests, the truth of Negritude, *our* truth, must come forward. We will never tire of repeating that it is not the vindication of a skin color, not even a race. We can do better than sow the hatred of the Other, which is the very antithesis of Negritude. We must vindicate cultural values that this world needs: the gift of emotion for a kinder world, the gift of image and rhythm, the gift of form and beauty, the gift of democracy and communion.

For us, in this part of the continent south of the Sahara, it is time to get a *futuristic* glimpse into our planet's future. Despite the eruption of antagonistic ideologies, the frenzy of clashing hatreds, despite the wars, spilled blood, and shed tears, despite everything, the world marches toward its "totalization," its "socialization." Here, I am with Father Pierre Teilhard de Chardin and his optimistic vision. What a shame it would be if Negro-Africans were to miss the call of History, the time for the fulfilment of the world, of mankind, in an age of grace where we will build the civilization of the universal. To be universal, civilization will need to bring together, in a dynamic symbiosis, the complementary values of all civilizations: of all races. It would be neither universal nor human if it lacked the kindness of Negritude. Indeed, to fight for Negritude is to fight for the civilization of the universal.

Governor General, I will conclude where I began. The few ideas I just shared will resonate, I am sure, with your own and those of the Nigerian people. Such is my hope. Your method and noble ideals are inextricable from those of the Senegalese people. Thus, the cooperation between our two countries, which has just begun, shall increase. With positive actions. The earlier, the better.

10

Negritude Is a Humanism of the Twentieth Century

LECTURE GIVEN IN BEIRUT,
LEBANON, MAY 1966

Reprinted in *Liberté 3* (Paris: Seuil, 1977), 69–79

Over the last thirty years of championing Negritude, we have routinely faced accusations of racism. Some critics went so far as to claim that "Negritude is an inferiority complex." But a single word cannot mean "racism" and "inferiority complex" without contradicting itself.

Negritude is nothing of the sort. It is neither racist nor self-negating. It is a rooting in and an affirmation of oneself: of one's *being*. Negritude is nothing more than what English-speaking Negro-Africans call *African personality*. It is the "Black personality" the American New Negro movement has discovered and defended. As Langston Hughes said in a statement released in the immediate aftermath of World War I, "We younger Negro artists who create now intend to express our individual dark-skinned selves without fear or shame.... We know we are beautiful. And ugly too. The tom-tom cries and the tom-tom laughs."[1] Our unique original contribution to this matter is, perhaps, our rigorous effort to define the concept, to make it a tool of combat, an instrument of liberation, a contribution to the humanism of the twentieth century.

So, what exactly is Negritude? Today's ethnologists and sociologists speak of "different civilizations." Evidently, different ideas, languages, philosophies, religions, morals, institutions, literatures, arts shape different peoples. Would anyone deny that Negro-Africans, too, have a certain way of conceiving and living their life? A certain way of speaking, singing, dancing, painting, sculpting, laughing, and even crying? "Negro Art" would not have survived for the last sixty years if someone did, and Black Africa would currently be the only continent without ethnologists or sociologists. But we are left with the question: What indeed is Negritude? It is *the set of civilizational values of the Black world*, a certain active presence in the world: in the universe. As John Reed and Clive Wake put it, it is a certain "way of relating oneself to the world and to the others."[2] In essence, it is about forming a relation with and a movement toward the world, engaging and participating with others. For Negritude as such is necessary to the world of today: It is a humanism of the twentieth century.

The Revolution of 1889

Let's backtrack to 1885, just after the Berlin Conference. European nations had just divided Africa, effectively dividing the planet. Only five or six of them, including the United States, were at the top, dominating the world. They proudly reveled in their material power, took even more pride in their science and, paradoxically, in their race. Back then, this was not considered a paradox. One recalls Gobineau, who had an osmotic impact even on Marx. While Marx was by no means a racist—after all, he married his daughter to a mixed-race man—he thought that colonization represented a step in India's progress. Disraeli declared himself the primary theorist of "this *Anglo-Saxon* race, the greatest governing race, so proud, so tenacious, self-confident and determined, this race which neither climate nor change can degenerate."[3] The emphasis is mine. As German ethnographer Leo Frobenius wrote in *Kulturgeschichte Afrikas* (A cultural history of Africa), "Every great nation that thinks of herself as personally responsible for the 'fate of the world' believes she alone holds the key to understanding the Whole and other nations. This is a behavior coming straight from the past."[a][4]

Indeed, this behavior "from the past" began to waver in the late nineteenth century with works like Bergson's *Time and Free Will: An Essay on the Immediate*

a Translated from the German as *Le Destin des civilisations*, 15.

Data of Consciousness, published in 1889. Since the Renaissance, the values of European civilization had essentially rested upon discursive reason and facts, upon logic and matter. Bergson, with his dialectical subtlety, appealed to an audience tired of scientism and naturalism. He showed that it was necessary to move beyond the superficial veneer of facts and matters—both objects of discursive reason—to develop, through intuition, a deeper vision of reality.

But the Revolution of 1889—as we shall call it—did not only affect art and literature: It shook the very foundations of science. In 1880, just a year before the term *electron* was coined, there was still a clear distinction between matter and energy. The former was inert and immutable, the latter was not. However, both were defined by their conservation and continuity, and both were subject to rigorous and mechanical determinism. Matter and energy were, in a word, eternal: They could change their form but not their substance. The only thing we lacked was accurate instruments to objectively know them in space and time.

Well, in less than fifty years, all those established principles were on the brink of obsolescence, soon to be discarded. Some thirty years ago, fresh scientific discoveries—quantum physics, relativity, wave mechanics, the uncertainty principle, spin—shook the concepts of matter and energy and the entire deterministic approach of classical physics. Broglie revealed the matter-energy—also known as particle-wave—duality that lies beneath the surface of things. Heisenberg taught us that objectivity was an illusion and that our observation of the facts inevitably altered them. Other scientists discovered that particles influence one another, both the infinitesimal realm and the macrocosmic scale. From then on, neither physicochemical laws nor the things themselves could be seen as immutable. Even within the sole domains and scales where those laws worked, they amounted to no more than rough approximation or probability. A mere scratch beneath the surface of things or facts opens unstable horizons that defy our measuring tools, most likely because these tools are mechanical: material.

It is through such discoveries that Pierre Teilhard de Chardin, merging dialectical coherence with dazzling intuition, scientific experimentation with personal experience, transcended classical dichotomies to reach a new dialectic. He showed us the thrilling and lively unity of the universe. Through these scientific discoveries, he moved beyond the age-old dualism between scientists and philosophers—a dualism that Marx and Engels had not ended when they asserted the primacy of matter over mind. Chardin posited that the fabric of the universe consisted not of two separate entities but of a single reality in a two-phenomenon form, that one should not speak of matter and energy or even of matter and mind, but of a mind-matter, much like we speak of space-time. To speak like Gaston Bachelard, matter and mind are nothing more than a "web of relations"; nothing more than energy, defined as a network of forces. In mind-matter, there exists only one energy split into two categories. The "external" or tangential energy is material and quantitative, tightly binding the corpuscles that make up matter. The "inside" or radial energy is psychological and qualitative. It is a centripetal force that organizes and complexifies the central association of particles within a corpuscle. Since energy is force, radial energy is the creative one, "the original fabric of things," while tangential energy is merely a residual product "triggered by the inter-reaction of elementary 'centers' of consciousness, imperceptible in the pre-living world but which we can experience clearly thanks to a sufficiently advanced degree of material organization."[b5] In the preliving world, it thus follows that physicochemical laws remain valid despite the limitations we highlighted earlier, whereas in the living world, as we move from plants to animals and from animals to men, the psyche gains in consciousness to self-develop and communicate freely. By *self-develop*, I mean self-actualize through—and beyond—material well-being and toward spiritual more-than-being. By *self-actualize*, I mean a harmonious development between the two complementary elements of the soul: heart and mind, intuitive reason and discursive reason.

What Is Negritude?

In trying to illustrate that the ontology, ethics, aesthetics of Negritude respond to a contemporary humanism shaped by European scientists and philosophers of the nineteenth century and presented by Teilhard de Chardin alongside writers and artists of our twentieth century, I might appear to be drawing out a paradox.

Let us first discuss Negro-African ontology. Regardless of how far we venture into our past, whether in the North-Sudan or the South-Bantu, Negro-Africans have consistently presented a worldview that stands in stark contrast to classical philosophy. The latter is essentially static, *ob-jective, dicho-tomous*, hence Manichean. It is built on opposition and separation, on conflict and analysis. Conversely, Negro-Africans think of the world beyond a diversity of forms, as a fundamentally moving reality, a singular yet synthetic one. This calls for some explanation.

It is significant that in Wolof,[c] there are at least three words to translate the word *mind*,[d] while imagery is necessary for the word *matter*.[e] Of course, Negro-Africans are sensitive to the external world: the matter of beings and things. Because they feel these entities with all their sensory qualities—forms,

b Teilhard de Chardin, *L'apparition de l'homme*, 363.
c Main language of Senegal.
d *Xèl, sago*, or *dégai*.
e *Lef* (thing) or *yaram* (body).

colors, scents, weight, and so on—more intensely than Albo-Europeans, they consider them as signs that must be interpreted and transcended to get to the reality of being. Like others, possibly more than others, they distinguish between a pebble and a plant, a plant and an animal, an animal and a man. But the accidents and appearances that make these kingdoms different are merely diverse modes of one shared reality. This reality is Being—in the ontological sense—as force. Therefore, for Negro-Africans, the *matter* of Europeans is nothing more than a system of signs translating the sole reality of the universe: Being, which is mind, which is force. From this perspective, the entire universe appears as an infinitely large and infinitely small network of forces that emanates from God and ends with God, the Force of all forces, who reinforces or deforces all other beings: all other forces.

We are not as removed from contemporary ontology as you might think. Ethnographers, Africanists, and European artists all use similar words and expressions to name the ultimate reality of a universe they are striving to know and articulate: "spiderweb," "network of forces," "interconnected vessels," "system of canals," and so on. We are not even that far from science: physics and chemistry. In African ontology, there is no such thing as dead matter; Every being, every thing, even a simple grain of sand, radiates a force: a sort of corpuscle-wave, which the wise men, priests, kings, doctors, and artists harness to further the fulfillment of the universe.

Contrary to widely held belief, Negro-Africans are not passive before the order—or disorder—of things. Their behavior is fundamentally ethical. The reason their ethics has long been overlooked is because it naturally emanates from their worldview: their ontology. So naturally, in fact, that both aspects have been overlooked, negated even, because they were not challenged across generations.

God grew weary of all the virtualities within Him, locked in, unexpressed, dormant, like dead. So, God spoke. He spoke a long, harmonious, and rhythmed word. All virtualities, all possibilities, spoken by God, came into existence and found the vocation to live: to express God, in turn, by performing the ordination, toward God, of those forces from God.

To better explain the acting ethics of Negritude, let us step back. Each identified force in the universe—from the grain of sand to the Ancestor—forms part of a network of forces. Modern physics and chemistry confirm this: a network of elements that seem to contradict but in fact complement each other. Hence, for Negro-Africans, the *man-person* is composed of both matter and mind, body and soul, but it also contains manly and feminine elements, even several "souls." The man-person is an unstable web of crossing forces: an interconnected world that seeks unity. By existing, he marks both a beginning and an end: the end of the three kingdoms—mineral, plant, and animal—and the beginning of the human kingdom. Let us set aside the first three kingdoms for now and focus on the human one. Beyond the man-person yet based on him, the fourth kingdom is layered in ever broader and higher concentric circles that ultimately extend to God and encompass the entire universe. Each circle—family, village, province, nation, humanity—forms a cohesive society designed to reflect the image of the man-person.

Indeed, for Negro-Africans, to live ethically means living with naturally opposing yet complementary forces. It is about enriching the fabric of the universe, tightening the threads that weave the web of life. It is about overcoming contradictions—especially those within oneself, within the man-person, but within any human society as a whole—to foster a complementarity of forces. By fulfilling those forces in alignment with their mutual complementarity, man reinforces them in their path toward God. Through this reinforcement, he reinforces himself, transitioning from just *existing* to *being*. I do not mean *to be*, for in truth, only God can *be* in all the fullness of creation, the fullness of existing beings whose actualization can only happen in Him.

What Negritude Brings

Ethnologists have often praised the unity, balance, and harmony of the Negro-African civilization—the communalistic yet personalistic Black society where the group, grounded in dialogue and reciprocal service, takes precedence over individuals without crushing them, as it nurtures them *personally*. I want to emphasize how these distinctive traits of Negritude facilitate the integration of individuals into contemporary humanism, thus empowering Black Africa to make her contribution to the Civilization of the Universal—a contribution that is vitally needed in a fractured yet interdependent world in the latter half of the twentieth century. This is particularly crucial for an international cooperation that must—and will—be the cornerstone of this civilization. It is thanks to the virtues of Negritude that decolonization in sub-Saharan Africa unfolded with minimal bloodshed and hatred, that a positive cooperation built on "dialogue and reciprocal services" developed between former colonizers and colonized, that a new wind blows at the United Nations where power no longer lies in loud voices or strong-arm tactics. Thanks to those virtues, peaceful cooperation could extend to South Africa, South Rhodesia, and the Portuguese colonies if only the Manichean mind of Albo-Europeans would open to dialogue.

In truth, the contribution of Negritude of the Civilization of the Universal is nothing new. In the realm of arts and literature, it came contemporaneously with the Revolution of 1889. Arthur Rimbaud had already proclaimed his ties to Negritude. Here, however, I only wish to evoke the "Negro Revolution"—to borrow the expression from Emmanuel Berl—that played a part in reshaping European plastic arts at the beginning of the century.

Art, like literature, always expresses a certain conception of life and the world: a certain philosophy and, above all, ontology. The scientific and philosophical movement of 1889 corresponded not only with a literary revolution—symbolism followed by surrealism—but also with an artistic one, with movements named Nabism, Expressionism, fauvism, and cubism. In lieu of a narrow-minded world of permanent and continual substances, we now inhabit a world of unstable and lively forces that require taming rather than preserving.

Western European art has been rooted in realism since the days of the ancient Greek *kouroi*. The work of art has been an imitation of the object ever since: a *physéôs mimesis*, Aristotle called it.[6] It was a kind of refined imitation—improved, embellished, rationally idealized, but still imitation. The medieval Christian era was a significant interruption, in part because of Christianity's Asiatic origins and the substantial influence of Augustine the African. Twentieth-century European artists like Kandinsky, for instance, assert that "art begins where nature ends." So, what would artists express? Not the matter-object but the mind-subject, their inner self, their spirituality, and by extension, the spirit of their era, using not the traditional tools of perspective, shaping, and chiaroscuro, but, as Bazaine wrote, "the most obscure instinctual and sensitive work."[f] And Masson further added, "by a simple play of forms and colors legibly organized."[g7] This play of forms and colors is indeed the play of vital "forces," as an artist like Soulages would name it.

The "play of vital forces" brings us back to Negritude. As Soulages confided in me, Negro-African aesthetics aligns with "[the aesthetics] of contemporary art." I find indirect evidence of this in the fact that, though the consecration and diffusion of the new aesthetic revolution happened in France, most of its proponents were Slavic or Germanic peoples who, like Negro-Africans, belong to those mystical civilizations that extoll meaning. Certainly, a revolution would have occurred even without the discovery of Negro Art, but perhaps not with the same energy, assurance, and depth of understanding of humanity. The fact that an art of the subject and of the mind blossomed there and among

f [Bazaine cited in] Bouret, *L'art abstrait*.
g Bouret, *L'art abstrait*, 45.

Negro-African peoples—even before ethnologists had begun to appreciate them—attested to the human relevance of their new message.

Beyond the aesthetic implications—we will return to that—the early explorers seeking Negro art were after its "human values," its unifying vision of the world and life, which has long steered toward monotheism. In Black Africa, art is not a separate activity—in itself or for itself. It is a social activity, a technique for life, indeed, a craft. It is a crucial activity that, much like prayer in the Christian Middle Ages, underpins all other activities: from birth and education to marriage and death, even sports and war. The point is to weave all human activities—to the smallest daily tasks—into the subtle play of vital forces: family, tribal, national, global, universal forces. The point is to facilitate this harmonious play by subjecting inner forces—mineral, plant, animal—to the play of *human be-ing*, and the forces of human society to the play of the divine Being through the mediation of ancestral beings.

Several years ago, I had the opportunity to attend a ceremony on the Bandiagara Escarpment in the Republic of Mali, which showed the microcosm of Dogon art. While the performance was merely a shadow of its historical grandeur, it was the most profound display of the Dogon cosmic vision. The ceremony was declaimed and sung, *unwalked* and danced, adorned, painted, and sculpted. The entire Dogon universe was on display in a symbiosis of art typical of Black Africa. The universe—heaven and earth—was represented by the mediation of man, whose ideogram could be mistaken for the universe itself. There was also the realm of masks, each one simultaneously representing a totemic animal, an ancestor, a Jinn, and other ones denoting nonindigenous peoples: nomadic Fulani and Albo-Europeans. Through a symbiosis of arts—poem, song, dance, sculpture, painting—used as means of inclusion, the goal of the ceremony was to re-create the universe and the contemporary world in a more harmonious light, with a distinct Negro humor that could reconcile distortions, even at the expense of Fulani migrants and White conquerors. But this ontological vision was more than a celebration; it was an artistic manifestation that *delighted the soul because it delighted the eyes*—a recreation because it was a re-creation.

Maybe, surely, the latter aspect of this aesthetic lesson appealed to Picasso and Braque when, around 1905, they discovered Negro Art in a Fang mask and drew inspiration from it. What struck me too at the very beginning of the Dogon performance, before I could even try to understand its meaning, was the harmony of forms and movements, the colors and rhythms that made it. This harmony, which made me, the spectator, *e-motional*, acted on invisible forces whose appearances were signs in this re-created reality. It aimed to subject those signs to one another in a complementary way and ordinate them toward God through the mediation of man. By *appearance*, I mean the properties of matter that strike our senses: forms, colors, timbre, tone, movements, and rhythms. I said that appearances are signs. They are more than that: They are signifying signs, "lines of force" of vital forces, used in their rawest form for the sole virtue of their forms, colors, sounds, movements, and rhythms. A few months ago, Mr. Lods, a professor at the National School of the Arts of Senegal, showed me the paintings his students were considering for display at the First World Festival of Negro Arts. I was immediately struck by the noble and elegant play of forms and colors. Upon learning that the paintings were not abstract but actual depictions of women, princes, and noble animals, I was almost disappointed. This information seemed unnecessary; the play of colored forms was enough to convey the elegant nobility typical of North Sudanese art.

That is indeed the aesthetic lesson: Art is not about reproducing nature, but about taming it. So does the hunter who imitates animal calls, so do two distinct beings—a couple, two lovers—striving to unite. The call is not merely a reproduction of the voice of the Other; it is a call for complementarity, a song: a *call-harmony seeking the harmony of a union that creates more-than-beings and enriches them.* To reiterate, the Negro lesson is that art is not a photograph, that images are rhythmic. I can suggest or create anything—a man, a moon, a fruit, a smile, a tear—through a simple assemblage of forms and colors (in painting, sculpting), of forms and movements (in dancing) as long as this assemblage is not rhythmic ag-gregation but rather organization. For it is rhythm, the defining virtue of Negritude, that endows a work of art with beauty. Rhythm is the magnetic push and pull that reflects the vitality of cosmic forces: symmetry and asymmetry, repetition and opposition, in other words, lines of force that ordinate forms, colors, timbres, and tones into signifying signs.

Before wrapping up, I want to address a seeming contradiction you may have noticed between contemporary European art, which underscores the subject, and Negro art, which emphasizes the object. Indeed, the Revolution of 1889 began with a necessary reaction against the fetishism of the object. While the existential ontology of Negro-Africans is based upon *subject-existing*, it makes God—the plenitude of Being—*object-centric*. Yet, for both Negro-Africans and contemporary Europeans, the work of art—like the act of knowing—expresses the confrontation, or embrace, of subject and object: "the penetration," Bazaine wrote, "this great common structure, this profound resemblance between man and the world, without which there cannot be any living form."[h]

h [Baizaine cited in] Bouret, *L'art abstrait*, 1.

Conclusion

The warm reception of Negritude at the First World Festival of Negro Art, held in Dakar from April 1 to 24, 1966, serves as the latest testament to its status as a humanism of the twentieth century. The great nations of Europe and America participated in the festival by contributing works of art from their collections or, in the case of the United States and Brazil, by sending their Black artists. It is worth noting that the "Arab" states of Africa also came to Dakar for the festival.

The relevance of the Civilization of the Universal, gradually built on the ruins of racial hatred and intercontinental wars since the dawn of the century, cannot be overstated. It is relevant because its development from its current form would not be possible without the valuable contributions of Negritude.

The Negroes of the twentieth century, Neo-Negros as my friend [Janheinz] Jahn would put it, aspire to make a twofold contribution to the Civilization of the Universal.[8] First, they want to introduce the wealth of their philosophy, literature, and traditional arts. Second, they seek to show how much they have borrowed from other civilizations since the Renaissance, especially European and Arabo-Berber civilizations. This was, indeed, the goal of the First World Festival of Negro Arts: to exhibit the humanism of the twentieth century.

TRANSLATOR'S NOTES

1. Hughes, "Negro Artist," 95.

2. Reed and Wake, *Senghor*, 68.

3. The quote is mistakenly attributed to Benjamin Disraeli. It was articulated by British statesman Joseph Chamberlain, as cited in Eldridge, *Imperial Experience*, 108.

4. Frobenius, *Kulturgeschichte Afrikas*, 62–63. The book has not been translated into English. The French translation—meaning "The destiny of civilisations"—differs significantly from the literal translation of the original German title, loosely translated as "A cultural history of Africa."

5. The content of the book significantly resembles Teilhard de Chardin's seminal work, *The Phenomenon of Man*, published a year earlier. The book has not yet been translated into English.

6. Aristotle, *Poetics*.

7. Masson, *Le plaisir de peindre*, 38.

8. Jahn, *Neo-African Literature*.

II

Francophonie as Culture

LECTURE GIVEN AT LAVAL UNIVERSITY,
QUEBEC, DOCTOR HONORIS CAUSA
CEREMONY, SEPTEMBER 22, 1966

Reprinted in *Liberté 3* (Paris: Seuil, 1977), 80–89

I cannot help but feel that this honor is not merely a tribute to me as an individual but also a choice to recognize the French-speaking writer, and thus Francophonie. This fills me with profound joy and pride. The best response I can offer is one in praise of Francophonie.

So, what exactly is Francophonie? It is not "a war-machine wielded by French imperialism," as some might believe. We, in Senegal, who were among the first African nations to champion a stance that veered away from "positive neutrality" and instead embrace what we call "cooperative nonalignment," would not have aligned ourselves with it otherwise. It was twenty years ago, in 1946, in France, when I first voiced our will to independence, "by force" if necessary, alongside our will to join a community bound by the French language. Our initiative toward Francophonie was not driven by economic or financial gain.

Surely, in a buyer's market, there are far more generous offers than France's. We sought highly skilled Francophone technicians because, for us, *Francophonie is culture.*

It is a way of thinking and acting: a certain way of framing problems and finding solutions. More than that, it is a spiritual community: a worldwide noosphere. In sum, Francophonie is more than just a language: It is French civilization or, more precisely, its spirit, which is French culture. This is what I will call *Francity.*

Before we delve further, I must clarify that Francophonie is not out to unsettle; it aims to settle and cooperate. In Francophone Black Africa, our nation—the first unitary republic—led the way to make English compulsory in secondary and vocational schools. We see it as a complementary language and civilization, also a means to avoid "Frenglish."

When we speak of Francophonie, *the one indisputable principle is its foundation in the French language.* It is safe to assume our bond to the language would not be so strong if it were not also a bond to French culture. These are the two facets I want to focus on.

The Virtues of the French Language

Why do we have a bond to the French language?

To begin with, there are two historical—and factual—reasons. The first is our determination not to deny who we are. We thus refuse to deny any part of our history, no matter how "colonial," that has become an element of our national personality. Taking my country as an example, the French presence has lasted for three centuries. It has brought both misfortune and fortune, the latter by empowering us to act effectively. We have been tested. And then, there was French, today an international language of communication. This serves as our second factual reason.

There are additional, deeper reasons rooted in the very qualities of the language itself. Whether in its morphology or syntax, French delivers both clarity and richness, precision and nuance.

The clarity of the vocabulary springs from its clear derivations and compositions—particularly those from ancient Greek and Latin. These do not preclude more colloquial modes of expression, which are necessarily more vibrant and spontaneous, resulting in an impressive diversity of words. For instance, there has been much debate, even disagreement, about whether we are "Francophone" or "Francolingual." The people could have settled it by simply referring to us as "French speaking," though some might have labeled this as

"Frenglish." Fortunately, the *Robert Dictionary* had already blessed the term *Francophone*.

Sometimes the language offers two or three synonyms, from which its precision and nuance stem, adding to its richness. There have thus been *serious* discussions about the properties of the term *Francophone* although there was minor risk of *severe* injuries. Indeed, Francophones—I do not mean just the French—who are accustomed to these grammatical debates rarely let them escalate into conflicts, and certainly never into fights.

French words are known for their clarity and precision. They gravitate toward abstraction, making them perfect tools for reasoning. It is inaccurate to say that abstraction ignores reality; instead, it reduces it to a minimum, its network of relations, which is its essence—at least, for the man of action. It is time we return to Descartes. While the concrete reality and details that so often inundate us these days might make us feel alive, they obstruct our ability to contemplate life, to see the forest for the trees. Because of the leaves and branches.

As for the forms of French, its morphology, I will focus here on the spoken language. In an article published in *Le Monde* on October 24, 1962, M. Robert Le Bidois writes, "The range of French tenses is astonishingly rich. To express the past, our language has five primary tenses, and I am only referring to the indicative mood: imperfect, pluperfect, present perfect, past historic, and past anterior—to which one must add three 'plus past perfect.'" Here, in addition to a wealth of forms, we see the same inclination toward abstraction: clarity over precision. In Wolof, one of Senegal's languages, there are about twenty equivalent forms to the French imperfect tense—further evidence, if needed, that our language is indeed precise. However, it is a *lived* precision. Wolof emphasizes the aspect of things: the concrete way in which an action occurs. Hence, the existence of five subcategories of the indicative mood, among other peculiarities. French, on the other hand, prioritizes the abstract notion of time. It is less concerned with how the action unfolds than with pointing to the exact moment it happens in its trajectory.

French syntax can be characterized as a syntax of subordination, of logic, more so than any other European language. Through its many *functors*, as my mentor Ferdinand Brunot would say, French conjunctions—the *hinge words*—link clauses together. Indeed, they subordinate the clauses—and thus, the ideas—to one another. Hence, a typical French sentence forms a synthetic whole where no element is overlooked, but rather where conjunctions—which signal a relation between ideas—invite analysis. Hence, becoming analysis and synthesis simultaneously, it positions itself as an effective instrument of reason.

"Sound reasoning," says Anatole France, "requires a rigorous syntax and exact vocabulary. I cannot help but believe that the most advanced people of the world will be found to possess the finest syntax."[1]

I spoke of sentences from the classical era: periodic sentences. Since the time of Descartes, the French language has benefited from the aforementioned processes, gaining enough flexibility to produce complex subordinations out of simple juxtapositions. A syntax of subordination and continuity was gradually replaced by a syntax of coordination and discontinuous juxtaposition, which the surrealists took full advantage of and even exploited. This evolution was facilitated by the extensive tool kit of the language, the flexible spectrum provided not only by nominal sentences or relative dependent clauses but also by the subtle play of participles, appositions, moods, and tenses. Here is an example that, I concede, does not encapsulate all the possibilities.

"In you, moving, we move, and we pronounce you the unnameable Sea: mutable and movable in her moultings, immutable and immovable in her mass; diversity in the principle and parity of Being, truth in the lie and betrayal in the message; all presence and all absence, all patience and all refusal—absence, presence; order and madness—license!"[2]

You might argue that this is the work of a poet. So, let me provide an excerpt from a philosopher:

> Our free will? What shall we choose? There are four possible paths, Father suggests. The first is pessimism. All is bad, being is bad, we must resist life, resist evolution, especially now that we understand the deception. How will the Father judge those who harbor such views, those who betray life? Let them be, he says. This is typical of Father Teilhard's approach, which I shall return to. He is not digressing, he does not seek to prove anything, he simply wants us to act, he wants to invite us to see things from a certain perspective, and I will return to that too when I discuss the importance of the phenomenological approach in Teilhard de Chardin's philosophy. As for those who betray existence, the wearied who renounce life and apathetically seek solace elsewhere, leave them be; let us turn to others and move on.[3]

This is where the French sentence truly thrives, navigating freely between these two extremes. The language yields to all demands of our thoughts and our emotions, flexing with agility from the rigidity of diamonds to the dramatic twists of twisters, from the slow and strong motion of the sea to the sudden brevity of a stab.

Just moments ago, I quoted a verse from a poet—that was Saint-John Perse. And a paragraph from a philosopher—that was Gaston Berger. This was no coincidence. Saint-John Perse is among the greatest French living poets, and Gaston Berger, who passed away four years ago, was the director of higher education in France. It was no coincidence because both were born overseas: a Guadeloupe Creole and a French-Senegalese mixed race.

Thus, we have ventured beyond mere grammar: into the *style* of the French language. Born of the development of linguistics, stylistics is, as you know, the study of the relations between our thoughts and their translation on the one hand, between individuals and their expression on the other. When Rivarol tackles the concept of *clarity* in his renowned *Discourse on the Universality of the French Language*, he frames it as a matter of stylistics. According to him, this clarity of the language serves diplomats and philosophers well, but less so poets and musicians. I beg to differ. Do read the French poets of the sixteenth century. They wrote in a language that was ripening yet not quite ripe. The great poets of that era? They are all musicians: Maurice Scève and Louise Labbé, Joachim du Bellay and Pierre de Ronsard, Agrippa d'Aubine and François de Malherbe. Can anything be more musical than these verses:

All my Muse, all my Grace,
My all, in whom my thoughts live,
All my all, all my everything,
Entirely my mistress Marie,
Entirely my sweet deceiver,
All my ills, all my good.[4]

It sounds like Aragon, or even Éluard. It is indeed Ronsard.

How can we explain the beauty of prose, especially in French poetry, when despite its richness, we have only unveiled rigor, abstraction, clarity, and precision? Its beauty lies not in its intellectual qualities, but perhaps more so in its sensitive or sensual ones. I recall being seven years old when I first discovered French; to me, it was nothing but musical charm. The beauty of French in its poetry does not arise from the imaginative power of words—they have been stripped of their concrete roots. It springs from the rhythm of words and the melody of sentences, lines, and verses.

I am aware of the crispness of French consonants that lends a certain melody to the words yet could also give an impression of scarcity. There is, however, the rhythm, the harmonious play of diverse and nuanced vowels: long or short, oral or nasal, open, mid, or closed vowels, not to mention semivowels, diphthongs, or triphthongs. And how can I forget the play of silent ⟨e⟩ that, with its nuances, brings the word, the sentence, or the line to life?

Music is powerful because of its power to suggest. The remarkable originality of hearing—the most abstract of all senses following sight—transcends sensuousness even as it delves deeper into sensitivity. This is why musicians do not just express a thought, contrary to common belief; they translate feelings through the evocation of images. During the surrealist period, we spoke of the "narcotic image." The beauty of language, of French poetry, is created by this musical charm. The influence of ultramarine poets, like Evariste Désiré de Parny or Saint-John Perse, is remarkable. Closer to cosmic forces, they harness the musical power of their lines to elevate images, like doves, like grasshoppers, like ardent lava. Listen to the voice of Aimé Césaire:

> Bareback on the river of blood of earth
> on the blood of broken sun
> on the blood of a hundred sun nails
> on the blood of the suicide of fire beasts
> on the blood of an ember the blood of salt the blood of bloods of love
> on the fire bird inflamed blood
> herons and falcons
> ride and burn[5]

We took a moment to dwell on poetry, to affirm that the French language is culture. It is the very spirit of civilization, the foundation of a humanism that has never felt more relevant than today. This will shape the second part of my lecture.

Francity

So, as I alluded to earlier, Francophonie—or more aptly, *Francity*—is a rational way of framing problems and finding solutions, with man at its core. I often share with my compatriots that what I learned in France, specifically in the Latin Quarter, is the spirit of *method*.

"Always your French rationalism, so abstract," an African friend of mine—albeit an Anglophone—once told me. "We prefer to stick with *pragmatism*, a method of action." His words seemed to dismiss the fact that the founder of modern rationalism indeed penned the *Discourse on Method*.

Is Cartesian rationalism an abstraction? Undeniably, we will circle back to that point. But it is first rooted—though not essentially so—in reality, at least in life. It is too easy to forget that before emerging as a philosopher, Descartes was a soldier stationed abroad. Note that the *Discourse on Method* begins with an autobiographical account.

Is Cartesian rationalism impractical? Descartes anchors metaphysics in physics and returns it to its roots, which do not negate but go beyond physics. In our technocratic and practical world today, isn't it mathematics that sits at the heart of science and thus material power? Lest we forget, Descartes made his mark with the discovery of the laws of universal mathematics.

His yearning for practicality is evident in the goal that he sets for his philosophical investigations: "to work in such a way for the good of our fellow men."[6] Consequently, an ethical dimension emerges: a concern for *man*.

I will be the first to admit that this does not entirely capture the essence of Cartesianism. According to Gaston Berger, that essence lies in the pursuit of an "absolute science" based upon an "unwavering certitude." It is found in the rigor of a research method that begins with doubting everything, relying on empirical evidence, and proceeds from one piece of evidence to another until it arrives at the only incontrovertible proof: the cogito, which claims "the very origin of objectivity in transcendental subjectivity."[a] It is absolutely correct that Descartes grounds reality—or more specifically, truth—on discursive reason, on logic, that seamlessly ties one evidence to another like links in a chain. Better yet, it links all evidence together, like a spiderweb with the cogito at its core.

Is Cartesian rationalism outdated? I believe it to be more relevant than ever. Gaston Berger, the philosopher of action and pioneer of futuristic studies, advocated for a return to Descartes. Edmund Husserl, the founder of phenomenology, acknowledged his debt to Descartes, as evidenced by his *Cartesian Meditations*. Rationalism becomes even more relevant when we contrast it with empiricism and intuitionism.

Empiricists or pragmatists, the proponents of such philosophy have always relied on experience. But it is evident that the realm of experience must be rational to make action possible; discursive reason must unveil the structures of experiential objects, their true relations. There is no action without method, without logic. In an article titled "Ideology and Experience," Arthur Schlesinger Jr. writes, "We must not necessarily reject abstractions. In fact, we could not reason without them."[7]

As for the relation between rationalism and intuitionism, I will attempt to demonstrate how Cartesian rationalism was enriched by the intellectual contribution of Blaise Pascal, which is a double symbiosis between theory and

a Berger, *Phénoménologie du temps et prospective*, 9.

experience, discursive reason and intuitive reason. This synthesis is distinctively French, as evident in the work of Teilhard de Chardin.

Pascal is undoubtedly a rationalist. In the *Provincial Letters* as in the *Pensées*, the power of his rigorous reasoning is deceptive. The *Provincial Letters'* originality lies in its exclusive reliance on the most common reasoning: common sense—a novelty for European literature written for a broad audience. In the *Apology for the Christian Religion*, the logic is airtight and builds a case for religion not as opposed to reason but conforming to it, as truth.

Yet, Pascal's originality resides elsewhere: beyond theory and argumentation; he lays out the facts. He goes beyond experience, he experiments. Like Descartes, he begins with scientific work: not with mathematics, which helps us understand the universe, but with physics, which confirms its existence through facts. In *Pensées*, the experimental facts are historical: They are, as we now call them, social facts.

Still, Pascal is also the man of faith who, with intense conviction in an era of Cartesian rationalism, delineated the limits of discursive reason and looked up to faith—or, in other words, the heart, the intuition: "It is the heart which *feels* God and not the reason." I emphasize the word *feel*, the linchpin that helps us understand the epistemology of Black peoples: peoples with intuitive reason.

Let us leap over three centuries of French history, during which the French steadfastly upheld rationalism despite foreign influence, assimilation, and racial mixing, and fiercely defended romanticism, symbolism, surrealism, indeed intuition through reason. André Breton's *Manifestos*, passionately written with a lucid passion, make this abundantly clear.

Starting with Pascal, then, if we leap over three centuries, we land on Teilhard de Chardin. The comparison is not arbitrary but necessary. The two authors share the same Celtic, Auvergne lineage, same scientific spirit, same fervent faith, same literary style. From Pascal to Chardin, French rationalism grew and deepened, propelled by scientific progress, subsequent technological and industrial development, and the burgeoning of interracial and intercontinental relations. The synthesis evolved into a symbiosis of theory and practice, argument and experiment, discursive reason and intuitive reason. In sum, analytic logic morphed into dialectical logic.

If we begin with Descartes, the work of Teilhard de Chardin—which profoundly shaped the twentieth century—is the most visible sign of this revolution. If we start with Pascal, I prefer to call it *evolution*. To sum up, Pascal's juxtaposition of argument and experiment, heart and reason, has evolved into Teilhard's conjunction of discursive reason and intuitive reason, transcending

Marxist dialectic. We must differentiate between discursive reason dialoguing with itself and a different dialogue intertwined with intuitive reason, a trend that emerged in the nineteenth century.

At the level of rationality alone, Teilhard's work rests on the two indomitable pillars of truth: theoretical consistency and practical utility. It is a true dialectic because it is not undermined by dogmatism—which is merely a regression to linear classical logic. At that level, dialectical logic is based on a total science, which makes it dialectical. Teilhard's work is not rooted in mathematics the way Descartes's and Pascal's are based on physics; he also relies on natural and social sciences just like Marx and Engels do. He goes a step further and integrates chemistry and biology—including his areas of specialty, paleontology and prehistory—into his research. Like Pascal and Descartes, Teilhard is a scholar before he is a philosopher, a point he clearly makes in his most important work, *The Human Phenomenon*, which he introduces as a "scientific memoir." "Nothing but the phenomenon," he writes, "but also, the whole of the phenomenon."[8]

Here, French rationalism has become both integral and universal. Teilhard indeed begins with "the whole of the phenomenon": a material matter, not a metaphysical one, with a "total matter," the properties of which—physical, chemical, mechanical, and biological—are measured and analyzed with state-of-the-art scientific instruments. It is during this analysis that the scholar perceives the trace of the spirit; and here, Teilhard, with a brilliant intuition, fearlessly turns dialectic around and introduces the spirit as a hypothesis not at the end but at the beginning—indeed, at the very heart—of matter, vitalizing matter with an eternally expanding vitality. It is intuition that permitted a scientific synthesis of incommensurable fruitfulness, giving us, in the twentieth century, the only worldview enabling us to understand everything. Especially, to dare anything, so we can act.

To discover the spirit is to discover man, if not God. The title of the book, *Human Phenomenon*, is telling. In Francophonie, man is ever-present: to save and improve, intellectually with Descartes, ethically with Pascal, holistically with Teilhard.

Some might argue that he is a theorist. My answer is that he is a scholar and a philosopher who revolutionized economics. No one can dismiss the French economy; on the contrary, the French plan is hailed as a "miracle." But French planning dispels econometrics to encompass humanism. Economics and humanism define the French economic movement led by the late Father Lebret, whose ambition was to achieve not just "economic growth" but also, through holistic development, the more-than-being that Pierre Teilhard de Chardin assigned as man's end.

Conclusion

My choice of Pascal and Teilhard de Chardin to complete and fulfill Descartes was no accident. I chose two individuals from Auvergne who retained not just the bloodline but also the temper of the Celtic people. A couple of years ago, I defined French culture as the grafting of Latin genius onto the Celtic genius: of Mediterranean clarity onto Alpine passion.

Last year, while visiting the Gaelic Art exhibit, I was struck by the affinities between their art and Negro art. The best explanation is the passionate undercurrent of intuitive reason. That day, I made two discoveries. First, that to us, Negroes, the Gauls may not be our ancestors, but they are our cousins. Second, that just like them, we can meet at the "rendezvous of giving and receiving," Francophonie, and reciprocate the Mediterranean genius, at least partially, for what it imparted to us.

Francophonie cannot be confined to the Hexagon. We are no longer "colonies": underage daughters that claim a part of a Heritage. We are now independent states, grown-ups who demand our share of responsibilities: to strengthen the community by expanding it.

I will not delve into the specifics of the International Organization of Francophonie. The member states will debate those freely. What matters is that France consents to cultural decolonization and that, together, we work toward a *Defense and Illustration of the French Language* just as we worked on its illustration. And indeed, France agrees, though she did not instigate this.

I recognize this praise falls short of my topic. My excuse is that our attachment to French language and culture is beyond any praise.

TRANSLATOR'S NOTES

1. France, "Latin Genius," 62; translation modified.

2. Saint-John Perse, "Seamarks," 551. Originally published as *Amers*.

3. Berger, *Phénoménologie du temps*, 242.

4. Ronsard, *Le second livre des amours de Marie (XXV)*. For an English translation, see Ronsard, *Poems of Pierre de Ronsard*. Cited in Senghor, *Liberté 3*, 84; translation modified.

5. Césaire, "Tom-Tom I," in *Miraculous Weapons*, 153. Originally published as "Tam Tam 1," in *Les armes miraculeuses*, 50.

6. The citation appears only once in print, in Lanson, *Manuel d'histoire de la littérature française,* 175.

7. Schlesinger, "Epilogue: The One Against the Many," originally in *Saturday Review,* 1962, republished in Schlesinger and White, *Paths of American Thought,* 532–33. The translation Senghor referenced is not definitively known. In the original work, the historian champions innovation and experimentation while warning against the use of abstraction as an ideological tool, which he sees as potentially serving the interests of communism.

8. Teilhard de Chardin, *Human Phenomenon,* ii.

12

For a Senegalese Tapestry

INAUGURAL STATEMENT FOR THE
NATIONAL MANUFACTURE OF TAPESTRY,
THIÈS, DECEMBER 4, 1966

Reprinted in *Liberté 3* (Paris: Seuil, 1977), 102–4

I have chosen to inaugurate the National Manufacture of Tapestry during the official visit of President Modibo Keita because his presence here today, as the Malian head of state, recognizes our shared North Sudanese past. Any national or regional initiative that overlooks this fundamental piece would be built on shifting sand. So, thank you again, Mr. President, for agreeing to preside over a ceremony that celebrates the North Sudanese civilization, which Mali has illuminated for centuries.

I would also like to recognize two influential figures in the world of French tapestry, who transformed contemporary tapestry into a major art form of the twentieth century: Michel Tourlière, the director of the Aubusson national training school and a highly respected tapestry designer, and François Tabard, a master weaver who, alongside the late Jean Lurçat, ignited this transformation.

Indeed, Jean Lurçat is not among us today. Several years ago, in Cotonou, he urged me to start a manufacturing facility like this in Senegal. If he were with us today, he would surely be thrilled to see that idea become a reality. Let us keep his memory alive.

I am grateful to Mr. Tourlière and Mr. Tabard for their valuable contribution in training the Senegalese in both modern techniques of tapestry as well as its spirit. Once again, France showed her true colors: her vocation as initiator of great things, to speak like Renan.

I would be remiss not to recognize Mr. Papa Ibra Tall: a man not only of exceptional artistic talent, who skillfully absorbed French teachings by only keeping their spirit—to rediscover and refine a distinct Negro style underneath—but also a man of character: a man of method, bravery, and steadfastness who successfully led a difficult endeavor. I am proud of Mr. Tall and his entire team.

So, we have recognized our Malian brothers, represented by their president, expressed our thanks to our French comrades, represented by the messengers of Aubusson, and applauded the director of our National Manufacture of Tapestry and his team. But what is the vision for our new venture? First, we aim to enhance our National School of the Arts by incorporating this decentralized department. The larger ambition here, as always, is the *creation of a new art for a new nation*. The minister of cultural affairs put it aptly when he said that our goal was to "pull off the miracle of harmoniously merging imported technical expertise with traditional culture felt from within."

Clearly, the creation of a national art requires a nation, moved by a common will for a common life, shaped not only by a common geographical space but more importantly by a community of thoughts and feelings. As such, we are already a nation, as we were before independence; but now we need to discover the most effective tools to articulate this community of thoughts and feelings with the diversity of individual temperaments. In a word, we must establish a *national* style that leverages modern techniques for our era.

As it happens, we already have this national style. It is the symbiosis of techniques imported from France and using our traditional cultures, just as our minister of cultural affairs has said. By "traditional cultures," I mean the "Atlantic facet of North Sudanese culture," from which Senegalese painting has retained "a sense of decoration and refinement," qualities that epitomize nobility and elegance. Further, the emerging Senegalese painting is increasingly committed to expressing, through plastic arts, the dreams fueling our people: the ancient repository of myths and legends that form the expressive core of Negro art. This sentiment is encapsulated by Irmeline Hossmann in the recent issue of the quarterly journal *Afrique*, which is dedicated to Senegal. She concludes that "should Senegalese painting successfully evade the trap of mere ornamentation, which is the flip side of its elegant, hieratic, and noble qualities, as well as its stylizing tendency, then it can aspire to be among the best in Africa."[1]

Indeed, these qualities, which can be viewed as flaws in painting, instead become blessings in the realm of tapestry—its primary role being, essentially, to embellish public monuments and invigorate bare walls. In the words of Lurçat, it is meant to serve as an "ornament" and an "exaltation" of the wall. As such it requires a simple and restrained drawing, yet with vibrant colors and a collective fervor: communal. This is particularly true today, in Africa, as we reshape our civilizations to fit our peoples and build new monuments for our new nations—monuments that embody a delicate strength and simple greatness to fit our time.

My choice to end with eternal Africa is no accident. With the inauguration of this National Manufacture of Tapestry, a place that welcomes all neighbors of the Senegal River and even artists residing beyond it, we do nothing more but return to Mother Africa. After all, the origin of tapestry is African, specifically Egyptian, in 3000 BC. We have retained the loincloth and its polyvalence, as all African things are. The loincloth, whether serving as garment or decoration, invariably functions as an ornament.

We see the same phenomenon, the same process, at every stage of our development. It must be *cultural*: both rooted in Africa and open to the world.

Let us thus celebrate the birth of this manufacture, Mother Africa, and raise a toast to the Civilization of the Universal.

TRANSLATOR'S NOTE

1. Hossmann, "Ibou Diouf."

13

The Problematic of Negritude

KEYNOTE FOR THE NEGRITUDE
COLLOQUIUM, DAKAR, APRIL 12, 1971

Reprinted in *Liberté 3* (Paris: Seuil, 1977), 268–89

In my opinion, whatever people may say, what we are witnessing today is the triumph of Negritude (as I conceive of it, at least).
—Léon Damas, "La négritude en question"

I choose to open this colloquium with the problematic of Negritude because our former colonizers were always confronted with it, at the dawn of our respective movements of emancipation and throughout their course, whether we be Negro-Americans or Negro-Africans.

We were cast as second-class citizens or subjects. Even more unsettling, we were denied the claim to possessing a civilization of our own—an equal civilization, albeit different. We were also denied the right to recognize and proclaim this difference, to demand an equality not of identity but of complementarity. Nothing illustrates this better than a document published by the US Senate in

1919, titled *Radicalism and Sedition Among the Negroes as Reflected in Their Publications*, which reads, "Underlying these more salient viewpoints is the increasingly emphasized feeling of a race consciousness, in many of these publications always antagonistic to the white race, and openly, defiantly assertive of its own equality and even superiority."[1] Note the expression "race consciousness."

What's worse, Whites have managed to frame the problematic of Negritude on behalf of the Negroes. I am not targeting those who debate us on the content or elements of Negritude. Indeed, it is good that the concept be studied, debated, researched, and expanded from generation to generation. I will return to this point. I am referring to those who spread it with a tone that sounds something like this: "Why talk about Negritude and define us according to race or skin color?" And then, reversing cause with effect and victims with perpetrators, they conclusively proclaim, "Racism breeds antiracism." We heard this sentiment echoed at the Pan-African Festival of Algiers conference, which, as is well known, was inspired by self-proclaimed "revolutionaries" aiming to bring down the Negritude movement, even Arabism.

The problematic of Negritude can thus be enunciated as such. One: Are there, for Negroes, problems that are specifically the result of their skin color or their affiliation to an ethnic group different from White and Asian peoples? Two, what are these problems and how are they articulated? Before going further, we must define the word.

What Is Negritude?

Negritude has often come under scrutiny as a word even before being scrutinized as a concept. Some have proposed substituting it with other words, such as *melanity* or *Africanity*—the list could go on. Why not *Ethiopianity* or even *Ethiopness*? I am all the more free to defend the term since it was not invented by me, as is often mistakenly claimed, but by Aimé Césaire.

First, Césaire followed the most orthodox rules in the French language when he created the term. If you are interested in the use of suffixes in *-ité* (from Latin *-itas*) and *-itude* (from Latin *-itudo*), I would recommend Maurice Grevisse's authoritative French grammar book, *Le bon usage*, and a couple of scholarly studies conducted at the University of Strasbourg, which my friend Dr. Robert Schilling kindly shared with me.[a] Both suffixes, starting from the Late Latin period, have been used to make adjectives more abstract. They can convey either a situation or a condition, a virtue or a flaw, even a way to express these. *Le Petit*

a Grevisse, *Le bon usage*.

Robert thus defines Latinity: "1. Way of speaking or writing in Latin; 2. (1835) Latin world, Latin civilization. *The spirit of Latinity.*"[2] Negritude emulates the Latin model: "The Negro's mode of expression. Negro character. Negro world. Negro civilization." Césaire, Damas, and I, while not the founders but the first advocates of Negritude, have consistently upheld this interpretation.

Césaire was often criticized for his choice of the word *Negritude* instead of *Negrity*. Let me repeat: Both words convey the same meaning because the two suffixes convey the same meaning. The suffix *-itude* might be seen as more academic, but according to Strasbourg's grammarians, it allows for less abstract words, often describing a condition more than a quality. Hence, I use *Arabity*, but favor *Berberitude*. Nonetheless, you can find *nigritudo* in the Latin of Pliny the Elder, with a concrete meaning: "The fact of being black, the color black, blackness." And according to the French-English Harrap's dictionary, *nigritude* exists in English with the same meaning. It is important to note that the meaning, in both contexts, has remained quite concrete. The originality of the French word lies in its transition from concrete to abstract: from materiality to spirituality.

Césaire thus defines Negritude as such: "Negritude is the simple recognition of the fact that one is black, the acceptance of this fact and of our destiny as blacks, of our history and culture."[3] This brief passage holds within it two complementary definitions of the concept. As I recently highlighted in my lecture "Negritude and Modernity," the word, and hence the concept, carries a dual meaning: objective and subjective.

Objectively, Negritude is a fact: a *culture*. It encompasses the whole set of values—economic and political, intellectual, ethical, artistic, and social—that resonate not only with the peoples of Black Africa but also with the Black minorities in America, Asia, and Oceania. Here I am referring to the peoples of Black Africa who forged civilizations and advanced arts that were only discovered and celebrated by historians, humanities scholars, and art critics at the dawn of the twentieth century. Leaving aside Negro-Americans—whose roots trace back to Africa—anthropologists, ethnographers, and sociologists have often observed that African Blacks, Asian Blacks, and Oceanian Blacks share civilizational affinities. This connection was already recognized by ancient Greek writers when they referred to them as Ethiopians, drawing only a distinction between "Eastern people" (Asians) and "Western people" (Africans). Isn't it remarkable that the earliest Indian civilization—Mohenjo-Daro and Harappa—thriving around 2500 BC, employed a script that expressed a Dravidian language, a language of the Blacks?

Subjectively, Negritude is the "acceptance of this fact" of civilization and its preservation, prospectively, through the shaping of history in a Negro civilization that seeks rebirth and realization. To summarize, this is the task that the activists of Negritude undertook: to claim the civilizational values of the Black world, to actualize them and make them fruitful, integrating foreign elements if necessary, to live by and for them, and to enable Others to do the same. In so doing, they aim to bring the Negro contribution to the Civilization of the Universal.

Thus, in my discussion, the term *Negritude* is utilized in its most encompassing sense. It includes all cultural movements initiated by a Negro figure or group: the Niagara and Negro Renaissance movements in the United States, the Haitian school movement in the Caribbean, the African Personality movement in Anglophone Africa, and the Negritude movement in both the Caribbean and Francophone Africa.

The *quarrel of Negritude*, despite its lexical focus, was born out of several reasons that go to the heart of things: to the problematic of the concept. And despite the ambivalence of the term, it is entrenched in the disputes between Anglophones and Francophones, Negro-Americans and Negro-Africans. A generational conflict is at play. But let us not forget that the quarrel was initiated and fueled by Whites from all quarters.

Anglophony and Francophony

Let me distinguish between pretext and other factors in the Anglophone-Francophone dispute. First, the pretext, fueled by the remembrance of the Fashoda Incident between Britain and France, a petty rivalry to keep Black Africa under a predominant cultural sway. I am not taking sides; I am merely observing. Some went so far as to criticize our use of a French word to depict the essence of Black civilization. As though we were not Francophones, as though we did not draw inspiration from Negro-Americans when we crafted the concept from Alain Locke's movement, at least partially, which he christened with a French word: *Renaissance*. You can see how the two languages and thus the two civilizations have influenced each other.

I will not dwell on the pretext, since it was initiated by Whites, also because the memory of Fashoda is gradually fading in Black Africa, as evidenced by this colloquium. I do want to raise, however, an argument that seems rather significant. Many times, in Senegal, when we encounter a problem, we look to our Negro-African civilization for solutions, questioning whether it might offer us the most efficient answer. More often than not, it does: in politics or economics, culture or health, as some of my subsequent lectures will illustrate. So therefore, I wondered whether our languages could present a concept akin to Negritude. Indeed, such a concept exists. For instance, in Pulaar. In this Negro-African language spoken uninterruptedly for three thousand miles from Mauritania to Chad, *pull-o* translates to "the Pulaar man." Many words are constructed on the root *pul-*, but I will focus on two specifically. First, there is *pul-aa-gu*, which according to Gaden means "Pulaar set of characteristics."[b] Second, *pul-aa-gal* means "ways in which any Pulaar conveys those characteristics." These two meanings align, respectively, with objective and subjective Negritude. Indeed, *pulaagu* belongs to the nouns whose suffix *-gu* lends an abstract level that indicates a condition or quality, whereas *pulaagal* belongs to nouns whose suffix *-gal* implies "a way of being or acting." There is even a verb, *fu-laa-de*, which means "to act like a Pulaar." The verb is interesting for many reasons, particularly because it has a reflexive voice, thus the three related words (*ful-aa-de, pul-aa-gu,* and *pul-aa-gal*) indicate that the incurred action reverts to its grammatical subject.

More seriously, English-speaking Negro-Africans have asked us, "Why would you create a term that alludes to color to express an idea that we hold so dear?" Our reply is rooted in facts: the laws of language and ethno-sociological realities. In nearly all languages, the term denoting a people's civilization refers to their country, ethnicity, or skin color. Terms like *Latinity, Germanness, Indianness, Europeanness* allude to either ethnicity or a country. Consider a few examples where a term corresponds to a people and is associated with a color: *Ethiopian* (derived from the Greek *aithiops*: burned, black); *Sudanese* (from the Arabic *Sudan*: black), *Beidane* for Moorish (from the Arabic *beidan*: white). From these, we derive *Ethiopianness, Sudaneseness, Beidaneness.* We, Black peoples, are seen by Whites as *Blacks,* and we, in our Negro-African languages, view and identify ourselves as such, unashamedly, even proudly.

Even more seriously, I am aware that our Anglophone brothers began with *African personality.* This expression can only translate into French as *Africanness*: the whole set of civilizational values of African peoples. But in simple terms, these African peoples are constituents of at least two civilizations: Arabo-Berber and Negro-African. Thus, the "African Civilization" is not a monolithic entity, contrary to Leo Frobenius's belief, who authored an entire book on the subject, but rather the symbiosis of two disparate facets. The African personality cannot legitimately be conflated with Negritude. To use plain language, we should emulate what Negro-Americans do: use the terms *Blackness*

b Gaden, *Le poular.*

or *Negroness*.[c] Indeed, the English suffix *-ness* aligns with the French suffix *-ité* or *-itude*. I did discover, as I said, the word *nigritude* in Harrap's French-English dictionary, but it carries a distinct, literal meaning: *darkness*.

The most credible criticism we receive from English-speaking Negro-Africans is that we too often succumb to abstraction, a consequence of our French training. True, as Francophones we are prone to drawing conclusions prematurely and formulating concepts for which we concoct new words without substantial research into our subjects. And it is also true that our Anglophone brothers, under the influence of Anglo-Saxon pragmatism and Black temperament, have focused on the more concrete study of the Negro-African Man, *Homo aethiopicus*: in his physical milieu, his anthropological and ethnographic features, his social life, and finally, his cultural manifestations. And they expanded the number of Institutes of African Studies at their universities, just like the Americans did with African Studies Centers.

Of course, all of this is true. But the truth is not that simple. The pioneers of the Negritude movement in the Francophone world of the 1930s and '40s were either pursuing or had delved into linguistics, ethnology, or prehistory. Their abstraction notwithstanding, the French established research institutes not only in North Africa but also in Black Africa, with the mission to study men and structures alongside characteristic elements of Arabo-Berber and Negro-African civilizations. I concede that, since independence, we, French-speaking Negro-Africans, have prioritized politics over economics, and economics over culture—instead of investing in this order of things, the order of themes and efforts. That much was clear at the Pan-African Festival of Algiers, where many sought to dismiss Negritude and Arabism as mere folklore museum exhibits.

As I was saying, the truth is hardly that straightforward. It is more nuanced. Thus, we Anglophone and Francophone Negroes must wage a dual battle: one for empirical studies rooted in fieldwork and laboratory research, and another for dialectic—by which I mean, specifically, conceptualizing. As I have showed with Pulaar, our languages also possess a series of processes to create abstract words or word-concepts. In our ideological struggle—for this is where the heart of the issue lies—we need both facts, which scientific research alone can give, and concepts, which form the other half of dialectical reasoning, simultaneously. For this reason, we do not restrict ourselves to *Negritude* or *Negroness*, we embrace and launch terms such as *negry* or *negrory* (global Black community), *Negrity* or the antiquated term *Nigritie* (homeland of Blacks), and *Negrism* (Black ideology in a subjective sense of Negritude).

c Cook and Henderson, *Militant Black Writer*.

Negro-Americans and Negro-Africans

The dispute between Negro-Americans and Negro-Africans is less contentious than it appears. It is, in truth, a simple gap—in time and in space. First, linguistic communality between Negroes in the United States and Anglophone Negroes in Africa and the Antilles has made reciprocal understanding—and by extension, cooperation—easier. I had the pleasure of meeting Alain Locke and Mercer Cook in the 1930s thanks to Paulette Nardal, the Martinican founder of the *Revue du monde noir*. It was the Guyanese Léon Damas who arranged a meeting with Langston Hughes and Countee Cullen. Meeting them, yes, but also reading their work. In the broadest sense, the Negritude movement—the discovery of Black values and the burgeoning self-consciousness of the Negro's situation—had its roots in the United States. The founders of Negritude in Francophony have consistently recognized this fact—Damas confirmed as much just last month in the March 16, 1971, issue of *Jeune Afrique*. The epigraph is taken from this interview.[4] Our movement, born in Paris, was catalyzed by the Niagara movement, the Negro Renaissance, even Garveyism.

Before continuing further, it is essential to analyze those three movements. That will help us elucidate the primary concerns and discern the similarities and disparities between Negro-Americans and Negro-Africans.

One must always begin with W. E. B. Du Bois, who is rightly considered "the father of the Negritude movement," as Lilyan Kesteloot writes.[d] Du Bois was the first to holistically conceptualize the movement in all its uniqueness, goals, aspects, and methods. For Du Bois, there is, above all, the plight of Negroes in the United States and the degrading perceptions created by Whites: a subhuman, intellectually and morally underdeveloped, stuck in childhood, flawed. This image stuck not only in the minds of White people but also, unfortunately, in those of the Negroes themselves. "It is a peculiar sensation," wrote Du Bois, "this double consciousness, this sense of always looking at one's self through the eyes of others, of measuring one's soul by the tape of a world that looks on in *amused contempt* and *pity*."[e] Such sentiments allowed for the institutionalization of "racial discrimination" in American society, piling on humiliation to deny Negroes a part of their rights in economic, political, cultural, and social well-being.

After analyzing the subjective and objective situation of Negro-Americans theoretically, Du Bois identified the necessary steps for their liberation. The

d Kesteloot, *Anthologie négro-africaine*, 15.
e Epigraph to Wagner, *Les poètes nègres des États-Unis*. The original is in Du Bois, *The Souls of Black Folk*, 8.

point was, above all, to erase the demeaning image of the *Negro-flawed-child* held in the Whites'—and especially Blacks'—mind and replace it with an image of a classic, authentic Africa as civilization: "Africa is not a country, it is a world, a universe of itself and for itself."[f] This might then inspire a desire and a sustained effort among Negro-Americans to "be themselves before all else," to project their authentic African image. The point was, also, to eradicate "racial discrimination" and the economic and political, cultural, and social struggles that relegated Blacks to second-rate citizenship. In short, Du Bois sought to transform Negro-Americans both inward and outward—the former through education and training, the latter by exerting pressure on both the American government and the public.

Du Bois's theoretical and practical actions were aligned with these two objectives. Look no further than *Black Souls*, his seminal work, the source from which Negritude erupted. For Du Bois was not only an intellectual but also a man of action. He also played a crucial role in the organization and life of the movement, not just in America, but in Europe and Africa as well. He was instrumental in the establishment of the National Association for the Advancement of Colored People (NAACP), stewarding its journal, *The Crisis*, and in the organization of the four Pan-African Congresses, most notably as the secretary-general of the first one.

The ideas of Du Bois's actions were discussed, debated, and developed not only in the United States but also in the Antilles and Africa. Nevertheless, their impact on us was indirect. By *us*, I mean Negro-Africans in general and the founders of the Francophone Negritude movement in particular. We felt their influence via the mediation of Marcus Garvey and the Negro Renaissance.

Garvey, by foregrounding Africa, her history, nobility, and beauty, and engaging not only Black intellectuals but also the masses, gave the movement a worldly resonance—as reflected in the mission-statement title of his weekly *Negro World*. Indeed, it was the combined impact of Garvey's movement and the Pan-African Congresses that most deeply influenced Black Africa's politicians: Senegal's congressmen Blaise Diagne and Galandou Diouf, as well as future Anglophone leaders like Nnamdi Azikiwe, Kwame Nkrumah, and Jomo Kenyatta. I do not want to forget the proletarian front, which was equally swayed by Du Bois and Garvey. I am thinking of *La Voix des Nègres*, the Parisian journal led by Tiemokho Garan Kouyaté and Lamine Senghor after World War I.

f Du Bois, "Little Portrait of Africa," 274.

Yet, in the Latin Quarter during the 1930s, we were highly tuned to the ideas and actions led by the Negro Renaissance, whose leading figures we sometimes met in Paris. Damas recalled this in his interview. For my part, I regularly read not only *The Crisis* and *Opportunity*, the National Urban League's review, but also the *Journal of Negro History* founded by Carter G. Woodson, which published numerous essays enriching our knowledge of Africa. *The New Negro*, edited by Alain Locke and hailed by Jean Wagner as the "Anthology-Manifesto," was my bedside book. Nancy Cunard's *Negro Anthology*, published in 1934, soon joined my collection. As we shall see, it was less the theory than the practice of Negritude, particularly the novel and especially the poetry of the Negro Renaissance, that shaped our vision.

Having analyzed the influence of Negro-Americans, it is time we examine the source of the gap, not conflict, between us. It arises from differences in historical, geographical, and cultural contexts. Essentially, Negro-American and Antillean peoples—even the Francophone ones—have inherited and continue to bear the profound burden of slavery. For centuries, they have been physically and, what is more, spiritually, cut off from the source that nourished and shaped their ancestors for millions of years: Mother Africa. In fact, current evidence suggests that the emergence of man took place in Africa, some 5,500,000 years ago.

For us, Negro-Africans, the situation was different. We were among the first ones to seek a university education in Europe. Many of us lived in rural areas, where White presence was minimal, our civilization still intact and having retained its moral foundation, humanity, and harmony. As I perused the opening pages of Leo Frobenius's *History of the African Civilization*, I was swept back into my Serer childhood in the kingdom of Sine—despite its eventual change into a protectorate.[5] I fondly remember, among other instances, a visit from King Koumba Ndofène Diouf to my father, where every sentiment was honorable, every gesture dignified, every word graceful. Later, in the Catholic School of Dakar, whenever the director sought to belittle our past and denied our civilization's existence, we never failed to meet his assertions with vigorous opposition, even as seminarians. That was the moment when the idea began to resonate within me: the *idea*, not the word, of a *different yet equal Black civilization*. From those transformative school years, the goal—or more accurately the meaning—of my life has been, I believe, to affirm and to live this idea. My experience is not exceptional; on the contrary, it is representative, which is why I shared it.

Black students of my generation thus left for Europe with their senses heightened and consciousness alert, eager to learn not only the arts and sciences of the Whites but also the evidence of the grandeur of Africa and her peoples. This explains our interest in ethnology and other sciences. The interwar era was a period when Europe finally discovered what Africa was. Historians and pre-historians, ethnographers and linguists, writers and artists alike, from England, Germany, and particularly France, all were exploring the original and ancient antiquity of Africa: the *Ur-Afrika*, as the Germans would say. This was the period Emmanuel Berl labeled the "Negro Revolution," where Negro-Americans also played a role, revolutionizing European music and fine arts, influencing European thought and literature more than many might admit.

European scholars, artists, and writers taught us to deepen our knowledge not only of vibrant African life but also her invaluable civilizational contributions. Negro-Americans played a different yet significant part. They did not just teach us to express moral indignation but inspired us to organize socially, and even politically, above all, to foster *creativity*. The Negro Renaissance poets who left an indelible mark on us included Langston Hughes, Claude McKay, Jean Toomer, James Weldon Johnson, Sterling Brown, and Frank Marshall Davis. They showed us, by forging ahead, that it was possible to spark a movement, that primarily through artistic creativity, it was possible to respect and breathe new life into African civilization.

Negro-Americans, I said, influenced Negro-Africans. Because their respective situation—thus their experience—was different, however, their Negritude took on a different color. To fully comprehend the nuances within the unity that exists between both groups, one should delve into *The Militant Black Writer*, published by the University of Wisconsin. In the first part of the book, "Voices of Protest," Mercer Cook explores contemporary Negro-African literature, while in the second part, "Survival Motion: A Study of the Black Writer and the Black Revolution in America," Stephen E. Henderson discusses Negro-American literature. In the latter part, a few lines penned by Leroux Bennett struck me as especially poignant: "The whole corpus of the tradition . . . is compressed into the folk myth of Soul, the American counterpart of the African Negritude, a distant quality of Negro-ness growing out of the Negro's experience and not his genes. Soul is a metaphorical evocation of Negro being as expressed in the Negro tradition. It is the feeling with which an artist invests his creation, the style with which a man lives his life. It is, above all, the spirit rather than the letter: a certain way of feeling, a certain way of expressing oneself, a certain way of being."[6]

Our entire definition of Negritude—as a condition and an expression—is here validated. Better yet, the very choice of the word—the idea of—*soul* echoes a certain African and popular perspective. I recall an incident from

1941, in a prisoner camp for "Senegalese." I was talking with comrades, farmers, about the respective qualities of European Whites and Negro-Africans, when one of them, Mbaye Diop, told me in Wolof: *Ñoo nu ëpë xel, noo leen ëpë fit*. Which means, "They have more spirit than us, we have more soul than them." Still, Negroes on the other side of the Atlantic, whether they be from the United States of America, the United States of Brazil, or the Antilles, insist on their specific situation because of their original experience: on social heredity more than biological inheritance. And some Antillean Marxists, like the Haitian René Depestre, go so far as to reduce Negritude to a historical experience. They speak of "mysticism" or even "mystification" about those who, like myself and many Negro-Africans, emphasize ethnicity.

It is because I am a Francophone that I understand them—although I do not share their views. Of course, the Francophone Negroes of Africa experienced neither deportation to America nor slavery on plantations. Yet, the French policy of assimilation has, to some degree, I mean morally, exiled and subjected us: depersonalized us. This is a trauma that Anglophone Africans did not experience. But to accuse us of "mysticism," as Depestre does, is narrow-minded.

We now transition to the final segment of my lecture, which concerns generational conflict.

Generational Conflict

As a famous writer once said, it is fitting and natural that the younger generation commences their life journey by "slandering." When I hear echoes of Damas, Césaire, or Senghor in poems that young French-speaking Black writers send me to read, I cannot help but yawn. And I think to myself, "This is not promising." When I read or hear a writer in their thirties proclaim, "The Negritude of Césaire, Damas, and Senghor is and must be overcome," I cheer enthusiastically or, as we say in Senegal, with all of my hands. Yes, each generation, each thinker, each writer, artist, politician, must, in their own ways and for their own good, go deeper and expand Negritude. They must overcome Negritude's predecessors. But overcoming does not mean negating, for to overcome is not to better something but to alter its quality: a new way to see, live, speak, aligning with changing circumstances. Of course, the Francophone and the Anglophone worlds are porous. For young poets, this would mean overcoming Countee Cullen, Claude McKay, even Langston Hughes. *That is the question.*

So, I begin with my agreement with Tchicaya U Tam'si, who, to the question "What is Negritude?," answers, "Negritude is a generational and intellectual business. I belong to a different generation and school of thought, and I cannot help but laugh when people try to instruct me about it." Tchicaya does not renounce Negritude, he simply seeks to contribute to it in his unique way, freely. And he does so with the marvels of his poetry, which is among the most groundbreaking on the continent, while still firmly Negro—indeed Congolese.

But here comes Wole Soyinka, who tells us, "A tiger doesn't proclaim his tigritude, it pounces." Just look at *Neo-African Literature: A History of Black Writing*, written by the German Janheinz Jahn.[7] On pages 242–43, in the French edition, he notes how swiftly White critics removed the fundamental proposition—"the tiger pounces"—to sow discord among African advocates of Negritude and proponents of the African personality, once again. Let us turn our attention to the Nigerian writer, as quoted by Jahn: "I was trying to distinguish between propaganda and true poetic creativity. I was saying in other words that what one expected from poetry was an intrinsic poetic quality, not a mere name-dropping."[8]

Truth be told, this debate is not a new one: It harkens back to the early days of the movement. Du Bois proudly called himself a "propagandist." Yet, his spiritual son, Alain Locke, leaned toward "choosing art and leaving propaganda alone."[g] We Francophones engaged in a similar debate in the 1930s and '40s. I then leaned toward Soyinka's solution. Here is what I wrote in 1948 about David Diop, who tragically left us too soon, and with him, friendship: "We do not doubt that Diop will become more humanist as he gets older. He shall understand that what gives a poem its Negritude is less its theme than its style, the emotional vigor that breathes life into words, that transmutes words into Word."[h] Jahn concurs with us and, after citing Soyinka, concludes, "Negritude theorists aspired to nothing less."

Therefore, the debate is not between "Negritude" and "tigritude," and when Mphahlele suggests an "individual realism," I am not too disturbed because we are talking about Negroes, and when Negroes are themselves, they cannot but express their "way of being Negro." Just as the zebra cannot shed its zebraness, and the tiger cannot renounce its tigritude, we can only overcome ethnic and historical determinations—the artist's work—by advancing in this direction.

The real debate lies elsewhere. It is between culturalists and politicians, between the ideology of Negritude and ideologies that, in Europe, Asia, and America, fuel the imperialist endeavors vying for world dominance. We saw it clearly at the Pan-African Festival of Algiers. There, major White-owned news-

g Quoted in Wagner, *Les poètes nègres des Etats-Unis*, who talks about this debate on pages 172–84.
h Senghor, *Anthologie de la nouvelle poésie nègre*, 137.

papers and journals glorified Negroes' attack on Negritude and blew them out of proportion. The responses from the Asian world were more subtle but no less poignant.

But let us examine the politicians' objections to Negritude, starting with the already-mentioned interview of Léon Damas: "None of Negritude's censors argue for melanism, quite the opposite. At the Algiers Festival, attacks against Negritude seemed to have a dual origin: from one side, a (Black) African one, from Guineans, Congolese (Brazzaville), etc.; on the other, an Arab one, who seemingly use it as a tool to foster continental division. Isn't it indeed counter-productive to emphasize the color factor at a time when Africa is seeking unity despite its internal differences?" That is the problem. Let us see how it unfolds.

Insofar as Arabs are concerned, it would be unfair to criticize the Negroes for accentuating their differences when the former began much earlier than the latter: first, with the Lebanese-inspired Nada (Renaissance) movement, and now with Arabism. Furthermore, to divide the African continent over language is only slightly better than doing so over color. Indeed, none of Negritude's founders brought attention to color but rather to ethnicity. And ethnicity, as we know, is not just about race and physical attributes but also about culture with its "civilizational values"—values that proponents of Negritude have always extolled. Today, the youth chant "Black is beautiful" because Whites began by insulting our skin color, and we had no choice but to respond to and uplift it. Each ethnic group, each people have praised their physical attributes as qualities, as canonized beauty. In Senegal, the Serer people celebrated the "tall and black" athletes in their athletic poems, while the Pulaar people, in their love poems, sang of the young girls with a "red copper complexion," much like the Greeks once lauded their goddesses with "white arms."

Speaking of the Arabs, far from railing against Arabism, I believe we were the first to speak objectively about Africanity, without any complex regarding Black culture, but as a testament to the "African civilization," which I defined not so long ago as the "symbiosis of Arabism—more precisely, Arabity—and Negritude."[i] The true strength of Africanity lies in the fact that this symbiosis dates back to prehistoric times, or at the least, protohistory, when it was perceived as a superior manifestation of man. When I speak about Arabs, I think about southern Mediterranean Whites: Berbers and Semites. Father Engelbert Mveng could teach us so much on this subject.

---

i Senghor, "Les fondations de l'africanité," 45–120; Senghor, Foundations of "Africanité" or "Négritude" and "Arabité."

Negritude and Marxism

The real problem, then, does not dwell in the opposition between Negritude and Arabism, but in the opposition between two concepts—I would venture to say, two ideologies—and the ideologies that currently drive the great European, American, and Asian nations, particularly those known as Marxist-Leninist. It is important to note that the delegations that attacked Negritude were from Guinea and Congo (Brazzaville). The official Arab delegations, stronger in the vindication of their national cultures, did not assail Arabism, but the young Turks readily consigned both Negritude and Arabism to the proverbial Museum of Antiquities. As Mr. Faouzi writes in *Jeune Afrique*, "Algiers proved the triviality and error of racialized thinking. It showed that African artists and intellectuals, far from contenting themselves with a naive historical admiration or uncritical glorification, take ownership of techniques that were developed in the very culture of the oppressor for the benefit of the national cause and the cause of Africa."

In sum, if we understand Mr. Faouzi well, the point is to take the essence of the former colonizer's European culture, their technicalized and discursive reason. And why? To uphold the "national cause" and the "African cause" understood as political independence—and I add: economic growth—and nothing more. Here, it is never a question of independence of the mind, which is the necessary premise to all independence, or cultural development, which should be the aim of any economic growth. Mr. Faouzi double-faults when he asserts the superiority of discursive reason—that Europeans prefer—over intuitive reason, that Negroes favor but not exclusively employ.

Indeed, the Europeans, maybe not for the past two thousand years but, let us say, since Descartes, have relied heavily on classical logic. But the kingdom of discursive reason is a mere three hundred years old in the more than five million years of human history—although, logic morphed into a dialectic, nonlinear form as early as the mid-nineteenth century. As you are aware, the past century has seen a radical revolution in epistemology, led by the advent of the human sciences: anthropology, ethnography, sociology, linguistics; fields that started with a dash of metaphysics and have become structural and functional. Today, to comprehend an object, we no longer isolate it from its temporal and spatial environment, nor do we draw out its most sensitive aspects—as one would its sap, stock, and blood. We certainly do not observe from a distance, like a detached God surveying an eternal world. Contemporary knowledge is a dynamic interaction between subject and object, a collaboration, a communion where both are concurrently observing and observed, acting and acted upon.

It is a romance between the eye of reason and the touch of reason. This is how ethnographers, with the terms *participation* and *communion*, have consistently defined the Negroes' way of knowing.

I know, the false-Marxist foes of Negritude have criticized me for my words: "Emotion is Negro as Reason is Hellenic." They inferred that I dismiss the power of reason, a reason for the Negroes. How would they know what I meant if they remove the sentence from its context? Evidently, here *emotion*, akin to the word *soul* used by Negro-Americans, means "intuitive reason," and *reason*, the European reason, means "discursive reason." The latter is not superior to the former. A glance at the triumph of the new epistemology shows as much—not to mention the views of the founders of rationalism. Aristotle, though not the creator but the architect of Greek rationalism, ranks intuitive reason above the discursive one, much like Plato, and Descartes, the founder of modern rationalism, ranks *feeling* next to *thinking* and *willing*, marking it as a means of expressing *reason*. Thus, these "Marxists" read their sources badly, Marx among them.

My other evidence is the precedence they grant to politics and economics over culture, to quantity over quality, confusing growth with development as the capitalists do—and contrary to the teachings of Marx and Lenin. In his *Differentialist Manifesto*, Henri Lefebvre—one of France's leading Marxist scholars—writes, "This dual aspect—the real priority of economics over the fictional yet acting primacy of politics—forms a social structure that is doomed to fail. Insofar as socialism, by forgoing differentiation, has adopted this structure (this model), it too is doomed to fail. How will it fail? By dissolving crucial social bonds."[j] Yet Marx, before Lenin, differentiated between growth and development. In a posthumous manuscript, titled "Alienated Labor" and published by *La Revue Socialiste*, the founder of "scientific socialism" developed that idea by showing that economic growth, though capable of satisfying "animal needs"—food, clothing, and shelter—was no more than a means to the ultimate end of man, whose "generic activity" and fulfillment is to create works of art to nourish himself and other men, his brothers.[k] And for Marx, what imparts a human touch to these works is their beauty: the coincidence, in these works of art, between man and the world, individual and universal. In the sense that the entire universe is reflected in and through individual work, whereas man, in his individual consciousness, is stretched to the size of the universe; also, in the sense that this coincidence is spiritual because it is a

j Lefebvre, *Le manifeste différentialiste*, 37.
k *La Revue Socialiste*, February 1947.

qualitative, not quantitative, equilibrium. The words of Marx that I read elucidate this in the twentieth-century failure of the primacy of economics over politics. This failure is as conspicuous in communist countries as it is in fascist or merely bourgeois ones. Hence, the youth in these regimes revolt in the name of culture: in the name of the *right to be different*. As Henri Lefebvre writes, "Development, fully restored, embodies more intricate and richer social relations that are far from being reduced. It is (one has to say *only*) qualitative. It is premised upon the *creation* of forms of social life, 'values,' ideas, ways of living, styles. In a word: difference."[1]

Among those who profess to be Marxist-Leninist so that they can rail against Negritude, one concern stands out above the primacy given to politics or even economics: their disdain for their national culture. They readily deny the accusation. Yet, at the dawn of European nations' rebirth was the birth of cultural movements that draw parallels with Negritude. Allow me to share three examples from Germany, Scandinavia, and Russia.

In Germany, the liberation movement surfaced as early as the mid-eighteenth century with Klopstock and Wieland, particularly with *Sturm und Drang* authors. The Germans are urged to follow their native folk poetry and Germanic myth, challenging the supremacy of (discursive) reason. In Hamann's words, "Reason discovers nothing more for us than what Job saw—the misery of our birth—the advantage of the grave—the futility and inadequacy of life, since we lack knowledge, and many passions and instincts, whose object is unknown to us."[m9] Undoubtedly, Goethe's genius extends beyond his own merits; he is a direct heir of the *Sturm und Drang*, which made him *German*. Indeed, he is the founder of modern German poetry.

Turning to Scandinavia, Erica Simon's *National Awakening and Folk Culture in Scandinavia* merits attention.[n] Simon shows how Scandinavian peoples, in the early nineteenth century, during and after the Napoleonic wars, confronted with invasions and humiliation by the great European powers, sought a "Northern Spirit" in their shared culture: values that enabled them to form a strong cultural and political entity through the awakening of their sister civilizations, with which they would move forward. It is worth noting that, like elsewhere, cultural awakenings often emerge from invasions, humiliations, conquests. A French journalist wrote not too long ago, "People are stirred into revolt not because of poverty but due to humiliation." It is also interesting to

l Lefebvre, *Le manifeste différentialiste*, 38.
m Mossé, *Histoire de la littérature allemande*, 387.
n Simon, *Réveil national et culture populaire*.

note the parallel Simon makes between Negritude and Nordicity in an article titled "Grundtvig University" published in the *Revue de la Société des études germaniques*.

Russia presents perhaps the most fascinating example. Much like in Scandinavia, the awakening happens in the face of foreign invasions and partial occupation of national territory. The initial resistance against foreign occupation, predominantly French, eventually morphs into a scholarly cultural movement postliberation: the Slavophilia movement. Alexis Stephanovich Khomiakov, one of its leaders, never forgot the hasty evacuation of his family when Napoleon's troops arrived and burned his family home. Still a child—he was born in 1804—he then proclaimed, "I will rally the Slavic people to revolt" against all Western Europeans. Much like in Scandinavia, the movement was primarily philosophical and literary, laying the groundwork for a Russian cultural renaissance, resulting in masterpieces across all intellectual and artistic fields: philosophy, literature, fine arts, and music.

Two observations on Slavophilia are worth mentioning. First, it too draws comparisons with Negritude.[o] Second, while the Russians, the Soviets, may claim to have "outgrown" Slavophilia, they have neither negated nor forgotten the cultural renaissance it engendered. They remain, in practice and theory, Slavophile or better yet: Slavic. Just look at some recent articles in *Molodaya Gvardia*, the official organ and vanguard of the Communist Youth.

By doing so, the Soviets have reconciled their loyalty to their ethnicity, their national culture, with their loyalty to the spirit—and the letter—of Marx. Marx himself wrote about ethnic determinations:

It is always the direct relationship of the owners of the conditions of production to the direct producers—a relation always naturally corresponding to a definite stage in the development of the methods of labor and thereby its social productivity—which reveals the innermost secret, the hidden basis of the entire social structure and with it the political form of the relation of sovereignty and dependence, in short, the corresponding specific form of the state. This does not prevent the same economic basis—the same from the standpoint of its main conditions—due to innumerable different empirical circumstances, *natural environment, racial relations, external historical influences*, etc. from showing infinite variations and gradations in appearance, which can be ascertained only by analysis of the empirically given circumstances.[p]

o Vaillant, "Encounter the West."
p Marx, *Capital*, vol. 3, 927.

This offers an explanation for the influence—and thus the role—of ethnicity, which can be defined by the words I have emphasized, as the result of a symbiosis, within man, of racial, geographical, and historical factors.

To those who dismiss the reality of race and ethnicity, and therefore their influence on civilization, I present these lines by Marx, whose relevance is vindicated by the rise of the new sciences of man—such as ethnology and characterology. Ethnology indeed focuses on the study of ethnic groups: not solely their physical traits but their behaviors and institutions. Meanwhile, characterology, a science born in the twentieth century, delves into the study of characters, the ways of feelings, thinking, and living that distinguish one person from another. Influenced by ethnology, characterologists soon expanded their analysis from individuals to ethnic groups, giving birth to a new discipline with scholars such as Paul Griéger at the helm: ethnic characterology. This science strives to underscore the irreducible originality of each civilization in a better way than the ethnologist could. As Griéger writes, "Natural human groups, just like individuals, possess their own psychobiological constitution. They do not feel, think, or act in the same way. Each has its distinctive way of conceiving existence and adopting a certain attitude about values. Insofar as psychological reality is concerned, *human unity* is a fact, it does not suppress another facet of truth, which is the *diversity* of collective and individual characters."q

Those who challenge the new human sciences will find it a formidable task. Perhaps, however, they will read Marx—and Lenin, whose comparable texts I could also quote—and consider him outgrown by Mao, their new idol. Yet, far from contradicting Marx and Lenin, the example of the Chinese leader, who professes to be their orthodox disciple, only corroborates their thinking.

Mao's originality as a thinker stems from his refusal to follow the Soviet model. In fact, although he does not explicitly state it, he wants to do to Lenin, the *Russian*, what he does to Marx, the *German Jew*. Challenging the Russian model, he seeks to encourage the Chinese people to interpret Marx by and for themselves—as free men, without any inferiority complex. In so doing, Mao Zedong remains loyal to the spirit of Marx, and even his letter. Engels, indeed, in his commentary on Marx, notes that Marxism is not a "dogma" but a "method," not a "model" but a "way," as Henri Lefebvre recently pointed out. He adds, "The Model, as obsession and phantasm of specialized political apparatuses, arrived after Marx and Lenin. It is not a 'Marxist' concept. This is how Marxism is dismembered, how dialectic is thrown out. The Model prescribes a

q Griéger, *La caractérologie ethnique*, xv.

specific growth that conforms to the demands and strategy of those in power. The Model is the same for all. It imposes identity or simulation. It manipulates people and allows them to be intimidated. The way does not impose, it proposes. The ways can be different; the way is that of difference."[r]

So, to our opponents, the leftists, the Maoists, I say this: The only true way to remain true to Mao is to reject the "Chinese model" for Africa and seek a sui generis model, in the way of the Chinese thinker himself, for Black Africa and for the Antilles—not to mention the United States of America or the United States of Brazil. The debate is not new. It began in the 1930s when we combated those among us who prioritized Marxism over Negritude. Our argument has always been that Culture supersedes Politics, serving both as premise and its objective. In other words, man is at the beginning and the end of development. Differently put, *Marxism must be not just revised but rethought by Black thinkers and aligned with the values of Negritude.*

Conclusion

It is true that we did not remain passive, like our so-called revolutionaries did, waiting for Marx, Lenin, or Mao to rethink our situation and forge a—cultural, political, economic, and social—model that combined the values of Negritude with those of modernity. We are not seeking to challenge the European, American, or Asian civilizations; nor are we rejecting the opportunity to draw from ideologies—be they liberal capitalism or democratic socialism, Russian or Chinese Marxism-Leninism—which serve those imperialist powers locked in a struggle for world dominance, particularly the dominance of Africa, and which we, as proponents of Negritude, must study and learn from. Much like the American management followed the old European capitalism, like Lenin followed Marx, so too must we take heed of Mao and Nehru and *think and act by and for ourselves, as Negroes.*

The philosopher Gaston Berger, a mixed-race man born in Saint-Louis, Senegal, at the turn of the last century, is one of our own. He founded Futurology, the science that allows us to anticipate the future evolution of the world to better predict it. It teaches us, essentially, that the civilization of the twenty-first century will be the civilization of the universal, to which each ethnic group and nation will be able to bring their contribution. I say "will" because not all will necessarily heed Aimé Césaire's call to the "rendezvous of giving and receiving." Only those ethnic groups and nations that believe they have a unique message

r Griéger, *La caractérologie ethnique*, 40.

to deliver and consciously wish to disseminate it will be there and contribute to building the Civilization of the Universal.

Here, Negritude as subject joins Negritude as object. Since the beginning of the century, indeed, advocates of Negritude have begun to disseminate our civilizational values, using their words as a form of action—for every art is a Word—to aid in the construction of a more humane civilization made of necessary differences: complementary differences among ethnic groups and nations.

TRANSLATOR'S NOTES

1. Contrary to Senghor's attribution to the US Senate, the original report was authored by FBI Director J. Edgar Hoover. It is an eighteen-page memorandum to Mr. Fisher at the Department of Justice, dated September 10, 1919, and archived in record group 60, file 9–12–725 at the National Archives in Washington, DC. A brief excerpt appeared in the *New York Times* on November 23, 1919 (section D, p. 1). The exact version Senghor referenced remains unclear. For further context on the media's role in politics and race relations, see Maxwell, *F. B. Eyes*; and Maxwell, "Editorial Federalism."

2. Robert, *Dictionnaire*.

3. Senghor adapted the quote originally given by Césaire to Lilyan Kesteloot: "I remained attached to a certain negritude, an extremely simple one, a very minimum credo that consists in saying in simple terms that I am a Negro and know it, that I am a Negro and feel a solidarity with every Negro, I am Negro and consider that I am a part of a tradition and I must give myself the mission to make a legacy fruitful." See Kesteloot, *Aimé Césaire*, 197–209.

4. Léon-Gontran Damas, "La négritude en question," interview, *Jeune Afrique*, no. 532 (March 16, 1971): 57–58; Léon-Gontran Damas, "Négritude Revisited: An Interview with Léon Damas," in *Critical Perspectives on Léon-Gontran Damas*, translated and edited by Keith Q. Warner (Washington, DC: Three Continents Press, 1988), 23–28. Although this interview is authentic, the passage Senghor attributes to Damas does not appear in the published texts.

5. Frobenius, *Histoire de la civilisation africaine*, originally published as *Kulturgeschichte Afrikas*.

6. Senghor provides his own French translation of the text. The original is in Cook and Henderson, *Militant Black Writer*, 115.

7. Jahn, *Neo-African Literature*.

8. Jahn, *Neo-African Literature*, 266. Based on a transcription from a tape owned by Jahn.

9. Herder, *Sämtliche Werke*, 147; Beiser, *Fate of Reason*, 31; translation modified.

Acknowledgments

At the heart of this intellectual odyssey stands Gayatri Chakravorty Spivak, my dissertation advisor, whose profound influence extends far beyond the pages of this book. She taught me to think, to challenge boundaries, to explore the depths of texts in ways I never thought possible, and to reside in the liminal spaces of thought where Senghor's ideas often unfold.

The present book would not be possible without Souleymane Bachir Diagne, whose insights illuminating the nuances of Senghor's philosophy are unmatched today, while Étienne Balibar helped me situate the philosophy within his unparalleled grasp of the broader tapestry of global intellectual history.

The nurturing environment of Stetson University, marked by a productive tension between teaching and research, has been crucial in bringing the work to fruition. My colleague and friend Yves-Antoine Clemmen, as chair of the Department of World Languages and Cultures, provided both intellectual companionship and the academic freedom to explore Senghor's world through pedagogical innovation that could directly inform my scholarly production.

The dedication of the DuPont Ball Library staff in tracking down obscure texts and facilitating interlibrary loans and other research tools has been nothing short of heroic. It made possible the reconstruction of the bibliographical landscape that shaped Senghor's thought for half a century.

Financial support came at critical junctures: The Ernest Hemingway Grant from the Cultural Services of the French Embassy, under the direction of Gaëtan Bruel, then cultural attaché, enabled the acquisition of vital copyrights. Stetson University's Summer Grants provided generous temporal and financial resources necessary for sustained research and writing.

Throughout this process, my wife, Hannah Sun, has been my most steadfast supporter and astute critic, patiently helping me untangle my thoughts across multiple drafts and often abstruse arguments. Her contribution to this work, while not always visible on the page, is woven into its very fabric.

At Duke University Press, Elizabeth Ault's early faith in this project and her guidance, along with the insights of peer reviewers, have been instrumental in refining and focusing the book you now hold.

To all those unnamed here—colleagues, students, and friends whose conversations and critiques have enriched this work—I extend my gratitude. This book is a testament to the power of intellectual endeavors and the enduring relevance of Senghor's thought in our contemporary moment.

Bibliography

Ackermann, Bruce. *We the People.* Vol. 1. Cambridge, MA: Harvard University Press, 1991.

"African Institute Named National Resource Center." *Columbia University Record* 19, no. 13 (December 10, 1993): 5. https://curecordarchive.library.columbia.edu/?a=d&d =cr19931210–01.2.19&e=————-en-20—1—txt-txIN————-.

Ako, Edward O. "'L'Étudiant Noir' and the Myth of the Genesis of the Negritude Movement." *Research in African Literatures* 15, no. 3 (1984): 341–53.

Alexander, Lewis. "Transformation." In *The Poetry of the Negro 1746–1949*, edited by Langston Hughes and Arna Bontemps. New York: Doubleday, 1949.

Althusser, Louis. "Ideology and Ideological State Apparatuses." Translated by Ben Brewster. In *Lenin and Philosophy and Other Essays*. New York: Monthly Review Press, 2001.

Amin, Samir. *Re-Reading the Postwar Period: An Intellectual Itinerary.* Translated by Michael Wolfers. New York: Monthly Review Press, 1994.

Aristotle. *Poetics.* Translated by Stephen Halliwell. Cambridge, MA: Harvard University Press, 1995.

Arthur, Paige. *Unfinished Projects: Decolonization and the Philosophy of Jean-Paul Sartre.* London: Verso, 2010.

Asi, Hakim. *The 1945 Manchester Pan-African Congress.* London: New Beacon, 1995.

Ayittey, George C. "The United States of Africa: A Revisit." *Annals of the American Academy of Political and Social Science* 632 (2010): 86–102.

Azikiwe, Nnamdi. *Renascent Africa.* London: Frank Cass and Company, 1937.

Baer, Ben Conisbee. *Indigenous Vanguards: Education, National Liberation, and the Limits of Modernism.* New York: Columbia University Press, 2019.

Baer, Ben Conisbee. "Léopold Sédar Senghor: The Species and Spaces of Impersonal Belonging." *Boundary 2* 47, no. 3 (2020): 31–54.

Balandier, Georges. "L'anthropologie sociale au XXe siècle" [Social anthropology in the twentieth century]. *L'Homme* 35, no. 134 (1995): 9–16.

Barthélémy, Pascale. "La formation des institutrices africaines en A.O.F.: Pour une lecture historique du roman de Mariama Bâ, 'Une si longue lettre.'" *Clio: Histoire, femmes et sociétés* 6 (1997). http://journals.openedition.org/clio/381.

Baudelaire, Charles. *Baudelaire on Poe*. Translated by Francis E. Hyslop Jr. State College, PA: Bald Eagle Press, 1952.

Baudelaire, Charles. *Œuvres complètes*. Edited by Marcel A. Ruff. Paris: Seuil, 1968.

Becker, A. L. *Beyond Translation: Essays Toward a Modern Philology*. Ann Arbor: University of Michigan Press, 2000.

Beiser, Frederick C. *The Fate of Reason: German Philosophy from Kant to Fichte*. Cambridge, MA: Harvard University Press, 1987.

Bennett, Gwendolyn. "To a Dark Girl." In *Voices from the Harlem Renaissance*, edited by Nathan Irvin Huggins. New York: Oxford University Press, 1995.

Benoist, Jules de. *L'Afrique Occidentale Française: De la Conférence de Brazzaville (1944) à l'Indépendance (1960)*. Dakar: Nouvelles Éditions Africaines, 1982.

Berger, Gaston. *Phénoménologie du temps et prospective*. Paris: Presses Universitaires de France, 1964.

Blum, Françoise. "Sénégal 1968: Révolte étudiante et grève générale" [Senegal 1968: Student revolt and general strike]. *Revue d'histoire moderne et contemporaine* 59, no. 2 (2012): 144–77.

Bonner, Christopher. "Alioune Diop and the Cultural Politics of Négritude: Reading the First Congress of Black Writers and Artists, 1956." *Research in African Literatures* 50, no. 2 (2019): 1–18.

Boone, Catherine. *Political Topographies of the African State: Territorial Authority and Institutional Choice*. Cambridge: Cambridge University Press, 2003.

Bouret, Jean. *L'art abstrait: Ses origines, ses luttes, sa présence*. Paris: Club français du livre, 1957.

Brawley, Benjamin. "The Negro Genius." In *The New Negro: Readings on Race, Representation, and African American Culture, 1892–1938*, edited by Henry Louis Gates Jr. and Gene Andrew Jarrett. Princeton, NJ: Princeton University Press, 2007.

Breton, André. "Golden Silence" (1946). In *Free Rein*, translated by Michel Parmentier and Jacqueline D'Amboise. Lincoln: University of Nebraska Press, 1995.

Breton, André. *Manifestos of Surrealism*. Translated by Richard Seaver and Helen R. Lane. Ann Arbor: University of Michigan Press, 1972.

Breton, André. *Premier manifeste du surréalisme*. Paris: Éditions du Sagittaire, 1946.

Brown, Sterling. "Tornado Blues." In *The Collected Poems of Sterling A. Brown*, edited by Michael S. Harper. Evanston, IL: Northwestern University Press, 2000.

Burbank, Jane. *Empires in World History: Power and the Politics of Difference*. Princeton, NJ: Princeton University Press, 2010.

Cabrera, Lydia. *Afro-Cuban Tales*. Translated by Alberto Hernandez-Chiroldes and Lauren Yoder. Lincoln: University of Nebraska Press, 2004.

Cabrera, Lydia. *Contes nègres de Cuba*. Paris: Gallimard, 1936.

Casswell, Nim. "Autopsie de l'Oncad: Politique arachidière du Sénégal, 1966–1980" [Autopsy of Oncad: Senegalese peanut policy]. *Politique Africaine* 14 (1984): 38–73.

Césaire, Aimé. "And the Dogs Were Silent." In *Lyric and Dramatic Poetry*, translated by Clayton Eshleman and Annette Smith. Charlottesville: University of Virginia Press, 1990.

Césaire, Aimé. *Cahier d'un retour au pays natal*. See Césaire, Aimé. *Journal of a Home-coming/Cahier d'un retour au pays natal*.

Césaire, Aimé. *Et si les chiens se taisaient*. 1946. Reprint, Paris: Gallimard, 1970.

Césaire, Aimé. *Journal of a Homecoming/Cahier d'un retour au pays natal*. Translated by N. Gregson Davis and Abiola Irele. Durham, NC: Duke University Press, 2017.

Césaire, Aimé. *Les armes miraculeuses*. 1946. Reprint, Paris: Seuil, 1970.

Césaire, Aimé. *The Miraculous Weapons*. Translated by Clayton Eshleman and Annette J. Smith. Berkeley: University of California Press, 1983.

Césaire, Aimé. "Nègreries: Conscience raciale et révolution sociale" [Negronesses: Racial consciousness and social revolution]. *L'Étudiant Noir* 3. Republished in *Les Temps Modernes*, no. 676 (2013/5): 250–51.

Césaire, Aimé. "Nègreries: Jeunesse noire et assimilation" [Negronesses: Black youth and assimilation]. *L'Étudiant Noir* 1. Republished in *Les Temps Modernes*, no. 676 (2013/5): 249–50.

Chevrier, Jacques. *Anthologie Africaine: La poésie de la Négritude*. Paris: Hatier International, 2006.

Cochrane, Laura. "The Growth of Artistic Nationalism in Senegal." In *Nations and Nationalism: Journal of the Association of Ethnicity and Nationalism* 17, no. 2 (2011): 377–95.

Cohen, Harvey G. *Duke Ellington's America*. Chicago: University of Chicago Press, 2010.

Coleman, James Smoot. *Sénégal: Évolution Politique et Organisation Administrative, 1954–1964*. Berkeley: University of California Press, 1964.

Coleman, James Smoot. "Tapisseries de Thies." *African Arts* 3, no. 2 (1970): 61–63.

Colin, Roland. *Sénégal notre pirogue: Au soleil de la liberté—Journal de bord 1955–1980*. Paris: Présence Africaine, 2007.

Collis-Buthelezi, Victoria J. "Peter Abrahams's Island Fictions for Freedom." *Small Axe* 25, no. 1 (64) (2021): 84–101.

Conrad, Joseph. *Heart of Darkness*. New York: Norton, 2016.

Cook, Mercer, and Stephen E. Henderson. *The Militant Black Writer*. Madison: University of Wisconsin Press, 1969.

Cooper, Frederick. *Citizenship Between Empire and Nation: Remaking France and French Africa, 1945–1960*. Princeton, NJ: Princeton University Press, 2014.

Coppet, Marcel de. *Physiologie et Médecine Traditionnelle à Madagascar*. Paris: Nouvelles Éditions Latines, 1963.

Corrothers, James David. "At the Closed Gate of Justice." In *Black Writing from Chicago: In the World, Not of It?*, edited by Richard Guzman. Carbondale: Southern Illinois University Press, 2006.

Cullen, Countee. *Collected Poems*. Edited by Major Jackson. New York: Library of America, 2013.

Damas, Léon-Gontran. *Graffiti*. Paris: Seghers, 1952.

Damas, Léon-Gontran. "La négritude en question" (interview). *Jeune Afrique*, no. 532 (16 March 1971): 57–58.

Damas, Léon-Gontran. "Négritude Revisited: An Interview with Léon Damas" In *Critical Perspectives on Léon-Gontran Damas*, translated and edited by Keith Q. Warner (Washington, DC: Three Continents Press, 1988), 23–28

Daniel-Rops, Henri. *Ce qui meurt et ce qui naît*. Paris: Plon, 1937.

Davis, Frank Marshall. *Black Moods, Collected Poems*. Urbana-Champaign: University of Illinois Press, 2002.

de Gaulle, Charles. *Mémoire de guerre: L'unité, 1942–1944*. Paris: Plon, 1954.

Delafosse, Maurice. *African Art*. New York: Parkstone International, 2012.

Delafosse, Maurice. *Haut-Sénégal-Niger: Le pays, les peuples, les langues; l'histoire; les civilisations*. Paris: Maisonneuve et Larose, 1972.

Delafosse, Maurice. *Les nègres*. Paris: Éditions Rieder, 1927.

Delas, Daniel. "Regard sur la politique culturelle de Senghor (1960–1980)." *Africultures* 2, no. 67 (2006): 239–43.

Delas, Daniel. "Rythme, culture et poésie dans *Éthiopiques de L. S. Senghor*." *L'École des Lettres* no. 12 (1998): 108–18.

Delavignette, Robert. *Soudan-Paris-Bourgogne*. Paris: Grasset, 1935.

Derrida, Jacques. *Aporias*. Translated by Thomas Dutoit. Stanford, CA: Stanford University Press, 1993.

Derrida, Jacques. *The Politics of Friendship*. Translated by George Collins. London: Verso, 2006.

Derrida, Jacques. *Rogues: Two Essays on Reason*. Translated by Michael Naas. Stanford, CA: Stanford University Press, 2005.

Dia, Mamadou. *Mémoires d'un militant du tiers-monde*. Paris: Publisud, 1985.

Diagne, Souleymane Bachir. "La leçon de musique." In *Le Sénégal contemporain*, edited by Momar Coumba Diop. Paris: Khartala, 2002.

Diagne, Souleymane Bachir. *Léopold Sédar Senghor : L'art africain comme philosophie*. Paris: Villeneuve, 2019.

Diagne, Souleymane Bachir. "Léopold Sédar Senghor: The Totalitarian Temptation." *Public Culture* 18, no. 3 (2006): 477–95.

Diop, Alioune. "Opening Discourse." *Présence Africaine*, June–November 1956, 22.

Diop, Alioune. "Opening Discourse." In *The First World Festival of Negro Arts*. Paris: Présence Africaine, 1966.

Diop, Boubacar Boris. *Tyaroye: Terre rouge*. Paris: L'Harmattan, 1981.

Diouf, Abdou. *Mémoires*. Paris: Seuil, 2014.

Diouf, Mamadou. "The French Colonial Policy of Assimilation and the Civility of the Originaires of the Four Communes (Senegal): A Nineteenth Century Globalization Project." *Development and Change* 29, no. 4 (1998): 671–96.

Diouf, Mamadou. "Senegalese Development: From Mass Mobilization to Technocratic Elitism." In *International Development and the Social Sciences: Essays on the History and Politics of Knowledge*, edited by Frederick Cooper and Randall Packard. Berkeley: University of California Press, 1998.

Disraeli, Benjamin. *Tancred: Or, The New Crusade*. London: Longmans, Green, 1880.

Dorsemaine, Michèle, Alfred Fierro, and Josette Masson, eds. *Léopold Sédar Senghor*. Paris: Bibliothèque Nationale, 1978.

Du Bois, W. E. B. "Little Portrait of Africa." *Crisis* 27, no. 6 (1924).

Du Bois, W. E. B. *The Souls of Black Folk*. Edited by Brent Edwards. New York: Oxford University Press, 2007.

Dunbar, Paul Laurence. *The Collected Poetry of Paul Laurence Dunbar*. Edited by Joanne M. Braxton. Charlottesville: University of Virginia Press, 1993.

Dunbar, Paul Laurence. *Oak and Ivy*. In *The Collected Poetry of Paul Laurence Dunbar*.

Dunbar, Paul Laurence. *When Malindy Sings*. New York: Dodd, Mead, 1906.

Eagleton, Terry, ed. *Ideology*. New York: Longman House, 1994.

Eagleton, Terry. *Marxism and Literary Criticism*. London: Methuen, 1976.

Eco, Umberto. "The Language of Europe Is Translation." Paper presented at the ATLAS assises de la traduction littéraire, Arles, November 14, 1993.

Edwards, Brent. *The Practice of Diaspora*. Cambridge, MA: Harvard University Press, 2003.

Eldridge, C. C. *The Imperial Experience: From Carlyle to Forster*. London: Palgrave, 1996.

Ellington, Duke. *The Duke Ellington Carnegie Hall Concerts: January 1943*. Berkeley, CA: Prestige Records, 1977.

Ellington, Duke. *Music Is My Mistress*. New York: Doubleday, 1973.

Engels, Frederick. *Anti-Dühring*. Translated by Emile Burns. Moscow: Progress Publishers, 1947.

Engels, Friedrich. *Ludwig Feuerbach and the Outcome of Classical German Philosophy*. New York: International Publisher, 1941.

Engels, Friedrich. *Ludwig Feuerbach et la fin de la philosophie classique allemande*. Paris: Éditions Sociales, 1946.

Engels, Friedrich. *M. E. Duhring bouleverse la science (anti-Duhring)*. France: Alfred Costes, 1946.

Engels, Friedrich. *Socialisme utopique et socialisme scientifique*. Paris: Editions Sociales, 1945.

Engels, Friedrich. *Socialism, Utopian and Scientific*. Translated by Edward Aveling. In *Selected Works*. Moscow: Progress Publishers, 1970.

Eschen, Penny von. *Satchmo Blows Up the World: Jazz Ambassadors Play the Cold War*. Cambridge, MA: Harvard University Press, 2004.

Fanon, Frantz. *Black Skin, White Masks*. Translated by Charles Lam Markmann. New York: Pluto Press, 1986.

Fanon, Frantz. *Towards the African Revolution*. Translated by Haakon Chevalier. London: Grove Press, 1988.

Fanon, Frantz. *The Wretched of the Earth*. Translated by Richard Philcox. New York: Grove Press, 2004.

Fischbach, Franck. *Manuscrits économico-philosophiques de 1844*. Paris: Vrin, 2007.

Fonds Emmanuel Roblès–Patrimoine méditerranéen. Université Paul Valéry, Montpellier 3, Montpellier, France.

Foucault, Michel. *This Is Not a Pipe*. Translated and edited by James Harkness. Berkeley: University of California Press, 2008.

France, Anatole. "The Latin Genius." In *The Works of Anatole France in an English Translation*, translated by Wilfrid S. Jackson. New York: Dodd, 1924.

Frobenius, Leo. *Histoire de la civilisation africaine*. Translated by Hanne Back and D. Ermont. Paris: Gallimard, 1952.

Frobenius, Leo. *Kulturgeschichte Afrikas*. Berlin: Phaidon-Verlag, 1933.

Frobenius, Leo. *Le Destin des civilisations*. Translated by Norbert Guterman. Paris: Gallimard, 1936.

Gaden, Henri. *Le poular: Dialecte du Sénégal*. Paris: Ernest Leroux, 1913.

Garavani, Giuliano. *After Empires: European Integration, Decolonization, and the Challenges from the Global South, 1957–1986*. New York: Oxford University Press, 2012.

Garrison, Lloyd. "Real Bursts Through the Unreal at Dakar Festival; Vitality and Diversity Last of U.S. Winners." *New York Times*, April 26, 1966.

Gates, Henry Louis, and Cornel West. *The African American Century: How Black Americans Have Shaped Our Country*. New York: Free Press, 2002.

Gautier, Théophile. *Mademoiselle de Maupin*. Paris: Charpentier, 1866.

Gautier, Théophile. *Mademoiselle de Maupin*. Translated by Claude Kendall. New York: Grosset and Dunlap, 1930.

Gellar, Sheldon. "Circulaire 32 Revisited: Prospects for Revitalizing the Senegalese Cooperative Movement in the 1980s." In *The Political Economy of Risk and Choice in Senegal*, edited by John Waterbury and Mark Gersovitz. London: Routledge, 2005.

Gide, André. *De l'importance du public: Conférence prononcée à la Cour de Weimar, le 5 août 1903*. Paris: Petite collection de l'Ermitage, 1903.

Gide, André. *Fruits of the Earth, Including Later Fruits of the Earth*. Translated by Dorothy Bussy. New York: Alfred A. Knopf, 1949.

Gide, André. *Le retour du Tchad*. Paris: Gallimard, 1928.

Gide, André. *Travels in the Congo*. Translated by Dorothy Bussy. Berkeley: University of California Press, 1962.

Gide, André. *Voyage au Congo: Carnets de Route*. Paris: Gallimard, 1927.

Glossaire du Parler français du Canada. Quebec City: Presses de l'Université Laval, 1968.

Grevisse, Maurice. *Le bon usage: Grammaire française*. 9th ed. Paris: Editions Duculot et Hatier, 1964.

Griéger, Paul. *La caractérologie ethnique: Approche et compréhension des peuples*. Paris: Presses Universitaires de France, 1961.

Grimoult, Cédric. "Créationnisme continuiste et transformisme limité: Les naturalistes français face à l'évolution biologique au XIXe siècle." *Archives Internationales d'Histoire des Sciences* 54, no. 3 (2004): 73–96.

Guéhenno, Jean. *Jeunesse de la France*. Paris: Grasset, 1936.

Guéhenno, Jean. *Journal d'une Révolution*. Paris: Grasset, 1939.

Guéhenno, Jean. *La France et les noirs*. Paris: Gallimard, 1954.

Guillaume, Paul, and Thomas Munro. *La sculpture nègre primitive*. Paris: Éditions G. Cres, 1929.

Guillaume, Paul, and Thomas Munro. *Primitive Negro Sculpture*. New York: Harcourt, Brace, 1926.

Guterman, Norbert, and Henri Lefebvre. *La conscience mystifiée*. Paris: Gallimard, 1936.

Hansen, Peo, and Stefan Jonsson. *Eurafrica: The Untold History of European Integration and Colonialism*. London: Bloomsbury, 2014.

Hardy, Georges. *L'art nègre: L'art animiste des noirs d'Afrique*. Paris: Henri Laurens, 1927.

Harney, Elizabeth. *In Senghor's Shadow: Art, Politics, and the Avant-Garde in Senegal, 1960–1995*. Durham, NC: Duke University Press, 2004.

Hegel, G. W. F. *Philosophy of Right*. Translated by T. M. Knox. New York: Oxford University Press, 1952.

Hell, Henri. "Poètes de ce temps: Pierre-Jean Jouve, René Char, Aimé Césaire, Jacques Prévert." *Fontaine*, no. 57 (1946–47): 803–16.

Herder, Johann Gottfried. *Sämtliche Werke*. Vol. 1, *Biblische Betrachtungen eines Christen*. Edited by Joseph Nadler. Freiburg im Breisgau: Herder, 1939.

Hiddleston, Jane. "Léopold Sédar Senghor: Politician and Poet Between Hybridity and Solitude." In *Decolonising the Intellectual: Politics, Culture, and Humanism at the End of the French Empire*. Liverpool: Liverpool University Press, 2014.

Hoover, J. Edgar. Memorandum to Mr. Fisher. September 10, 1919. Record group 60, file 9–12–725. National Archives, Washington, DC.

Hossmann, Irmeline. "Ibou Diouf: Le grand peintre africain de demain." *Afrique 62* (1966): 35–38.

Hughes, Langston. *The Collected Works of Langston Hughes: The Poems, 1921–1940*. Columbia: University of Missouri Press, 2001.

Hughes, Langston. "The Negro Artist and the Racial Mountain." In *The Portable Harlem Renaissance Reader*, edited by David Levering Lewis. New York: Penguin, 1995. Originally published in *The Nation*, June 1926.

Hughes, Langston. *Selected Poems of Langston Hughes*. New York: Vintage Classics, 1990.

Hutchinson, George, and John K. Young, eds. *Publishing Blackness: Textual Constructions of Race Since 1850*. Ann Arbor: University of Michigan Press, 2013.

Irele, Abiola. *The African Experience in Literature and Ideology*. London: Heinemann, 1981.

Irele, Abiola. *The Negritude Moment: Explorations in Francophone African and Caribbean Literature and Thought*. London: Africa World Press, 2011.

Jahn, Janheinz. *Neo-African Literature: A History of Black Writing*. New York: Grove Press, 1968.

Jaji, Tsitsi. *Africa in Stereo: Modernism, Music, and Pan-African Solidarity*. Oxford: Oxford University Press, 2014.

Johnson, G. Wesley. *The Emergence of Black Politics in Senegal: The Struggle for Power in the Four Communes, 1900–1920*. Stanford, CA: Stanford University Press, 1971.

Johnson, James Weldon. *God's Trombones: Seven Negro Sermons in Verse*. 1927. Reprint, New York: Viking, 1964.

Jones, Donna V. *The Racial Discourses of Life Philosophy: Négritude, Vitalism, and Modernity*. New York: Columbia University Press, 2010.

Joseph-Gabriel, Annette K. "Beyond the Great Camouflage: Haiti in Suzanne Césaire's Politics and Poetics of Liberation." *Small Axe*, no. 50 (2016): 1–13.

Kelley, Robin D. G. *Freedom Dreams: The Black Radical Imagination*. Boston: Beacon, 2003.

Kesteloot, Lilyan. *Aimé Césaire, l'homme et l'œuvre*. Paris: Présence Africaine, 1993.

Kesteloot, Lilyan. *Anthologie négro-africaine*. Paris: Marabout Université, 1967.

Kesteloot, Lilyan. "L'après-guerre, l'anthologie de Senghor et la préface de Sartre." *Éthiopiques*, no. 61 (1998).

Keyserling, Hermann von. *America Set Free*. London: Harper and Brothers, 1929.

Keyserling, Hermann von. *Amerika: Der Aufgang einer neuen Welt*. Stuttgart: Deutsche Verlags-Anstalt, 1930.

Keyserling, Hermann von. *Diagnostique de l'Amérique et de l'Américanisme*. Translated by Germain d'Hangest. Paris: Stock, 1941.

Kringelbach, Hélène Neveu. "Dance at the 1966 World Festival of Negro Arts: Of 'Fabulous Dancers' and Negritude Undermined." In *The First World Festival of Negro Arts, Dakar, 1966*, edited by David Murphy. Liverpool: Liverpool University Press, 2016.

Lambert, Fernando. *"Éthiopiques" de Senghor*. Paris: Présence Africaine, 1997.

Langellier, Jean-Pierre. *Léopold Sédar Senghor*. Paris: Perrin, 2021.

Lanson, Gustave. *Manuel d'histoire de la littérature française*. Paris: Hachette, 1933.

Laplanche, François. *La bible en France entre mythe et critique*. Paris: Albin Michel, 1994.

Lefebvre, Henri. *Le manifeste différentialiste*. Paris: Gallimard, 1970.

Le Houx, Troubat. *L'esprit et la paix*. Paris: Éditions des Amis de l'Institut international de la paix, 1945.

Lenin, V. I. *Materialism and Empirio-Criticism*. New York: International Publishers, 1927.

Lenin, V. I. *Materialisme et Empirio-Criticism*. Paris: Editions Sociales, 1937.

Lévi-Strauss, Claude. *Race and History*. In *Race, Science, and Society*. New York: Columbia University Press, 1975.

Lévi-Strauss, Claude. *Race et histoire*. 1952. Reprint, Paris: UNESCO, 2001.

Lewis, Roy. "Commonwealth et Empire Britannique." In *Civilisations*. Brussels: Institut International des Civilisations Différentes, 1955.

Lewis, Shireen K. *Race, Culture, and Identity: Francophone West African and Caribbean Literature and Theory from Négritude to Créolité*. Lanham, MD: Lexington, 2006.

Locke, Alain. *The Negro and His Music*. Washington, DC: Associates in Negro Folk Education, 1936.

Lumumba, Patrice. *Lumumba Speaks: The Speeches and Writings of Patrice Lumumba, 1958–1961*. Introduction by Jean-Paul Sartre. Edited by Jean van Lierde. Translated by Helen R. Lane. Boston: Little, Brown, 1972.

Malraux, André. *La condition humaine*. Paris: Gallimard, 1933.

Malraux, André. *Malraux: A Collection of Critical Essays*. Edited by R. W. B. Lewis. Englewood Cliffs, NJ: Prentice-Hall, 1964.

Maran, René. *Un homme pareil aux autres*. Paris: Éditions Arc-en-ciel, 1947.

Maritain, Jacques. *Art et scholastique*. Paris: Louis Rouart et Fils, 1920.

Maritain, Jacques. *Art and Scholasticism*. Translated by Joseph W. Evans. New York: Scribner and Sons, 1962.

Maritain, Jacques. *Integral Humanism*. Translated by Joseph W. Evans. Notre Dame, IN: University of Notre Dame Press, 1973.

Maritain, Jacques. *Humanisme intégral*. Paris: Aubier, 1936.

Marquet, Marie-Madeleine. *Le métissage dans la poésie de Léopold Sédar Senghor*. Dakar: Nouvelles Éditions Africaines, 1983.

Marx, Karl. *Capital*. Vol. 3. Translated by David Fernbach. New York: Penguin, 1991.

Marx, Karl. *A Contribution to the Critique of Political Economy.* Translated by
S. W. Ryazanskaya. New York: International Publishers, 1970.

Marx, Karl. *Der historische Materialismus.* Leipzig: Kröner, 1932.

Marx, Karl. *Economic and Philosophical Manuscripts (1844).* In *Early Writings,* translated
by Rodney Livingstone and Gregor Benton. New York: Penguin, 1992.

Marx, Karl. *Economie politique et philosophie.* Paris: Alfred Costes, 1937.

Marx, Karl. "For a Ruthless Criticism of Everything Existing." In *The Marx-Engels
Reader,* edited by Robert C. Tucker. New York: Norton, 1978.

Marx, Karl. *Free Trade: A Speech Delivered Before the Democratic Club.* Translated by
Florence Kelley Wischnewetzky. Boston: Lee and Shepard, 1888.

Marx, Karl. *Le capital.* Translated by M. J. Roy. Paris: Maurice Lachatre, 1872.

Marx, Karl. "Le travail aliéné." *La Revue Socialiste,* May 11, 1947, 154–68.

Marx, Karl. "Lettre à Vera Zassoulitch du 8 Mars 1881." *La Revue Socialiste,* May 11, 1947,
544–59.

Marx, Karl. *Misère de la philosophie.* Paris: Editions Sociales, 1947.

Marx, Karl. *Œuvres philosophiques.* Vol. 5. Paris: Alfred Costes, 1937.

Marx, Karl. "Postface to the Second Edition of *Capital.*" In *Capital, a Critique of Political
Economy,* Vol. 1, translated by Ben Fowkes. New York: Penguin, 1990.

Marx, Karl. *The Poverty of Philosophy.* Translated by Harry Quelch. New York: Cosmo
Classics, 2008.

Marx, Karl, and Friedrich Engels. *The German Ideology.* New York: International Publishers, 1960.

Marx, Karl, and Friedrich Engels. *The Holy Family or Critique of Critical Critique.*
Translated by Peter Byrne and Andy Blunden. Moscow: Foreign Language Publishing
House, 1956.

Marx, Karl, and Friedrich Engels. *L'idéologie allemande.* Paris: Alfred Costes, 1937.

Masse, Guirdex. "A Diasporic Encounter: The Politics of Race and Culture at the First
International Congress of Black Writers and Artists." PhD diss., Emory University,
2014.

Masson, André. *Le plaisir de peindre.* Paris: La Diane française, 1950.

Maximin, Daniel. "Sartre à l'écoute des sauvages." *Le Nouvel Observateur,* May 5, 1980, 63.

Maxwell, William J. "Editorial Federalism: The Hoover Raids, the New Negro
Renaissance, and the Origins of FBI Literary Surveillance." In *Publishing Blackness:
Textual Constructions of Race Since 1850,* edited by George Hutchinson and John K.
Young. Ann Arbor: University of Michigan Press, 2013.

Maxwell, William J. *F.B. Eyes: How J. Edgar Hoover's Ghostreaders Framed African
American Literature.* Princeton, NJ: Princeton University Press, 2015.

Mazower, Mark. *No Enchanted Palace: The End of Empire and the Ideological Origins of
the United Nations.* Princeton, NJ: Princeton University Press, 2009.

M'Baye, Babacar. "Richard Wright and African Francophone Intellectuals: A Reassess-
ment of the 1956 Congress of Black Writers in Paris." *African and Black Diaspora: An
International Journal* 2, no. 1 (2009): 29–42.

Mbembe, Achille. *Critique of Black Reason.* Translated by Laurent Dubois. Durham, NC:
Duke University Press, 2017.

Mbow, Cheikh, Ole Mertz, Awa Diouf, Kjeld Rasmussen, and Anette Reenberg. "The History of Environmental Change and Adaptation in Eastern Saloum-Senegal—Driving Forces and Perceptions." *Global and Planetary Change* 64, no. 3 (2008): 210–21.

McKay, Claude. *Banjo: A Story Without a Plot*. New York: Harper and Brothers, 1929.

McKay, Claude. *Complete Poems*. Edited by William Maxwell. Urbana: University of Illinois Press, 2004.

McKay, Claude. *Songs of Jamaica*. In *Complete Poems*.

Memmi, Albert. *The Colonizer and the Colonized*. Preface by Jean-Paul Sartre. Translated by Howard Greenfeld. Boston: Beacon Press, 1991.

Miller, Christopher L. "The (Revised) Birth of Negritude: Communist Revolution and the 'Immanent Negro' in 1935." *PMLA* 125, no. 3 (May 2010): 743–49.

Miller, F. Bart. *Rethinking Négritude Through Léon-Gontran Damas*. Amsterdam: Rodopi, 2014.

Monson, Ingrid. *Freedom Sounds: Civil Rights Call Out to Jazz and Africa*. Oxford: Oxford University Press, 2007.

Morand, Paul. *New York*. Translated by Hamish Mills. New York: Henry Holt, 1930.

Morgenthau, Ruth Schachter. *Political Parties in French-Speaking West Africa*. London: Oxford University Press, 1964.

Mossé, Fernand, ed. *Histoire de la littérature allemande*. Paris: Montaigne, 1959.

Mudimbe, Valentin Y. *The Invention of Africa: Gnosis, Philosophy, and the Order of Knowledge*. Bloomington: Indiana University Press, 1988.

Murphy, David, ed. *The First World Festival of Negro Arts, Dakar, 1966*. Liverpool: Liverpool University Press, 2016.

Nardal, Paulette. "Internationalisme noir." *La Dépêche Africaine*, January 1932.

Nehru, Jawaharlal. "Asia and Africa Awake." In *Jawaharlal Nehru Speeches, Volume 3 (1953–1957)*. Delhi: Publications Division, Ministry of Information and Broadcasting, Government of India, 1983.

New York Times. "Radicalism and Sedition Among the Negroes." November 23, 1919.

Ngũgĩ wa Thiong'o. *Decolonising the Mind*. Nairobi: East African Educational Publishers, 1981.

Noland, Carrie. *Voices of Negritude in Modernist Print: Aesthetic Subjectivity, Diaspora, and the Lyric Regime*. New York: Columbia University Press, 2015.

Panassié, Hugues. *Hot Jazz: The Guide to Swing Music*. Translated by Lyle Dowling and Eleanor Dowling. New York: Witmark and Sons, 1936.

Panassié, Hugues. *Le Jazz Hot*. Paris: Éditions Corrêa, 1934.

Perse, Saint-John. *Amers*. Paris: Gallimard, 1957.

Perse, Saint-John. "Seamarks." In *Collected Poems, Bilingual Edition*, translated by W. H. Auden. Princeton, NJ: Princeton University Press, 1971.

Plato. *The Republic*. Translated by Paul Shorey. Loeb Classical Library. Cambridge, MA: Harvard University Press, 1930.

Popescu, Monica. *At Penpoint: African Literatures, Postcolonial Studies, and the Cold War*. Durham, NC: Duke University Press, 2020.

Popper, Karl. *The Open Society and Its Enemies*. London: Routledge, 1945.

Puccini, Paola. "Le fonctionnement du mot 'francophonie' dans la revue *Esprit*, novembre 1962: À la recherche d'une définition." *Documents pour l'histoire du français langue étrangère ou seconde* 40/41 (2008): 101–19. http://journals.openedition.org/dhfles/99.

Rabaka, Reiland. *The Negritude Movement: W. E. B. Du Bois, Leon Damas, Aimé Césaire, Léopold Senghor, Frantz Fanon, and the Evolution of an Insurgent Idea*. Lanham, MD: Lexington, 2015.

Rabemananjara, Jacques. "Europe and Us." *Présence Africaine*, June–November 1956, 12.

Rappaport, Joanne. *The Disappearing Mestizo: Configuring Difference in the Colonial New Kingdom of Granada*. Durham, NC: Duke University Press, 2014.

Reed, John, and Clive Wake, eds. *Senghor: Prose and Poetry*. London: Heinemann, 1965.

Renault, Emmanuel. "Introduction." In *Comment lire les manuscrits de 1844?* Paris: Presses Universitaires de France, 2008.

Ripert, Yohann C. "Decolonizing Diplomacy: Senghor, Kennedy, and the Practice of Ideological Resistance." *African Studies Review* 64, no. 2 (2021): 292–314.

Ripert, Yohann C. "Rethinking Négritude: Aimé Césaire and Léopold Sédar Senghor and the Imagination of a Global Postcoloniality." PhD diss., Columbia University, 2017.

Ripert, Yohann C. "When Is Poetry Political? Césaire on the Role of Knowledge in 1944." *Small Axe*, no. 64 (2021): 1–14.

Rivarol, Antoine de. *De l'universalité de la langue française*. Paris: Obsidiane, 1991.

Robert, Paul. *Dictionnaire alphabétique et analogique de la langue française*. France: Société du Nouveau Littré le Robert, 1965.

Ronsard, Pierre de. *Le second livre des amours de Marie (XXV)*. Edited by Jean Céard, Daniel Ménager, and Michel Simonin. Paris: Gallimard, 1993.

Ronsard, Pierre de. *Poems of Pierre de Ronsard*. Translated by Nicholas Kilmer. Berkeley: University of California Press, 1979.

Rougemont, Denis de. *Écrits sur l'Europe: 1948–1961*. Paris: Christophe Calame, 1994.

Rougemont, Denis de. *L'amour et l'occident*. Paris: Plon, 1939.

Rougemont, Denis de. *Passion and Society*. Translated by Montgomery Belgion. London: Faber and Faber, 1956.

Sartre, Jean-Paul. "Black Orpheus." *Massachusetts Review* 6, no. 1 (1964): 13–52.

Sartre, Jean-Paul. *Black Orpheus*. Translated by S. W. Allen. Paris: Présence Africaine, 1951.

Sartre, Jean-Paul. "Orphée Noir." In Senghor, *Anthologie de la nouvelle poésie negre*.

Sauvage, Marcel. *Les secrets de l'Afrique noire*. Paris: Éditions Denoël, 1937.

Schlesinger, Arthur, Jr., and Morton White, eds. *Paths of American Thought*. Boston: Houghton Mifflin, 1963.

Schmidt, Elizabeth. "Anticolonial Nationalism in French West Africa: What Made Guinea Unique?" *African Studies Review* 52, no. 2 (2009): 1–34.

Séances de la Commission de la Constitution comptes rendus analytiques imprimés en exécution de la résolution votée par l'Assemblée, le 2 octobre 1946. Paris: Imprimerie de l'A.N.C., 1947.

Sedgwick, Eve. *Touching Feeling: Affect, Pedagogy, Performativity*. Durham, NC: Duke University Press, 2003.

Sembène, Ousmane. *God's Bits of Wood*. Translated by Francis Price. London: Heinemann, 1962.

Sembène, Ousmane. *Les bouts de bois de Dieu*. Paris: Pocket Press, 1960.

Sembène, Ousmane, and Thierno Faty Sow, dirs. *Le camp de Thiaroye*. Enaproc, 1988.

Senghor, Léopold Sédar. *Anthologie de la nouvelle poésie nègre et malgache de langue française*. Paris: Presses Universitaires de France, 1948.

Senghor, Léopold Sédar. "Apport de la poésie nègre au demi-siècle." In *Témoignages sur la poésie du demi-siècle*. Brussels: Éditions de la Maison du Poète, 1952.

Senghor, Léopold Sédar. *Ce que je crois*. Paris: Grasset, 1984.

Senghor, Léopold Sédar. *Chants pour Naëtt*. Paris: Seghers, 1949.

Senghor, Léopold Sédar. *The Collected Poetry*. Translated by Melvin Dixon. Charlottesville: University of Virginia Press, 1998.

Senghor, Léopold Sédar. "Debate: September 20th." *Présence Africaine*, June–November 1956, 215–16.

Senghor, Léopold Sédar. *Éducation et culture*. Edited by A. Raphaël Ndiaye and Doudou Joseph Ndiaye. Paris: Fondation Léopold Sédar Senghor, 2014.

Senghor, Léopold Sédar. *Éthiopiques*. Paris: Seuil, 1990.

Senghor, Léopold Sédar. *The Foundations of "Africanité" or "Négritude" and "Arabité."* Translated by Mercer Cook. Paris: Présence Africaine, 1971.

Senghor, Léopold Sédar. "Langage et poésie négro-africaine." In *Poésie et langage*. Brussels: Éditions de la Maison du Poète, 1954.

Senghor, Léopold Sédar. *La poésie de l'action: Conversations avec Mohamed Aziza* (The poetry of action: Conversations with Mohammed Aziza). Paris: Stock, 1980.

Senghor, Léopold Sédar. "Les fondations de l'africanité." In *Négritude, arabité, francité*. Beyrouth: Dar Al-Kitab Allubnani, 1967.

Senghor, Léopold Sédar. "Les négro-africains et l'Union française." *Réveil*, April 24, 1947.

Senghor, Léopold Sédar. "Les noirs dans l'antiquité méditerranéenne." In *Éthiopiques*, no. 11 (1977): 30–48.

Senghor, Léopold Sédar. *Letters in the Season of Hivernage*. Translated by Melvin Dixon. Charlottesville: University of Virginia Press, 1991.

Senghor, Léopold Sédar. "L'humanisme et nous: René Maran." *L'Étudiant Noir*, no. 1 (1935). https://catalogue.bnf.fr/ark:/12148/cb452723875.

Senghor, Léopold Sédar. *Liberté 1: Négritude et humanisme*. Paris: Seuil, 1964.

Senghor, Léopold Sédar. *Liberté 2: Nation et voie africaine du socialisme*. Paris: Seuil, 1971.

Senghor, Léopold Sédar. *Liberté 3: Négritude et civilisation de l'universel*. Paris: Seuil, 1977.

Senghor, Léopold Sédar. *Liberté 4: Socialisme et planification*. Paris: Seuil, 1983.

Senghor, Léopold Sédar. *Liberté 5: Le dialogue des cultures*. Paris: Seuil, 1993.

Senghor, Léopold Sédar. "L'intégration des pays d'outre-mer dans la Communauté Européenne" [Integration of overseas countries in the European Community]. *Le Monde*, October 6, 1953.

Senghor, Léopold Sédar. *Nocturnes*. Paris: Seuil, 1961.

Senghor, Léopold Sédar. *Œuvre poétique*. Paris: Seuil, 1964.

Senghor, Léopold Sédar. *Poésie complète.* Edited by Pierre Brunel. Paris: CNRS, 2007.

Senghor, Léopold Sédar. "Review of *La paix nazaréenne* by Delavignette." *L'étudiant de la France d'outre-mer: Chronique des foyers,* no. 8 (1944): SOLTFOM—V / 6. Archives nationales d'outre-mer, Aix-en-Provence.

Sharpley-Whiting, T. Denean. *Negritude Women.* Minneapolis: University of Minnesota Press, 2002.

Simon, Erica. *Réveil national et culture populaire en Scandinavie.* Paris: Presses Universitaires de France, 1960.

Smith, Andrew W. M., and Chris Jeppesen, eds. *Britain, France, and the Decolonization of Africa: Future Imperfect?* London: UCL Press, 2017.

Snipe, Tracy. *Arts and Politics in Senegal, 1960–1996.* Trenton, NJ: Africa World Press, 1998.

Somerhausen, Luc. *L'humanisme agissant de Karl Marx.* Paris: Richard Masse, 1946.

Spivak, Gayatri Chakravorty. *Critique of Postcolonial Reason: Toward a History of the Vanishing Present.* Cambridge, MA: Harvard University Press, 1999.

Sylla, Abdou. *Arts plastiques et état: Trente ans de mécénat au Sénégal.* Dakar: IFAN, 1998.

Sylla, Abdou. "Le mécénat de Léopold Sédar Senghor." *Éthiopiques,* no. 59 (1997): 76–84.

Táíwò, Olúfẹ́mi. *Against Decolonisation: Taking African Agency Seriously.* London: Hurst, 2022.

Táíwò, Olúfẹ́mi. *How Colonialism Preempted Modernity in Africa.* Bloomington: Indiana University Press, 2010.

Teilhard de Chardin, Pierre. *The Human Phenomenon.* Translated by Sarah Appleton-Weber. Eastborne, UK: Sussex Academic Press, 1999.

Teilhard de Chardin, Pierre. *L'apparition de l'homme.* Paris: Seuil, 1956.

Teilhard de Chardin, Pierre. *Le phénomène humain.* Paris: Seuil, 1955.

Teilhard de Chardin, Pierre. *The Phenomenon of Man.* Translated by Bernard Wall. New York: Harper and Row, 1959.

Thiam, Cheikh. *Return to the Kingdom of Childhood: Re-Envisioning the Legacy and Philosophical Relevance of Negritude.* Columbus: Ohio State University Press, 2014.

Thiam, Doudou. *La portée de la citoyenneté française dans les territoires d'outre-mer.* Paris: Société d'Éditions Africaines, 1953.

Toomer, Jean. "Harvest Song." In *Cane.* New York: Penguin, 2019.

Toomer, Jean. "Song of the Son." In *The Collected Poems of Jean Toomer,* edited by Robert B. Jones and Margery Toomer Latimer. Chapel Hill: University of North Carolina Press, 1988.

Twinam, Ann. *Purchasing Whiteness: Pardos, Mulatos, and the Quest for Social Mobility in the Spanish Indies.* Stanford, CA: Stanford University Press, 2015.

Ulmann, André. *Humanisme du XXe siècle.* Paris: Éditions à l'Enfant poète, 1946.

United States Committee for the First World Festival of Negro Arts. Press Agent's Files. Sc MG 220. Schomburg Center for Research in Black Culture, New York Public Library.

Usher, Phillip John. *Epic Arts in Renaissance France.* New York: Oxford University Press, 2014.

Vaillant, Janet G. *Black, French, and African: The Life of Léopold Sédar Senghor*. Cambridge, MA: Harvard University Press, 1990.

Vaillant, Janet G. "Encounter the West: The Ideological Responses of Alexis S. Khomiakhov and Léopold Sénghor." PhD diss., Harvard University, 1985.

Valentinov, N. *The Philosophical Constructions of Marxism*. Moscow, 1908.

Valéry, Paul. *Regards sur le monde actuel et autres essais*. Paris: Gallimard, 1945.

Verges, Françoise. "Métissage, discours masculin et déni de la mère." In *Penser la créolité*, edited by Maryse Condé. Paris: Khartala, 1995.

Vergès, Françoise. *Monsters and Revolutionaries: Colonial Family Romance and Métissage*. Durham, NC: Duke University Press, 1999.

Wagner, Jean. *Les poètes nègres des États-Unis: Le sentiment racial et religieux dans la poésie, de P. L. Dunbar à L. Hughes (1890–1940)*. Paris: Librairie Istra, 1963.

Warner, Tobias. *The Tongue-Tied Imagination: Decolonizing Literary Modernity in Senegal*. New York: Fordham University Press, 2019.

Washington Post. "The Right Policy on Zaire." May 21, 1978, p. B6.

Westermann, Diedrich. *The African Today and Tomorrow*. London: International Institute of African Languages and Cultures, 1939.

Westermann, Diedrich. *Noirs et blancs en Afrique*. Paris: Payot, 1937.

Wilder, Gary. *Freedom Time: Negritude, Decolonization, and the Future of the World*. Durham, NC: Duke University Press, 2015.

Wright, Richard. *The Richard Wright Reader*. Edited by Ellen Wright and Michel Faber. New York: Harper and Row, 1978.

Wynter, Sylvia. *After Man, Towards the Human: Critical Essays on Sylvia Wynter*. Kingston: Ian Randle Publishers, 2006.

Zischka, Anton. *Afrika, Europas Gemeinschaftsaufgabe*. Oldenburg: Stalling, 1951.

Zischka, Anton. *Afrique complément de l'Europe*. Translated by Christine Croizard. Paris: Robert Laffont, 1952.

Index

Blackness, xv, xvii, xxix, 50, 59, 135; Afro-diasporic consciousness, xx–xxi

Black Orpheus (Sartre), xviii, xlin22, 82; preface and, ix, xiii, xxxixn8

blues, xxxi, 49, 55, 57; origin in folk poetry, 49; as identity, 133. *See also* poetry; rhythm

Brazzaville Conference, 67

capitalism, xix–xx, 20, 33, 35, 40–42, 84, 149. *See also* colonialism; federalism; Marx; socialism

Caribbean, 21nm, 134

Cartesianism, 75, 121. *See also* Francity; rationalism

catholicism, 32, 35, 139

Ce que je crois (Senghor), xxxviii

Césaire, Aimé, 10, 21nm, 77–79, 81–82, 84, 120, 141, 149; role in Negritude, xiv, 132–33; contrast with Senghor, xv, xvii

civil disobedience, xii

civilization, 2, 4, 8, 10, 14, 16, 39, 57, 75, 98, 103, 111, 120, 129, 132, 135, 139, 146, 148–50; African, 140, 143; Black, 134–35, 139; crisis of, 23, 62, 102; European, 14, 107, 114; French, 75, 116; and Negritude, 106, 133; Negro-African, 4, 50, 110, 133–34, 136; Negro contribution to, 50, 59–60, 131, 134, 143; renewal of, 16. *See also* culture; humanism, Negritude

civilization of the universal, xxviii, xxxvii, 97, 101, 103, 110–11, 114, 129, 134, 150

colonialism, xviii, xxv, 6, 66, 68, 75, 100; critique of, xxxixn8, xlin22, 67, 100; and decolonization, xxx; and epistemic violence, xii–xiii, xxv, 98, 102, 116; and neocolonialism, xi, xxvi, 70. *See also* decolonization; Negritude

commonwealth, 74, 98, 100. *See also* federalism; independence

communism, 15, 33, 69, 102, 125n7, 146–47; Marx and, 35, 39; and revolution, 43–45; in Shanghai, xx; in the Soviet Union, 35.

confederation, xxvii, xlivn62, 66, 71–72, 100. *See also* federalism

cooperation, xiv, 42, 72, 75, 97, 99, 102–3, 110, 137

Coppet, Marcel de, xvi

cosmos, 15, 60, 84

Council of Europe, 101

Cullen, Countee, xxi, 18, 59–60, 62, 137, 141

culture, xii, 1, 11, 62, 72–73, 82, 85, 88, 100, 120, 124, 138, 146; bicephalic, xvi, definition of, 2–4, 7, 14nb, 28n1, 124; and decolonization, 124, 136; in education, 5–6; and identity, xiv, xvii, 128; Negritude as, xxvii, xxix, 133, 143; Negro-African, xxiv, 14, 89; as movement, 39, 50, 66, 116, 124, 146–47; and politics, xxiii, xxxii–xxxiv, xxxviii, xlvin91, 75, 95, 142, 145, 149; production, xxii, 98, 103, 129, 144. *See also* civilization; education; France; Negritude

Dakar, xvi, xxxi–xxxii, 6, 89, 91, 94–95, 139, 114; cathedral of, xlvn82; colloquium in, 131

Damas, Léon-Gontran, 10, 83–84, 133, 141; and Harlem Renaissance, 137, 139; and Negritude, 133, 143

dance, 3, 26, 48, 54, 55, 84, 106; as African ballet, 92–93; performance of, 80, 86; traditional, xxxi, 94, 112. *See also* performance; rhythm

decolonization, xi, xxxiii, 98, 101; meaning of, xxx; of the mind, xvii, xxvi; and Negritude, 110; project, xxii, xxvi, xxxi, 124; Senghor's vision of, xiii. *See also* colonialism; Francophonie; nation

Delafosse, Maurice, 17, 20, 26, 50

Delavignette, Robert, xvii, xlin21, 3

deracinalization, xxiv

Descartes, René, 117–18, 120–23, 145; return to, 117, 124

determinism, xii, 107

Dia, Mamadou, xxii, xxvi, xxix, 100; and French citizenship, xxi; and independence, xxviii, xlivn62

dialect, xi, 8–9, 18, 60; school, 51–58. *See also* dialect school

dialectical materialism, 37, 123. *See also* Marx, Karl

dialect school, 51, 55, 58

Dikē (Plato), xxix, xxxvi

Diop, Alioune, xvii, xxiii

Diop, Birago, 79

Diop, David, 142

Diop, Mbaye, 141

Diop, Ousmane Socé, xvii, 101

diplomacy, xxvii, xxxii, xxxvi, 37; treaties of, 71

Dogon, 79, 112

drum, 54, 85nn, 92–93

Du Bois, W. E. B., xvi, xxxvi, 138, 142; and double consciousness, xvi; as father of Negritude, 137; *The Souls of Black Folk*, 138

Dunbar, Paul Laurence, 9, 48, 54–55

École Normale Supérieure, x, 10, 21nm, 31, 82

education, 3–5, 11n3, 19, 89, 112, 119, 139; colonized, xvi, xviii, 10; and culture, 2; as tool for decolonization, 8, 10, 90, 138; Senghor's idea of, xvi, 2, 6–8. *See also* bilingualism; colonialism; culture

elections, xviii, xxi, 22, 70

Ellington, Duke, xxxi–xxxiii, xlvn82

Éluard, Paul, x, 119

emotion, 14–16, 25, 53–54, 61, 91, 93, 102–3, 118, 142; "is Negro as Reason is Hellenic," 15; and rhythm, 83

empire, xiv, 18, 66

Engels, Friedrich, 33, 36–37, 41, 45n5, 107, 123, 148

epistemic violence, x–xi, xiii, xxiv–xxv. *See also* colonialism; empire

essence, xxiv, xxvii, 2, 16, 28, 48, 81, 92, 117, 144; of Black Civilization, 134; of Cartesianism, 121; of poetry, 84

Éthiopiques (journal), xxv, xxxvi; postface to, 77

ethnicity, 47, 135, 141, 143, 147–48

ethnographer, x, xv, xxiv, 8, 14, 102, 106, 109, 133, 136, 140, 144–45

ethnology, 23, 136, 148

Étudiant Noir (journal), 14–15, xln10

Faidherbe, Louis, 7

family, xlin18, 2, 5, 18–19, 21–23, 42, 99, 110, 147; definition of, 19; as connection to the past, 17, 20

Fanon, Frantz, ix, xii, xxxixn8

Fauré, Gabriel, 26

federalism, xvii, xxvii, 68, 72–73, 75, 88–89, 97–99; or balkanization, 87; or confederation, xlivn62, 66; failure of, 99–100; against imperialism, xviii, xxii, 18, 74; as solution, xxi, xxiv, 65, 67, 76, 88. *See also* black Africa; confederation; France

France, 8, 65–66, 71, 74–75, 79, 85, 88, 100, 111, 115–16, 120, 128, 134, 140; education in, 2, 7, 11n2, 11n3, 119; role in federalism, 68, 71–72, 76; influence of, xxiii–xxiv, 4, 67, 69, 124. *See also* colonialism; federalism; Francophonie

France, Anatole, 116

Francity, 116, 120

Franck, César, 26

Francophonie, xxxiii, xxxvi–xxxviii, 115–16, 123–124; creation of, xxvii, xxix; definition of, xxx, xxxv, 120; as evolution of Negritude, xiv. *See also* Francity; French language

freedom, xii, xiv, xix, xxvii, xxx, xlviin101, 21, 22, 32, 44, 74, 83, 98, 151; individual, 43; from labor, 39; and nationalism, xxiv, 67

French Federal Republic, 66, 72–73, 88–90. *See also* federalism

French language, xiv, xxxviii, 9, 79–80, 85, 115–16, 118–20, 124; and Negritude, 132. *See also* Francophonie

French Union, xxi, 65, 67–69, 71, 75, 76n8, 90

French West Africa, xxiii, 1, 4, 7, 88–90, 99; unity in, 87

Gautier, Théophile, 24

Gide, André, 13, 26–28, 53, 55

god, xxi, 17–18, 26, 28, 35, 52, 58, 63, 78, 84, 109–10, 113, 122, 144. *See also* ancestor worship; religion

Guéhenno, Jean, 18, 79

Harlem, xi, xx

Hausa, xi, 8

Hughes, Langston, xxi, 9, 51, 55–56, 58, 60–63, 105, 137, 140–41

humanism, xv, xix, 9, 31–34, 43–44, 108, 110, 120, 123; colonial, 7; Marx's, 38–39; and Negritude, xxix, 106, 114. *See also* civilization of the universal; Negritude; Marx, Karl

humor, 9, 16, 51, 56–57, 83, 94, 112

idealism, 34, 37, 44. *See also* materialism

identity, x, xii–xv, xix, xxii, xxiv, xxix, xxxii, xxxiv, 36, 131, 149

imagination, x, xiii, xviii, 2, 15–16, 51, 92; creative, xxx, xxxv, xxxviii; decolonized, xxx–xxxi, xxxiii–xxxiv; Negro, xx, 52–53; poetic, xii, 54

imperialism, xi, xvii–xviii, 97, 115, 142 149

independence, xii–xiv, xix, xxii, xxvi, xxviii, xxx, xxxii, xxxvii, xln14, xliin39, xlivn62, 38, 69, 74–75, 97–103, 115, 128, 136, 144; cultural, 95; after federalism, 71–72; national, 98. *See also* confederation; decolonization

Indochina, 8, 68–69, 71–72

integration, xvi, xxiii, xliin33, 110

International Congress on the Cultural Evolution of Colonial Peoples (1937), xvi

jazz, xxxi, xlvn82, 9, 27, 50, 54–55, 85–86. *See also* music

jinns, 16–19, 21, 42, 81ng, 112

Johnson, James Weldon, xx–xxix, 51, 54, 140

Keita, Fodéba, 91–85

Keita, Modibo, xxviii, 127

labor, xix, 5, 17, 20–22, 28n1, 40, 42, 49, 78, 89, 145, 147; division of, 19; forced, 41; manual, 6; Party, 101. *See also* Marx, Karl; property

La Condition Humaine (journal), xix, xxii

La Nef (journal), xxii, xliin39, 65

language, x–xi, 5, 8, 18, 34, 40, 54, 66, 73, 80–82, 90, 92–93, 99, 106, 120, 134, 143; as dialect, xi, 8, 60; native, 7–9, 85; Negro-African, xxv, 48, 79, 133, 135; poetic, x. *See also* French language; syntax

Lefebvre, Henri, 145

Lenin, Vladimir, 38, 145, 148–49; and Leninism, 144, 146, 149; critique of Marxism, 34

liberation, 16, 33, 44, 65–66, 68, 79, 97–98, 106, 137, 146

Libermann, Father, 14

Lurçat, Jean, 127

Malagasy, federation, 74

Mali Federation, 95, 99–100, 112, 127; breaking up of, xxviii, xlivn65, 99

Mandinka, xi, 8

Mao, Ze Dong, 149

Maritain, Jacques, 18, 25 32–35; and personalism, 44

Marx, Karl, xix–xx, xxii, xlvn76, 33, 35, 38–39, 43–44, 106, 145–46, 148; *Capital,* 41, 147; and Engels, 36–37, 107, 123; *German Ideology,* 43; *Holy Family,* 33, 41; humanism of, 33, 38; manuscripts, xi; and Marxism, xv, xx, 32, 44–45, 141, 145, 148; and Negritude, 144, 149; philosophy, 33–34. *See also* communism; idealism; materialism

mask, 25, 55, 80, 85, 92–93, 12

materialism, 14–15, 34, 36, 38, 43–44; historical, 37, 41. *See also* idealism

McKay, Claude, xxi, 9, 11, 21nm, 58, 61–63, 140–41; inventor of Negritude, 63

metaphor, xliiin43, xlivn61, 53, 79, 80, 88, 140

métissage, xiii, xv–xviii, xxiv, xxx, xxxviii, 14, 67, 75, 84–85; as mixthreading, xln16. *See also* identity
Miller, Christopher, xiv, xln10
mind, xv, xx, xxvi, xxx, 2–3, 5–6, 19, 22, 28, 34, 36–37, 40, 47, 108–9, 111, 137–38, 144; and matter, 107–9; colonization of the, xii, 103. *See also* independence; Negritude
Morand, Paul, 13
Morocco, xxiii, 67, 69, 72
mother tongues, xi, 8
Mounier, Emmanuel, 43–44
music, xxii, xlviii89, 24, 26–27, 50, 79, 81, 86, 92, 119–20, 140, 147; Negro, 26, 47, 54–55; and rhythm, 93; Senegalese, xxxi–xxxii, xlivn54, 85
mysticism, xx, 52, 102, 141
myth, xii, xiv, xxxiv, 28, 77, 102, 128, 140, 146

Nardal, Jane, xv
Nardal, Paulette, xvii, 137
nation, xxviii, xxxiii, xxxvii, 31, 42, 65–66, 73, 75, 84, 88, 99, 106, 112, 114, 116, 147, 149–50; decolonized, xxxii, 98, 128, 144, 146; nationalism, xiv, xviii, xx, xxiv, xxx, 66–69, 73, 75, 98, 101. *See also* balkanization; independence; race
National Liberation Front, 101
nature, xxiii, xxxiii, 6, 16, 18, 21–22, 26, 31–32, 43–44, 69, 71, 77, 93–94, 107, 111, 113; in Marx, 34, 38–41, 123, 147; and Negritude, 63; resources, 20; and the supernatural, 18, 23. *See also* humanism; labor
Negritude, 18, 53, 56, 59–60, 78, 83, 85, 89, 101–3, 105–11, 113, 132–34, 141; Damas, 143; definition of, 105–6, 133, 140; inventor of, 56, 137–38; in poetry, 60–63, 79, 139. *See also* Africanity; Césaire, Aimé; civilization of the universal; Francophonie; race; rhythm; soul
Ngũgĩ wa Thiong'o, xi
Niagara movement, 134, 137
Nigeria, xii, xxviii, xxxi, 97–100, 103; Federation, 74
Nkrumah, Kwame, 101, 138
Normandity, xxxviii

ontology, 108–9, 111, 113
Orphée Noir (Sartre). See *Black Orpheus* (Sartre)

Pan-African Festival, 132, 136, 142–43
Pan-Africanism, xlivn67, xlvin88, 102, 138
Pascal, Blaise, xxxiv, 122–23
performance, x–xi, xix, xxxixn1, xlvn82, xlvin88, 26–27, 40, 51, 85, 92–94, 112
peri-racialism, ix, xvii, xxi
personality, xx, 14–15, 18, 21, 39, 41, 51, 43, 73, 84, 89, 116, 135; African, xxxiii, 105, 134, 142
Plato, ix–x, xv, xix, xxxiii, xxxvi, xxxixn1, 145
poetry, x, xii–xiv, xxxvii, 9; ethnic, 53, 58, 63, 79, 81, 86, 139, 146; French, 119–20; Negro-African, xx, xxv, 84–85, 142; written, 51, 78

Pompidou, Georges, xvii
postcolonial, ix, xiv, xviii, xxi, xxiv, xxix–xxxi, xxxiv
Présence Africaine, xxii, xxiii, xliiin43
property, 20–21, 34, 42–43
poular, 136

Rabemananjara, Jacques, xxiii
race, ix, xv, xix–xxi, xxiv, 2–3, 8, 11, 62, 68, 84, 98, 106, 132, 143, 148; and culture, 14; and Negritude, 103, 132; in poetry, 59, 61, 150n1; and politics, 90, 131; xviii; and racism, xiv. *See also* Africa; ethnicity; nation; Negritude; women
rationalism, xxv, xxxv, 14, 36, 80, 98, 111, 120–23, 145. *See also* Cartesianism; Descartes, René; Francity
realism, 16, 24–25, 111, 142
religion, xix, xxix, 14, 16–18, 33, 35, 38, 68, 73, 106, 122; and art; 24, 48. *See also* ancestor worship; god
Renaissance, 32, 93, 107, 114; Harlem, xxxvi; Negro, 50, 95, 134, 137–40
revolution, xii, xliin27, 42–43, 66–67, 72, 76n1, 111, 122–23, 132, 144, 149; communist, 43, 45; of 1848, xviii; of 1870, 65; of 1889, 106–7, 111, 113; Marxist, xliiin30, 33, 35, 38, 42; Negro, 111, 140
rhythm, xxv, xlvn83, 13, 15, 21–22, 26, 60, 77–78, 80, 82, 86, 103, 109, 112–13; and labor, 49; musical, 92–93; Negro, 25, 27; poetic, 10, 54–55, 81, 83–84, 119. *See also* art; music; Negritude; performance

Samba-Linguer, 4
Sartre, Jean-Paul, ix, xviii, xxxixn8, xlin22, 43, 82, 84
sculpture, xxxviii, 24–25, 26–27, 39, 54, 70, 85, 92, 94, 106, 112
segregation, 48
self-determination, xii, xvi, xix, xxv, 67, 101
Senegal, xviii, xxi, xxvi, xxix, xxxiv, xlvn82, xlvin90, xlvin91, 88, 90, 95, 98, 99–101, 103, 117, 119, 134, 141, 143, 149; arts in, 113; politics in, xiii, xxxviii, xxx–xxxi, xxxvii, 100, 115, 128–29, 138. *See also* black Africa
Serer, 17, 19, 22, 80, 139, 143
SFIO (French Section of the Workers' International Socialist Party), xviii, xx, xliiin29
Shadow Songs (Senghor), 77
socialism, xix, xx, xxxv, 34, 44–45, 98, 145, 149; African, xxvi, xxxviii. *See also* independence; confederation
Sorbonne, x, xxiii, 39nm,
soul, xii, xv, 3, 5, 9, 15–16, 18–19, 24, 27, 53, 55, 60–61, 84, 108–9, 112, 140–41; Negro, 14, 16, 21, 23; Negro-American, 51, 145. *See also* Negritude; race; rhythm
Soyinka, Wole, xxxiv, 142
spirituals, xx, 48–49, 51
state poïesis, xiv, xxxiii

strike, xlvn84, 70; Sembène's depiction in *God's Bits of Wood*, xx

Surrealism, x, 24, 80–82, 111, 118, 120, 122

sustainable independence, xi, xxiv, xxvi, xxx

symbiosis, xxx, 103, 112, 121–22, 128, 135, 143, 148

syntax, xxv, 116–18. *See also* French language

Tall, Papa Ibra, 128

Teilhard de Chardin, Pierre, 103, 107–8, 114n5, 118; and Pascal, 122–24

Thiam, Doudou, xxi

Tigritude, 142

tom-tom, 10, 22, 26–27, 49, 51, 55, 75, 77–79, 81, 84–85, 105

tradition, xv, xx, xxv, xxxi, 5–6, 14, 19, 21, 26, 88, 111, 114, 128; Negro-African, 22, 48, 93–94, 140, 150n3; oral, xxi–xxii, 81, 85nm, 119; poetic, xiv, 51, 63n4, 85

translation, xi, xvii, xxiv, xxxi, xxxv, xxxixn5, xxxixn6, xlin26, 28, 80, 108–9, 119–20, 135

transnationalism, xii, xiv, xx, xxiv, xxix, xxxii, xxxiv

Tropiques (journal), xvii

Tukulor, 17

Tunisia, xxiii, 67, 69, 72

Ulmann, André, 32

unitary republic, 73, 76, 116

United Nations, xx, 110, xliin34

United States of Africa, xxix, xlivn67, 101

United States of America, 3, 13–14, 16–17, 23, 47, 50, 66, 99, 138, 140–41, 149

universal, xix, 6, 38, 43, 51, 84–85, 102, 112, 121, 123, 145

Westermann, Diedrich, 19, 22

Wolof, xi, xvii, xxiv, xxxixn6, 4, 8, 20, 23, 94, 108, 117, 141

women, 59–60, 78–79, 92; role in African society, 19; artistic depiction of, 113

World Festival of Negro Arts, xxvii, xxxi–xxxiii, 113–14

Year of Africa, xii

Yoruba (language), xi, 8

www.ingramcontent.com/pod-product-compliance
Lightning Source LLC
Chambersburg PA
CBHW030822270326
41928CB00007B/860